MILLER'S

ceramic
figures

MILLER'S

ceramic figures

MILLER'S CERAMIC FIGURES BUYER'S GUIDE

Created and designed by
Miller's Publications
The Cellars, High Street,
Tenterden, Kent TN30 6BN
Tel: 01580 766411
Fax: 01580 766100

First published in Great Britain in 2006 by Miller's, a division of Mitchell Beazley,
imprints of Octopus Publishing Group Ltd,
2–4 Heron Quays, London E14 4JP
Miller's is a registered trademark of Octopus Publishing Group Ltd
Copyright © 2006 Octopus Publishing Group Ltd

ISBN-13: 978-1-84533-213-X
ISBN-10: 1-84533-213-X

A CIP record for this book is available from the British Library

Set in Frutiger

Colour Origination: Apex Press, Whitstable, Kent
Printed and bound in China by Toppan Printing Company Limited

Managing Editor: Valerie Lewis
Production Co-ordinator: Philip Hannath
Editorial Co-ordinator: Deborah Wanstall
Editorial Assistants: Melissa Hall, Joanna Hill
Production Assistants: Florence Buswell, Mel Smith, Charlotte Smith,
Ethne Tragett, Alexandra Wortley, Harriet Wortley
Advertising Executive: Emma Gillingham
Advertising Co-ordinator & Administrator: Melinda Williams
Designer: Nick Harris; **Advertisement Designer:** Kari Reeves
Indexer: Hilary Bird
Production: Jane Rogers
Jacket Design: Rhonda Summerbell
Additional Photography: Emma Gillingham, Robin Saker

Front cover illustration:
l. A Samson figural group of dancers, after Meissen, c1880.
£360–400 / €520–580 / $630–700
r. A Doulton figure, by Leslie Harradine, entitled 'Sunshine Girl', 1929.
£2,600–3,100 / €3,750–4,450 / $4,550–5,400 ↗ C
br. A pair of Staffordshire models of camels, c1900.
£1,800–2,000 / €2,600–2,900 / $3,150–3,500 ⊞ DHu

Contents

Contributors

British Pottery 18th & 19th Century
John Howard has been a dealer of English pottery for 30 years. His specializations are creamware, lusterware and animal figure groups manufactured in the British Isles in the 18th and 19th centuries. He has a showroom in Woodstock, near Oxford, and is a member of the British Antique Dealers Association and the Cotswolds Antique Dealers Association. John also exhibits at major antiques fairs in the UK and USA, such as Olympia in London and the New York Ceramics Fair. He is Chairman of the Ceramics Vetting Committee at Olympia and is a member of the vetting team at many UK and USA fairs.

British Porcelain 18th & 19th Century
Daniel Bray MRCIS is a senior auctioneer at Dreweatt Neate, Tunbridge Wells, Kent. He has been an auctioneer for six years.

Continental 18th & 19th Century
Christina Prescott-Walker is Vice President and Director of European Ceramics, Sotheby's, New York. She transferred to the United States from her native England eight years ago, having worked for Sotheby's in London and Sussex as a Ceramics auctioneer and valuer since 1989 after completing her BA in History of Art at the Courtauld Institute, London. She has written a book on collecting china as well as numerous short articles, and is a member of the American Ceramic Circle, the English Ceramic Circle and the French Porcelain Society.

Decorative Arts and 20th Century
Mark Oliver, a graduate of Warwick University, joined Bonhams, New Bond St, London in 1981, where he developed an enthusiasm for Lalique glass. In the mid-1980s he joined the Art Nouveau department as a cataloguer with special responsibility for Doulton sales. Oliver oversaw the sale of Royal Doulton's own collection which made record-breaking results. In 1998 he was appointed Head of the Design department, and in 2002 became Departmental Director. The department holds nine specialist sales a year, including Clarice Cliff, Moorcroft and, recently, a Sally Tuffin sale, the first of it's kind. With an ever younger crowd to please, sales held cover everything from Arts & Crafts stalwarts William Morris and Archibald Knox to the radical new breed of designers embodied by Ron Arad and Danny Lane.

How to Use

Every collector asks two key questions: "What should I look for?" and "What should I pay?". Both are answered in these pages. Five main collecting categories are covered in both sections of the book which can be navigated by the colour-coded tabs. If you are looking for a particular item, turn to the contents list on p.5–6 to find the appropriate section, for example, Decorative Arts. Having located your area of interest, you will see that the larger sections may be further sub-divided by subject, such as Denby, Gallé or Martin Brothers. If you are looking for a particular factory, maker or object, consult the index, which starts on p.285. Cross references also direct the reader to where other related items may be found. An explanation of some of the terms mentioned in this book and information on the care of ceramic figures is included on pp.12–13.

FINDING YOUR WAY AROUND
Use these running heads to see what sub-section you are in within each collecting category.

WHAT TO LOOK FOR
Key background and collecting information is covered in this section of the book.

INFORMATION BOXES
Additional historical, collecting or practical information is highlighted in these tint boxes.

Royal Crown Derby

Several factories were established in the Derby area at the end of the 19th century. The Derby Crown Porcelain Company, which later became Royal Crown Derby, was established in Osmaston Road in 1876, specializing in Imari wares. These were very successful and reached a peak between 1890 and 1915.

Figure production was increased from the 1930s, 'Marjorie', below right, was made c1933, and included reissued models from the 1880s, such as Don Quixote, Robin Hood and characters from Dickens. In 1935 Royal Crown Derby acquired the King Street

works, headed by Samson Hancock. The factory was originally a rival and made similar pieces based on the patterns and shapes produced by the first Derby company in the early 19th century.

During WWII output was largely restricted to useful wares, although by 1946 animal models, fancies, figures and statues were included in the catalogue. After the war production deteriorated and later pieces from the two factories are far less sought after today. In 1964 Royal Crown Derby was acquired by the Lawley Group.

LATER PIECES
• **Robert Jefferson** Employed during the 1960s as a sculptor, Jefferson later modelled a series of animal and bird paperweights, six of which were launched in 1981.
• **Other popular Jefferson models** These include Les Saisons, a group of figures inspired by Alphonse Mucha, and The Great Lovers, depicting Antony and Cleopatra, Romeo and Juliet, Lancelot and Guinevere and Robin Hood and Maid Marian.
• **The Classic Collection** Was created by Jo Ledger and modelled by Jefferson was launched in 1986. The first figures represented Persephone, Dione, Penelope and Athena.
• **Later models** These include the aristocratic cats, brought out in

1987. These, each wearing royal headgear, symbolize the crowned heads of Abyssinia, Siam, Persia, Egypt, Russia and Burma.
• **Paperweights** These are among the greatest successes in the firm's recent history and are avidly collected. The cat paperweight shown below was produced c1990.
• **Decoration** has continued with

the tradition of adapting old Oriental colours and motifs, and gold is used lavishly.
• **New editions** Designs by John Ablitt and some of Jefferson's earlier models, such as Cat, Rabbit, Duck, Badger and Hedgehog have recently been remodelled.

Marks
• Derby pieces are nearly always clearly marked, usually in red, with a printed crown and cipher and normally a year code; these marks are rarely faked.
• The King Street factory used the original Derby painted mark with the initials 'SH' on each side. Sometimes these initials have been ground away in an attempt to make the piece look older than it really is.

Market information
• Derby wares were traditionally considered the poor relation of Worcester and Minton, and until recently, items have been be undervalued.
• Price increases have been seen in the last few years, particularly for fine cabinet pieces with signed decoration.

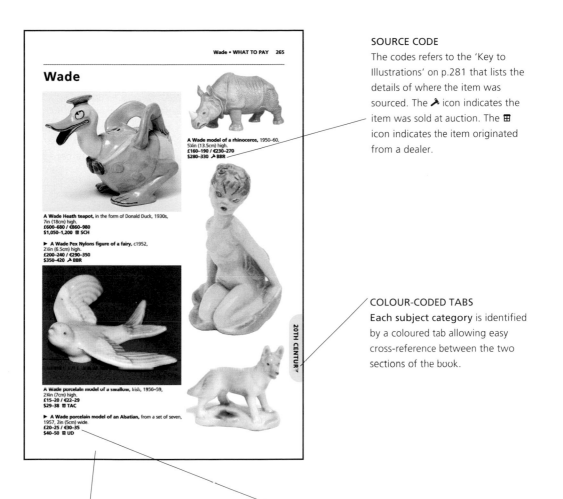

Wade • WHAT TO PAY   265

Wade

A Wade Heath teapot, in the form of Donald Duck, 1930s,
7in (18cm) high.
£600–680 / €860–980
$1,050–1,200 ⊞ SCH

▶ A Wade Pex Nylons figure of a fairy, c1952,
2½in (6.5cm) high.
£200–240 / €290–350
$350–420 ⋏ BBR

A Wade model of a rhinoceros, 1950–60,
5¼in (13.5cm) high.
£160–190 / €230–270
$280–330 ⋏ BBR

A Wade porcelain model of a swallow, Irish, 1956–59,
2¾in (7cm) high.
£15–20 / €22–29
$29–38 ⊞ TAC

▶ A Wade porcelain model of an Alsatian, from a set of seven,
1957, 2in (5cm) wide.
£20–25 / €30–35
$40–50 ⊞ UD

20TH CENTURY

SOURCE CODE
The codes refers to the 'Key to Illustrations' on p.281 that lists the details of where the item was sourced. The ⋏ icon indicates the item was sold at auction. The ⊞ icon indicates the item originated from a dealer.

COLOUR-CODED TABS
Each subject category is identified by a coloured tab allowing easy cross-reference between the two sections of the book.

PRICE GUIDE
Prices are based on actual prices realized at auction or offered for sale by a dealer, shown in £sterling, €, and $US. Remember that Miller's is a PRICE GUIDE not a PRICE LIST and prices are affected by many variables such as location, condition, desirability and so on. Don't forget that if you are selling, it is quite likely you will be offered less than the price range. Price ranges for items sold at auction tend to include the buyer's premium and VAT if applicable. The exchange rate used in this edition is 1.75 for $ and 1.44 for €.

WHAT TO PAY
Each collecting area includes a cross-section of items, each one captioned with a brief description of the item including the maker's name, medium, date, measurements and in some instances condition.

Introduction

Ceramic figures of animals and people have been appreciated for their significance and beauty since ancient times. Ceramic figures could be very simple in form, or very complex in style and were made for a whole host of reasons. One can only marvel at ceramic figures made for spiritual inspiration and ceremony found, for example, in the pyramids and those that were made in ancient China.

There are as many reasons why people collect ceramic figures as there are subjects to choose from. Inspiration and a desire to focus on a particular theme arises from countless sources. My own collecting passions were formed in childhood, influenced by my grandparents' copper lustre and Gaudy Welsh items, but most of all, the giant pair of Staffordshire pottery dogs with their brown glass eyes. I later purchased a Staffordshire pottery model of a cat, just like one my grandparents owned, and vividly remember coming across it in a junk shop, the owner of which sold it to me at a reduced price because it had a chip. This memory of my childhood demonstrates that nostalgia and sentiment are part of the collecting process. Every piece that I collect serves as a reminder of a time and place as evocatively as a photograph or video.

I have been dealing in antiques for over 30 years and the range of collecting fields never ceases to impress, amaze and sometimes amuse me. The chapters in this book reveal several collecting areas in ceramic figures, but there are many others – you are only restricted by your imagination. One enthusiast I know has over 300 cow creamers, another has over 2,000 relief-moulded jugs and a collector in the USA has over 5,000 Staffordshire pottery figure groups.

Utimately collectors should relate to and enjoy their chosen area of collecting for a variety of reasons. There are few serious collectors who are motivated purely by investment – the main criteria are much more complex and compelling, although many collections have increased significantly in value in recent years such as Staffordshire pottery jungle animals, illustrated by the model of the leopard on p.90 and the pair of camels on p.119. One can admire the detail on a Meissen figure – see pages 160–65, be amused by a

naïvely modelled and decorated Prattware duck, moved by a sentimental model of young child such as the girl on p.264 or appreciate the work of a genius such as Josiah Wedgwood or Thomas Whieldon. Collecting springs from a heart-felt response to an object as well as a need for intellectual satisfaction, but all collectors have one thing in common, and that is a passion for their subject.

Good advice when starting out is to buy the best you can afford. Acquire items that have an extra special appeal that make them stand out from other similar examples. This special factor could be a beautiful glaze, exquisite modelling, good decoration or humour. A serious collector of ceramics would benefit from establishing contact with a good dealer who will help to develop your collection, offer advice and make contact when that elusive figure comes their way. A dealer can also help with upgrading the collection as your taste and understanding of your subject become more focused and developed. (See our Key to Illustrations on pp281–83 for dealers in your area.)

Also consider where your chosen item will be placed and how it will look. Creative and thoughtful display will integrate a collection into room settings with striking impact. Assemblages of similar items displayed together work very well, and this is an art interior designers have used to great effect. One collector I know used the colour palette associated with Staffordshire pottery for her wall and floor colouring. It looked stunning and every figure introduced into that room looked at home. Lighting is also important and can be used strikingly to enhance the impact of your collection.

As collectors indulge their passion they are able to appreciate the journey that some of these often very fragile figures must have made through the passage of time and acknowledge the circumstances that allowed it to survive. Each figure has its own story and has earned the right to be cherished in order to give joy to future generations.

John Howard

what to look for

Materials

The term 'ceramics' refers to anything that is shaped from wet clay and then fired in a kiln to make it look hard. Different consistences and colours of clay, mixed with a variety of other ingredients, produce different types of finished ceramic body, from coarse-grained, porous earthenware and the harder stoneware to the finest porcelain.

Pottery

The earliest ceramics were made from earthenware, that is, clay fired at a relatively low temperature of under 2,200°F (1,200°C). Pottery, made from an earthenware body, can be white, brown, buff, grey, red or black in colour, according to the minerals contained in the clay. It has a coarse texture and the body is opaque. Unglazed earthenware is porous and in order to be made waterproof it must be coated with a glaze.

Stoneware

Fired at a high temperature, the body is water-resistant. Some stonewares are translucent and can resemble porcelain. There are two distinct types of stoneware: a fine white-bodied variety such as Sieburg and later Staffordshire; the other, a grey-bodied ware, was produced in Cologne, Westerwald and Fulham, London.

Porcelain

Porcelain bodies can be divided into two categories: hard paste and soft paste. This difference can be an aid when identifying unmarked pieces. Porcelain may be semi-translucent if held to the light, and if tapped, gives a musical note.

• **Hard-paste porcelain** has a smooth texture resembling icing sugar. It was first developed using a combination of kaolin, petuntse and quartz.

• **Soft-paste porcelain** is slightly more granular and any chips may have a rougher appearance. The colour can vary from white to grey according to the minerals used but this can help with identification as certain factories are associated with bodies of a particular shade.

Bone China

Bone china is pure white in appearance. It is a less expensive method of porcelain making as it contains calcified bone and is the most common type of porcelain made in England after c1820.

Glazes

Glazes are used to make a porous body watertight and are also decorative. They are usually made from powdered minerals mixed with water and washed over the ceramic body. When fired they fuse with the body, producing a glassy film. Glazes can be matt or shiny, soft or hard, coloured or colourless.

There are three main types of pottery glazes: salt, lead and tin. Glazes used on hard-paste porcelain have a typically glassy, thin appearance. Glazes used on soft-paste porcelain are thicker and often soften the detailed modelling and pool in the curves and crevices of a piece.

• **Lead glaze** is shiny and transparent and may be coloured with metal oxides. It is used on most European earthenwares including pearlware and creamware and also on Chinese Tang ware.

• **Tin glaze** contains tin oxide which gives a pure white surface resembling porcelain. It is found on maiolica, delftware and faïence, where it is used to give a pure white finish to an earthenware body. Tin glaze was applied to the fired body which was then decorated with enamels and finally coated with clear lead glaze, before the piece was returned to the kiln for refiring.

• **Salt glaze** has a distinctive pitted surface. It was formed when salt was thrown into the kiln during the high-temperature firing process. The sodium in the salt fused with silicates in the clay to form a glassy surface. Salt-glazed wares were made in England and Germany and also in the United States.

Care of your collection

Cleaning Figures

Over time, ceramic figures that are on display will incur an amount of dust and dirt. This needs be dealt with on a regular basis and in a variety of ways.

• **Unglazed figures** are porous and if washed the dirt will soak into the body, causing discolouration. Such pieces should only be dusted. If in doubt, consult a specialist dealer or restorer for advice.

• **Hard-paste porcelain and high-fired stonewares** are waterproof and can be washed by hand in mild soapy water. However, this is not the case if the item has been restored in any way.

• **Soft-paste porcelain, bone china and low-fired earthenwares** should not be washed, but gently wiped with a damp cloth.

Handling Figures

It is necessary to handle figures in order to appreciate, examine and identify them, but this is also the time when most damage can occur. There are certain guidelines that should be remembered when handling figures:

• **Two hands** should be used when lifting hollow figures and this provides better support.

• **Gilding** should not be touched if possible as it is easily worn.

• **Gently replace** figures back on the surface they came from, avoiding close proximity with other pieces.

Displaying Figures

Figures have high visual impact and to be fully appreciated need to be displayed with consideration and care. They should be supported securely and placed out of the way of danger that can include accidental knocks and vibration.

A collection can be enhanced by the furniture in which it is displayed, especially if it is of the same period. However, it is not usually appropriate to customize antique furniture by adding lights, whereas modern display cabinets often have lighting built into them. Porcelain is at its best when lit but be aware that it can crack if over-heated, so ensure there is plenty of ventilation. When displaying figures at different levels by using Perspex stands or wooden blocks, always make sure these are secure.

Repairing/Restoring Figures

There are arguments for and against restoration and previously negative attitudes are changing as the skills of professional restorers improve. If sympathetically undertaken, restoration can enhance a piece. Previous restoration techniques have included:

• **Riveting** – using a process of inserting red-hot staples across a crack to prevent it increasing.

• **Enamel paste** – used to fuse broken pieces together.

• **Silver replacements** – enabling a piece to be used when vital elements were broken or lost.

• **Transparent varnishes** – sprayed and fired for a smooth finish.

Modern restorers now concentrate on restoring imperfections that detract from the beauty of an object and halting damage that will deteriorate over time. This can be achieved using a process of over-painting and spraying, which may be expensive, so it is worth considering the overall value of a piece before consulting a restorer.

Restoration that is not declared is also something to be aware of. Never be afraid to ask a seller to describe any damage and restoration and always examine a purchase thoroughly. Look at fragile parts such as fingers and necks and examine gilding closely, as this is often poorly matched.

Glossary

basalt
Unglazed, very hard, fine-grained stoneware stained with cobalt and manganese oxides, developed by Wedgwood c1768.

biscuit (bisque)
Unglazed porcelain or earthenware fired once only. Popular for porcelain figures because it suggests classical marble sculptures.

bocage
Encrustations of flowers, grass and moss generally used to decorate the bases and supporting plinths of ceramic figures.

cow creamer
Milk jug modelled to resemble a cow. The tail would be the handle, the mouth the would be the spout, and milk was poured into the body though an opening in its back.

crazing
Tiny, undesirable surface cracks caused by shrinking or other technical defects in a glaze.

creamware
Cream-coloured earthenware with a transparent lead glaze, developed by Wedgwood c1760.

Delftware
Tin-glazed earthenware from Delft, in the Netherlands; refers to British ware when it does not have a capital latter.

enamel
Metallic oxides applied to metal, ceramics, or glass in paste form or in an oil-based mixture, which is then usually fired for decorative effect.

flambé
Glaze made from copper, usually deep crimson, flecked with blue or purple, and often faintly crackled.

flatbacks
Pottery figures with flat, unmodelled and undecorated backs, designed to be viewed from the front only. They were intended as mantelpiece decorations and produced mainly in the 19th century by Staffordshire potteries.

gilding
The use of gold to create a decorative effect. Gilding can be applied in a variety of ways: mixed with honey or mercury and fired or applied wafter firing.

incised
Mark or decoration that is cut or scratched into the suface.

underglaze
Colour or design painted before the application of the glaze on a ceramic object.

British Pottery 18th & 19thC

Ceramic production in Britain as we know it today began when tin-glazed pottery from Delft in Holland was introduced in the 16th century. The techniques employed by the Dutch were soon copied by British potters and significant factories were founded in London, Liverpool and Bristol. The new processes employed to produce delftware enabled potters to decorate wares with underglaze blue and polychrome colours, with startling impact at the time. Apart from the usual domestic ware for the table, figures and animals were also made. These items are now very rare, as production was limited and few have survived from the 1750s.

It was during the 18th century that the ceramics industry fully emerged in Britain with the birth of the Staffordshire Potteries, the collective name for the towns of Hanley, Burslem, Stoke-on-Trent, Longton, Shelton and Fenton. The development of the world's largest ceramic industry commenced in the area through a combination of local access to coal and clay, aided by the entrepreneurial skills of potters such as Thomas Whieldon (1719–95) and Josiah Wedgwood (1730–95), who took full advantage of the new pottery methods and ever increasing demand from a wealthy new market that had emerged with the advent of the industrial revolution. These factories introduced new techniques and methods that led to the development of creamware, pearlware and salt-glazed pieces in the latter half of the 18th century. Such was the success of these new ceramics that production of slipware and delftware had almost ceased by 1800.

By the 19th century mass-production had been established and there were over 300 factories producing ceramics. The spending power of the working and middle classes had increased, resulting in ornamental – as opposed to purely functional – ceramics being an increasingly affordable option for the growing population. At this time the British Empire was at the height of its power and the demand for representation of associated political, religious, military, theatrical and social issues resulted in an ever expanding home market, as well as a burgeoning export market. Royal coronations, famous murders, theatrical triumphs, military operations, religious dignitaries and celebrities were all portrayed, and these figures provided a social commentary on events much as television or newspapers do today. A demand also existed for large and costly figure groups; some reflected successes in farming, others were of more general interest.

Exploration of foreign countries and the discovery of animals such as zebras and giraffes gave rise to the production of many exotic animals. All types of domestic animals were represented, and farm animals must have evoked a feeling of nostalgia for the old days – a time before the vast majority of working folk resided in smoke-filled cities. However, the spaniel is the animal that is perhaps the most representative of Victorian England. It was produced in large numbers and almost every home had a pair of these dogs adorning the mantelpiece.

The demand and enduring appeal of figure groups and animals was such that many other potteries were established. Factories in the North East of England, Scotland, Yorkshire and South Wales all contributed to the output of the Staffordshire potters.

Some of these items have found their way into the collections of the major museums but countless items from the 18th and 19th centuries can still be found in private collections where they continue to give joy to their owners and are treasured both for their decorative appeal and their significance in history. Each piece has its own story, and if these figures could speak what a story they would tell.

Minton

This Staffordshire pottery was founded by Thomas Minton (1765–1836), who trained as an engraver at the Caughley China Works. In 1793, he established his own pottery that has continued under various titles and ownership until the present day. The Minton factory was one of the 19th century's biggest and most varied producers of every type of ceramic: porcelain, stoneware, china, earthenware, Parian and majolica. Most Minton majolica is figural and one of the foremost modellers commissioned by the firm was the Frenchman Albert-Ernest Carrier de Belleuse. Minton's greatest period spans from the mid– to late 19th century, although the company is still in production today.

WHAT TO LOOK FOR

• **Collecting** Minton figures fall into three main collecting areas: porcelain, Parian and majolica.

Marks
Nearly everything produced by the firm is marked 'Minton' or 'Mintons'; pieces also have shape and pattern numbers and date codes. Individual years have special symbols.

1842	1843	1844	1845	1846
✳	△	☐	✕	⬭
1847	1848	1849	1850	1851
⌒	—	⋈	♧	⋰
1852	1853	1854	1855	1856
V	⌂	₰	※	☡
1857	1858	1859	1860	1861
◇	ϒ	♉	♒	人
1862	1863	1864	1865	1866
✛	◈	Ƶ	≋	⋉
1867	1868	1869	1870	1871
⋇	⸦	⊡	Ⓜ	Ⓝ
1872	1873	1874	1875	1876
⊗	⋈	↓	Ɛ	⊖
1877	1878	1879	1880	1881
⊡	⟁	⟁	⚠	⊞
1882	1883	1884	1885	1886
⊗	⊘	⊠	⋈	B
1887	1888	1889	1890	1891
⚓	⊗	S	T	Ⓤ
1892	1893	1894	1895	1896
②	③	④	⤸	⤸
1897	1898	1899	1900	1901
⤸	⤸	⤸	⤸	①

Shown below is a majolica figure of a man with a wheelbarrow, c1851.
Colours When buying it is worth remembering that the muddier brown pieces are less commerical than the well-coloured examples that are decorated with a larger palette of colours such as turquoise, green and blue.
Marks Collectors of majolica are always pleased to see the Minton date marks on the base.
Condition Large models in good condition are very sought after but damage affects the price of pieces dramatically.
• **Restoration** When purchasing Minton figures check for restoration, as they seem particularly vulnerable to damage. However, minor restoration is more acceptable on pottery than on porcelain figures.

Market Information
• The Minton majolica market is very strong although prices probably peaked in 2005.
• This market is especially buoyant in the US.
• Large and imposing pieces can command five- or six-figures sums.
• Centrepieces and unusual and dynamic models in vibrant colours represent the top end of this market.

Prattware

Prattware takes its name from the Pratt family whose pottery in Fenton, Staffordshire developed a distinctive type of lead-glazed earthenware decorated with high-fired colours. The factory was founded c1780 by William Pratt and was taken over by his elder son Felix in 1810. The impressed name 'Pratt' ocasionally appears, but it is difficult to state with certainty which member of the family employed this mark. Wares of this type were also made in vast quantities by numerous other factories elsewhere in Staffordshire, Yorkshire and Scotland from 1775–1835 and the term Prattware has become a generic term used to describe pearlware earthenwares decorated in a distinctive palette of blue, green, yellow, orange, brown and purple and different themes include rustic subjects such as milkmaids, classical figures, political and royal subjects and animals, often decorated with a crude, daubed effect, which is typical of Prattware. Figural groups were very popular at the beginning of the 19th century, some bearing an impressed title to the base, which was a common feature at this time. Figures made later in the century were decorated with low-fired enamel colours, which created a wider and more subtle palette. Novelty and decorative items such as money boxes and figural groups are rarely marked and value relies heavily on the elaborateness of the decoration and the rarity of the form.

SUBJECTS
A number of different figures and groups were manufactured. These range from those with a neo-classical influence to groups emblematic of the four seasons. There is a host of figures in rural settings as well as animals, cow creamers and Toby jugs.

IDENTIFICATION
• **Fakes and copies** These are rare in early Prattware figures.
• **Research** It is important to be familiar with the range of colours used in the Prattware palette – attending auction viewings and museums, and using reference books can be very helpful.
• **Flaking** The colours are underglaze, so do not flake as enamel colours often do.
• **Identification** Buyers should note that some Continental factories made figures in a similar colour palette. However, these colours are usually more vibrant and look harsh and quite often they are tin-glazed, whereas English Prattware has a pearlware glaze.

Market Information
• Figures from the late 18th and early 19th century are quite rare and consequently good examples command high prices. In general animals, such as the cockerel, c1790, shown above, are more popular than the neo-classical figures, which can be rather stiff.
• When buying animals several factors should be considered: finesses of modelling, quality of colouring and decoration and, perhaps most importantly, artistic appeal. The best examples are pieces that reflect the creative spirit and expression of the artist who created them. Quite often there is comedy or humour in the model and such pieces have extra value.
• Figures of people are less expensive than animal groups, and appeal and decorative effect are factors that mainly affect prices. A complete set of the Four Seasons, for example, would be worth much more than an assembled set of the four, just as true pairs of figures have a higher value than singles which make up matched pairs.
• It is advisable to buy the best examples you can afford. Collectors tend to be more discriminating after they have purchased several items at the lower end of the market and, with hindsight, often wish they had started collecting a little higher up the scale.

Staffordshire

By the 19th century, porcelain figures had captured the top end of the market and pottery pieces were produced to a lower standard in order to achieve mass appeal. In the early 19th century over 300 small potteries in the north Staffordshire region produced a range of decorative pottery figures, some of which had secondary uses such as spill vases, pastille burners, watch holders and candlesticks. Shortly after 1837 a major change occurred in the manufacture of Staffordshire figures. Until then these figures had been made mainly by hand, using many 'secondary' moulds over and above the three basic moulds which were required to make a standard figure, and the whole piece, front and back, was then decorated. These figures were time-consuming and expensive to produce. In the mid-1840s, however, a new design called the 'flatback' was developed. All that it required was a three-part mould comprising a front, a back and a base. Clay was pressed by hand into the front and back moulds which were then tied together and fired with the base attached. After firing,

the unglazed figure would be decorated and fired again. This was an innovative concept because the figure was to stand on the mantelpiece or against a wall and thus there was no need to decorate the back. Labour-saving production lines were then introduced so that this new type of figure could be made at a low cost in quantities never before seen. The majority of pieces were produced in the Victorian era with the 1850s to 1870s witnessing their heydey in terms of quality of production.

Over the following 40 years more than 5,000 figures were made, some in great quantity. Figures of famous, contemporary and historical personalities, were popular; religious, musical and theatrical figures were produced, as were figures of children, soldiers, sailors, shepherds and hunters, animals and domestic buildings. Some versions were made in three or four sizes and some, such as dog models, in up to six sizes. Despite their primitive qualities Staffordshire figures are hugely popular with present-day collectors, and have an international following.

MARKS
Virtually all Victorian Staffordshire figures are unmarked, so it is not possible to identify the maker. Occasionally decorator's marks are found but these are of no real significance in terms of dating or identification. Figures are usually judged on quality rather than maker.

COLLECTIBILITY
• **Quality** The huge price range of Staffordshire figures is affected by quality of modelling and enamelling, as well as subject matter. Generally the best quality figures were produced prior to 1860.
• **Subject matter** Collectors' favourites include sporting and theatrical subjects and rare exotic

animals such as elephants and lions. Most collectors concentrate on specific areas of interest, which include John Wesley, Admiral Lord

Nelson, the Crimea War, theatre, circus and royalty.
• **Animal collecting** categories can range from the iconic Staffordshire spaniels to pugs, poodles, whippets, lions, elephants and farm animals such as cows, chickens, horses and ducks. One of the main criteria of choice with these figures is sentimental and decorative appeal.
• **Specific factories** also provide a more focused collecting area. The most famous are 'The Alpha Factory' Lloyd of Shelton, Dudson & Co and the Thomas Parr factory, to which the rifle volunteer NCO, c1860, shown left, is attributed. These companies had unique styles that enabled attribution even though their models were unmarked.

Market Information

• Collections of miniatures and simply modelled and decorated items approximately under 3in (7.5cm) high can give a varied and interesting view of the Staffordshire potters' work and can often be purchased for under £100 / €145 / $175.
• Restored pieces are common and best

avoided. It always possible to find a piece in good condition.
• A degree of restoration on early and rare examples is acceptable.
• Rarity, condition and quality of modelling and decoration are all features to take into account as there is a discriminating collectors' market.

Wemyss

Wemyss ware, made at the Fife pottery in Scotland from 1880, covers a range of useful and ornamental wares which vary in size from buttons to garden seats. As well as producing pieces such as wall plaques, jugs, preserve pots, vases and commemorative souvenirs, the factory made ornamental wares such as garden seats and a popular range of moulded animal models that included pigs, cats and rabbits – a rare Wemyss cat once sold for a five-figure sum. Wemyss ware was only sold through Thomas Goode & Co's Mayfair shop which created an air of exclusivity for the Wemyss pieces.

PIGS
• Ornamental pieces in the form of pigs are popular with collectors. They are often decorated in a variety of flowers and made in a range of sizes that enabled the pieces to be used as door-stops or ornaments on nursery shelves.

DECORATION
Wemyss ware hand-painted motifs vary widely but the most common form of decoration consists of brightly-painted floral sprays and fruit with the firm's most popular motif depicting cabbage roses.

The soft clay body and rather semi porous glaze of Wemyss tends to suffer from staining. Wemyss has such a decorative impact that it is important to buy good clean examples as obvious blemishes detract significantly.

Marks

Authentic Wemyss ware bears the maker's mark of the retailer's mark of Thomas Goode & Co. Some pieces show the initials 'RH' for Fife's owner Robert Heron, as well as 'Wemyss'. On those pieces produced by the Bohemian artist Karel Nekola the letter 'Y' of the word Wemyss is elongated.

Market Information

• Prices have peaked for standard items such as bowls, mugs and trays etc decorated with the familiar rose pattern.
• The more common examples of flowers, roosters, damsons and thistles used as assemblages or as adornments in the home are by far the weakest area of the Wemyss market. The rather chintzy look of these wares is currently out of fashion and now would be a good time to acquire pieces as, relatively speaking, good clean examples will be difficult to find in the future.
• Unusual and rare shapes command very high prices, fuelled by a strong collectors' market and new record prices are still achieved. The paperweight of a sleeping piglet and the comical cats with glass eyes, for example, have all commanded very high prices recently.
• The strongest area of the market is for items produced in Scotland between 1880 and 1930. The work of Karel Nekola is keenly sought after by serious collectors.
• Later Items produced from the original Wemyss patterns and designs at Bovey Tracey after 1930, or those by Jan Plichta, never captured the organic feel of the originals from Scotland.

Ralph Wood

The Wood family, Ralph I (1715–72), and his son Ralph II (1748–95) ran the Hill factory in Burslem in Staffordshire, making a series of earthenwares from c1765.

They were mainly well- but simply-modelled figures of pastoral and animal subjects in cream-coloured earthenware, initially decorated in rich underglaze colours similar to earlier Whieldon-type wares. Some figures were glazed only with a colourless lead or 'china' glaze. The blue used on Wood wares is purer than the grey tone found on Whieldon and Wedgwood pieces, and the yellow is paler. Later Wood wares were painted more carefully, keeping the coloured washes separate. Enamelled figures were a more expensive innovation involving more work and an extra firing.

WHAT TO LOOK FOR
• **Subject matter** Wood figures vary in subject and there are many well-modelled equestrian figures including St George, William III and Hudibras.
• **Characteristics** Look for plump cheeks, large hands and slightly protruding eyes.
• **Quality of work** Wood figures were usually made to a high standard, as shown by the

shepherd, made c1785, below left. Fine modelling, attention to detail and the application of glazes are all things to consider.
• **Restoration** This is often inevitable on pottery from the late 18th century and, if professionally executed and stated at the time of purchase, is acceptable if reflected in the price of the item.

TOBY JUGS
So-called after Toby Philpot, who featured in *The Brown Jug*, in 1761, the Wood family are credited with introducing the Toby jug, (although some medieval and Roman ware was decorated with faces). Toby jugs were extremely successful, being copied by many potteries and are still being made today. They were modelled with a multitude of different personalities, (mainly male, but some female), generally being of stout, bucolic character, although there are the more refined types: the Squire, Lord Howe, the Thin Man and Prince Hal. John Wood's sales ledger of 1785 is the first surviving documentary evidence of a Toby jug.

Marks
• Wood wares were among the first coloured English pottery figures to be marked.
• Look for the early 'R. Wood' mark and the later 'R. A. Wood, Burslem', used from c1780. Marked wares comprise mainly figures, reliefs and Toby jugs.

Market Information
• The distinctive figures produced by Ralph Wood and his son are increasingly difficult to find on the market. Consequently good examples of their work maintain a steady value and it is likely that prices will significantly increase in the next few years.
• The rather academic and classical nature of the Woods' work tends to narrow its commercial appeal. Their figures are seen in many quarters as fine art and its form, quality of modelling and superb signature coloured glazes are appreciated by academics, art lovers and ceramic collectors, mainly in the UK and US.
• The classic Wood Toby jugs are somewhat out of favour as the Toby jug niche collecting area has declined in the last year or so.
• Rural groups such as shepherds or country folk are currently undervalued. However these items have the strongest general appeal and will be increasingly valuable.

British Porcelain 18th & 19thC

Porcelain has been produced for over 1,000 years, having been invented in China long before it was discovered in Europe. The earliest English porcelain figures were probably made at the Chelsea factory which first produced wares from 1744, but it was not until 1750 that they manufactured figures in larger numbers. Longton Hall was established around 1749 and closed in 1760, so their figures, even in damaged condition, start at around £500 / €720 / $870. Worcester 18th-century figures are extremely scarce.

Hard-paste porcelain was developed in Britain by William Cookworthy of Plymouth, who discovered a source of china-clay and china-stone in Cornwall and started producing hard-paste porcelain at Plymouth in 1768. After about two years the factory was moved to Bristol and taken over by Richard Champion in 1773 but closed in 1781. The figures produced are often primitive looking with a discoloured smoky glaze but have a following among collectors because of the achievement they represent.

In the mid-19th century Parian figures and busts became very popular. Vast numbers of pieces were produced by manufacturers such as Copeland, Minton, Robinson & Leadbeater, J. & T. Bevington and, to a lesser degree, Goss. The art unions of the day helped to promote Parian by offering items modelled on classical sculptures as prizes to their subscribers. They were trying to educate the masses as to what they considered to be aesthetically correct. In the 1840s and '50s porcellaneous figures of animals and people were also produced by anonymous Staffordshire factories.

Generally speaking, the market for porcelain figures is currently depressed, so now is a good time to buy. Derby figures, for example, are worth less than they were ten years ago, and although rare figures from all factories are expensive, they are still good value and prices will probably rise. The exception to this are the niche interest areas, where the strong competition among collectors has kept prices high.

LONGTON HALL

Established in Staffordshire in 1749 by William Littler, Longton produced a series of figures that became known as 'snowmen' because of their blurred outline due to the thick glaze. After 1753 the factory concentrated on moulded tableware decorated in cobalt, or 'Littler's blue'. The factory closed in 1760.

SAMUEL ALCOCK & CO

Samuel Alcock owned the Hill Pottery at Burslem in Staffordshire. The combined pottery and porcelain works employed some 400 people producing table and tea services, vases and figures from history and romance.

A range of animal models was also produced, such as the wolf c1840, shown right, and these have impressed numbers on their bases. Apart from some portrait busts and other figures made in unglazed biscuit china, most of Alcock's porcelain of the 1830s and 1840s appears to be unmarked. This is why the firm is so little known and is often confused with Rockingham or Coalport.

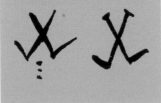

Longton Hall mark
This Longton Hall mark, while clearly attempting to imitate a Meissen crossed-swords mark, is in fact a pair of entwined 'L's used probably because the owner's name was William Littler.

MOORE BROTHERS

The Moore Brothers came to fame in the 1880s and early 1890s with their distinctive figures. They were also known for their figural centre-pieces such as the example shown right. Some, inspired by Dresden, were often in the form of cherubs supporting various items such as lilies.

Bernard and Samuel's inexpensive but highly decorative porcelain proved to be popular. Susceptible to damage, it is now rare to find pieces in perfect condition.

The 1890s saw Bernard Moore become more experimental with ceramic glazes, and his colourful models of animals were very successful.

Belleek

Established in 1863 by David McBirney and Robert Williams Armstrong in County Fermanagh, Northern Ireland, Belleek specialized in producing an incredibly thin high-quality white porcelain, using a glazed Parian body. Warm and creamy in appearance Belleek resembled the texture and translucence of sea shells.

Before long the factory began making wares in the forms of shells decorated with an iridescent glaze, as well as finely-woven baskets.

Belleek has always been popular in the United States, and in fact, workers from the Irish factory emigrated and set up rival establishments there; their products are termed 'American Belleek'.

The factory is still in production and the same designs have been produced throughout its existence.

BELLEEK PERIODS

Production is divided into the following periods, all of which carry slightly different marks:
- **First Black Period** 1863–90.
- **Second Black Period** 1891–26. Mark changed to comply with the 1891 McKinley Tariff Act and amendments to the British Merchandise Act of the same year, which required the country of origin to be specified on the piece.
- **Third Black Period** 1926–46. Possibly changed to mark the 1926 Wembley Exhibition; included a stamp with the Celtic words 'Deanta in Eireann' (Made in Ireland).

- **Fourth Period/First Green** 1946–55. Mark identical to previous except that green was used because it was thought to be less obtrusive than black on the translucent china.
- **Fifth Period/ Second Green** 1955–65. An upper case 'R' was added to signify that the Belleek mark was registered in the United States.
- **Sixth Period/Third Green** 1965–80. The size of the mark was reduced so that it could be accommodated on smaller pieces.
- **Seventh Period/ First Gold** 1981–92 Produced in gold to commemorate

Marks

The first date of production in 1863 saw the introduction of a transfer-printed mark of a round tower with an Irish harp and an Irish Wolfhound above the name 'Belleek' in a ribbon with shamrock leaves at either end. After 1891 the words 'Co Fermanagh Ireland' were added to the mark, and from around 1900 the marks changed again.

the centenary of the gold medal won at the Melbourne Exhibition of 1880.
• **Eighth Period/First Blue** 1993–96.Mark similar to Second Period, but printed in blue.
• **Ninth Period/ Second Blue** 1997–99. Changed for technical reasons as the first blue mark burnt off the porcelain during firing.
• **Tenth Period/Black** 2000 only. This mark was used to commemorate the Millennium and limited to pieces produced in that year.
• **Eleventh Period/Green** 2001–Present. Designed to match the green used on the first earthenware pieces.

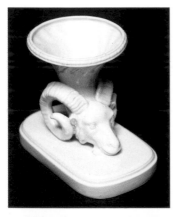

at the same rate, and coated with powder to prevent adhesion. The model is then left to dry for 24–36 hours so that cracking does not occur during the biscuit firing – an average figure can contract by up to 15 per cent. After firing for 60–70 hours at a high temperature, the oven is gradually cooled. When cold, the props are removed from the figure and any flaws erased. The figure is then refired for vitrification, supported by sand-filled saggers.
• **Damage** to the delicate Parian body is likely and many pieces will therefore have restoration. This will greatly reduce the value of a figure, depending on its rarity and the extent of the damage.

BELLEEK PARIAN FIGURES
• **Production** of Parian figures is labour-intensive and, in the early days of coal-fired ovens, it would have been difficult to control the temperature of the firings.
   Each figure requires many slip-cast moulds that are liable to distort. These casts are assembled and those parts liable to movement during the firing process are supported on props made of slip-casting so that any contractions during firing will be

AMERICAN BELLEEK
William Bromley, the creator of Irish Belleek, travelled to America in the 1880s to supervise the manufacture of the Belleek formula by American potteries, including the Willets Manufacturing Co in Trenton, New Jersey.
• **Willets Belleek** Also called Art Porcelaine, was first made in 1887, and produced delicate white ware inspired by Irish prototypes.
• **Other wares** The company also made a range of porcelain decorated with ormolu and gilding.
• **Mark** The printed mark on Willets Belleek was a twisted serpent with the word 'Willets'.

Market information

• Nineteenth-century Belleek figures are less common than other items produced by the factory, such as the First Period ram's-head spill vase, above. The First and Second Period figures that come under this heading vary in value according to rarity, condition and glaze finish. Many were produced in pairs, such as First Period 'Affection' and 'Meditation', above. A pair of these rare figures will cost over £3,000 / €4,300 / $5,200.
• There are many variations in the glaze finish on individual figures which make it difficult to match an individual figure to another. Therefore a single example can be purchased for as little as £200 / €290 / $350. Some of the rare Belleek figures such as 'Crouching Venus' and 'Prisoner of Love' occasionally appear on the market with unusual coloured or bronzed finishes. These rare variations have been known to fetch in excess of £10,000 / €14,400 / $17,500 for an individual figure.
• Some of the early Belleek figures, such as First Period figural candlesticks in the form of a boy and girl each carrying a basket (shown right) were produced well into the 20th century, so it is important to check the marks before making a purchase.

Bow

Bow was founded by Thomas Frye and Edward Heylyn in Stratford-le-Bow, Essex, and was one of the earliest porcelain factories in England. Although the patent was granted in 1744, wares were not available for sale until c1748.

The porcelain made at Bow was coarser than hard-paste porcelain, and the bone ash that was a principal ingredient created a body that was prone to staining. At first, Bow concentrated on household items in the Chinese and Japanese style, but competition from other makers forced them to concentrate on ornamental wares, especially figures. They successfully copied Meissen figures, although unlike their elegant Chelsea counterparts, Bow figures were less refined. However, the bright colours on later figures, combined with a strong underglaze blue, resulted in highly decorative ornaments that sold well at the time.

The Bow factory was also called 'New Canton' as it was based on a Chinese design. At its peak it employed 300 people and continued for 30 years until a recession. Figures became unfashionable and the rococo style that Bow incorporated gave way to neo-classical taste. The factory closed in 1776.

MANUFACTURE

Bow figures were press-moulded rather then slip-cast. This gave them a much heavier body, and in order to prevent them collapsing during firing, they were constructed almost architecturally.

• **White figures or early figures** Most of the early figures were left in the white. The exceptions were copies of Meissen or Oriental-inspired pieces. The most popular of the early figures were portraits of theatrical personalities.

• **Glazes** Bow figures were also covered in a heavy glaze, which tended to obscure the details.

• **Enamelled or later figures** By 1755 the figures were coloured

Marks
This hand-painted anchor and dagger mark was the standard Bow mark from c1760–76, and is usually found on figures and groups.

with enamels, as seen by the figure of Air, c1765, left; they still stood on relatively simple bases which were sometimes applied with flowers. However, after 1760, bases were moulded in the rococo style and were often elevated on high scroll feet.

Market information
The market for Bow porcelain figures has remained steady in recent years.

• Slight damage or restoration will not affect values very much as perfect figures are rare.

• Early Bow figures of the 1748–55 period are most prized by collectors.

• The majority of early figures, other than the Meissen copies and Oriental inspired pieces, are left glazed in the white. Restored pieces from this period start from around £300 / €430 / $520. The rarer enamelled examples are fetching four- or five-figure sums, around three or four times the amount for a standard figure.

• The later and more common pieces, which date from c1760 onwards, are quite affordable.

• For instance, a small figure of a putto (angel) may cost £150 / €210 / $260 and a larger figure with some restoration from c£200 / €290 / $350.

• Individual figures that originally formed part of a set or a pair will start from around £400 / €570 / $700 in reasonable condition.

• Elaborately modelled pairs of ornamental figures from 1765 onwards, such as a shepherd and shepherdess holding flowers, may cost from £1,500 / €2,150 / $2,600 if in reasonable condition.

Chelsea

Chelsea, an early and important porcelain factory, was founded in 1744 by Nicholas Sprimont, a French Huguenot silversmith. Aimed at the top end of the market, pieces were made in limited numbers and so were expensive to buy. The earlier figures are among the most sophisticated and well-modelled ever produced by a British porcelain factory and prices will reflect this.

Chelsea's soft-paste porcelain is dated and classified according to the various marks used.

The most sought-after pieces are those of the red anchor period, such as the Hans Sloane wares decorated with botanical specimens. In 1769 Sprimont suffered failing health and the following year the factory was taken over by William Duesbury of the Derby Porcelain Works. The company was known as Chelsea-Derby until it finally closed in 1784.

Chelsea pieces are very popular today. Their copies of Meissen pieces can fetch more than the originals.

GIRL IN A SWING
Also known as St James' factory. It is believed that Charles Gouyn ran the concern from his house in St James' Street, London between 1749 and 1759. The production from this factory had previously been incorrectly attributed to Chelsea as the porcelain body is very similar. Gouyn managed the Chelsea factory between 1745 and 1748 and used a similar paste at his St James' factory. Some figures were made at St James', but most items are found in the form of figural scent bottles and seals.

Marks

Production at the Chelsea factory falls into five periods, four of which are named after marks used at the time:

TRIANGLE PERIOD 1744–49
• **Mark** Usually incised or painted in underglaze blue.
• **Body** White, glossy, translucent body, often left uncoloured.

RAISED ANCHOR PERIOD 1749–52
• **Mark** Embossed on a raised pad.
• **Body** Milky white, silky body, containing impurity specks.
• **Decoration** Based on Japanese porcelain, Vincennes and Meissen.

RED ANCHOR PERIOD 1752–56
• **Mark** Very small mark in red enamel on the backs of figures and bases of plates and cups.
• **Body** Creamy white body with dribbling glaze, often decorated with Meissen-style flowers.

• **Chelsea Moons** When held up to strong light, so-called Chelsea 'moons' can be seen – bubbles trapped in the paste, which appear as light spots in the body.

GOLD ANCHOR PERIOD 1756–69
• **Mark** Painted in gold and often found on reproductions of Chelsea Porcelain; on genuine pieces the mark should never be more than ¼in height.
• **Creamy body** Prone to staining. Clear, thickly applied glaze which tends to craze. Rococo decoration, influenced by Sèvres. Use of gilding significantly increased.

CHELSEA-DERBY PERIOD 1770–84
• **Mark** 'D' with an anchor conjoined, usually in gold. Gold anchor mark also continued to be used.
• **Decoration** Predominantly neo-classical decoration with a new French look.

Triangle period

Raised anchor period

Red anchor period

Gold anchor period

Chelsea-Derby period

Market information

• Rare, early Chelsea figures of the 1744–56 period are the most coveted. The majority are closely based upon original Meissen models covering the triangle, raised anchor and red anchor periods. They show great skill in modelling and are normally decorated in restrained enamel colours.

• Prices can exceed £20,000 / €28,800 / $35,000 for the rarest figures with attractive decoration and in good condition.

• From an artistic point of view, the finest figures date from the red anchor period. The modeller famous for these figures is Joseph Willems. He worked at the factory from 1750, also producing allegorical and peasant models such as the figure of a carter, c1755, left. Prices are affected by quality of decoration, colouring, attributable period and condition. For instance, 'La Nourrice' is normally found with a red anchor mark, but a rare and earlier example with a raised anchor mark has sold for twice as much at auction. The rarest and most expensive figures reached a peak in 2002 and are now selling for less astronomic sums.

• Figures from the gold anchor period start at around £300 / €430 / $520 for examples with restoration.

• Figures from the Chelsea-Derby period are very similar to those produced at Derby, complete with patch marks, and prices for restored pieces start at £150 / €210 / $260.

Copeland

Copeland & Garrett of Stoke-on-Trent, bought Spode in 1833 and began developing a statuary porcelain called Parian. It was named after the Greek island of Paros where it was found, and developed as a substitute for the white biscuit porcelain produced by factories such as Sèvres.

Statuary Parian incorporates a glass frit – which adds density – and classifies it as soft-paste porcelain. Parian is capable of being moulded without losing any details which enabled full-sized statues by Victorian sculptors to be reproduced in smaller sizes and large numbers, using a device known as Cheverton's Reducing Machine, patented by Benjamin Cheverton in 1844. These smaller busts were of various subjects, including royalty, politicians, philanthropists, poets, composers and characters from antiquity. They were greatly desired by middle-class Victorians and displayed on mantel pieces or as dining table centrepieces, alongside vases and candlesticks. In 1847 Copeland & Garrett became W. T. Copeland & Sons.

PRODUCTION

Parian statues were made by slip-casting. The liquid porcelain, or slip, was passed into a mould and allowed to harden enough to coat the walls of the mould. They then poured out the excess, creating a thin-walled hollow form such as the 'Prodigal's Return', c1855, right.

ART UNIONS

Copeland was one of numerous firms who made figures for art unions. To raise funds for the Arts, 'art unions' ran lotteries in which art lovers could win an original work such as a specially commissioned Parian figure. Parian figures are often stamped with names such as 'The Crystal Palace Union' or 'Art Union of London'.

PARIAN MARKS

Parian figures are usually marked by their maker on the base or on the back of the model. Some pieces may also be titled and have a date code.

Market information

The Copeland factory produced a large number of Parian wares throughout the second half of the 19th century.

• A bust of a common model such as 'Hope' or a little known Victorian gentleman might cost as little as £80 / €115 / $140 whereas a rarer models such as 'Night', c1862, left, and 'The Veiled Bride', c1860, may cost £1,000 / €1,450 / $1,750 and £2,500 / €3,600 / $4,350 respectively.

• Busts of famous or patriotic 19th-century figures such as Admiral Lord Nelson are generally more expensive (in the mid hundreds) as they have a wider appeal to collectors.

• Parian is prone to firing cracks in production which can affect the price if they are in a very visible area; from an investment point of view it is best to buy items in good order.

Derby

The Derby factory was founded in 1750 by a Frenchman, André Planche and was the most prolific manufacturer of porcelain figures in the 18th and 19th centuries. It is now known that William Duesbury decorated some of the figures from this period. In 1757 Derby was bought out by John Heath and William Duesbury, who had been decorating pieces for Chelsea. Their early Derby figures were simple, but sharply modelled. In 1770 Heath and Duesbury bought the Chelsea factory, and for the next 14 years, in a phase known as Chelsea-Derby, the two concerns operated together.

In 1811 the business was acquired by Robert Bloor who, despite the decline of his mental health in 1826, continued to manage the factory until it closed in 1848. The quality of the figures declined – most were over-decorated, had sombre colours and square, octagonal or even debased rococo-style bases.

Several other factories were established in Derby in the 19th century. The most successful was the so-called Crown Derby company, which survives today as the Royal Crown Derby Porcelain Company.

EARLY FIGURES
Derby's earliest figures, dating from 1750–55, are among the rarest and most valuable, and are known as 'dry-edge' figures because of the characteristic dry appearance of the edge of the base. This was the result of the glaze being wiped away before firing to prevent it from sticking to the kiln.
• **Modelling** This was simple but sharp.

LATER FIGURES
• **Style** Derby's later figures were very rococo in style, standing on wide, scrolled bases, such as the figure of a tailor c1830, shown on p.27, and

often backed with intricate bocage.
• **Copies** A number of 18th-century figures were reproduced, such as Pierre Stephan's 'The Four Seasons' c1775, remodelled with circular bases by William Coffee around 1815.
• **Most famous figures** These are known as the Mansion House Dwarves. Dating from around 1825–30 a good pair of these figures will cost from £800 / €1,150 / $1,400 upwards.
• **Decoration** The colours were sombre and figures often had heavily rouged cheeks.
• **Patch marks** To prevent kiln adhesion during firing, the unglazed bases of figures were supported on

raised clay pads that left distinctive 'patch marks'.
• **Later reproduction** It is important to note that a number of

Marks
• Early Derby figures were not marked and are identifiable only by the 'patch marks' on the base.
• From 1775 an incised crowned D and crossed batons was used, but only on biscuit porcelain figures.
• From c1800 an iron-red crowned D and crossed batons mark was used.

the Derby figures were reproduced from the original moulds in the latter half of the 19th century by the partnership of Stevenson & Hancock at the Derby King Street works. These are worth far less than their originals, a pair of figures can be bought for as little as £50 / €70 / $90. King Street figures are marked on their bases with a crowned 'D' and crossed batons mark which is flanked with an 'S' and 'H'.

Market information
- Recently at auction Duesbury-decorated 'dry edge' figures of 'Spring' and 'Winter' sold for £7,000 / €10,000 / $12,200 and £5,000 / €7,200 / $8,800 respectively. A part set of four, from a complete set of five figures of 'The Senses' sold for over £8,000 / €11,500 / $14,000 despite damage to the backs of each base.
- Sets of figures from 1758 onwards have a premium over individual figures. For instance, a set of 'The Four Quarters of the Globe' start from around £800 / €1,150 / $1,400. However, a pair of Derby putto figures dating from around 1765–70 may cost as little as £80 / €115 / $140.
- A rare Derby Royal Family biscuit group c1773 recently sold at auction for £7,200 / €10,400 / $12,600.
- Derby figures produced in the first half of the 19th century are generally less expensive.

Minton

The Minton factory produced figures in bone china from around 1830 to 1850. These mid-19th century figures often copy contemporary Meissen hard-paste porcelain examples and some even bear a pseudo crossed swords mark, such as that used by the German factory. An enamel-decorated Meissen-style Minton figure will start at around £150 / €220 / $260 in reasonable condition. Between 1830 and 1840 unmarked biscuit porcelain figures were produced, some depicting historical figures of the time, such as William Wilberforce.

These figures are not so popular today and can be purchased from as little as £50 / €70 / $90. Between 1840 and 1850 the production of Parian took over from biscuit porcelain. Some Parian busts were produced which range from £200 / €220 / $260 upwards, but in the main Minton concentrated on producing figures that today sell for around £100 / €145 / $175 upwards. The larger scale figures of 15¾in (40cm) high or more, such as 'Miranda' often sell in excess of £350 / €500 / $610. Generally, Minton Parian wares bear the impressed factory mark.

Robinson & Leadbeater

The factory of Robinson & Leadbeater was founded in Stoke in 1865 by partners Edward James Leadbeater and James Robinson. The company produced high-quality Parian wares that included a large number of busts as well as figures. It also produced centrepieces, baskets, flower holders and jugs.

The factory worked in close competition with the likes of Copeland, Minton, Worcester and Goss. Most Robinson & Leadbeater wares are unmarked. Robinson & Leadbeater differed from other factories in that it concentrated its whole production on Parian wares and continued long after the others had ceased production.

CONDITION

Although small chips are incidental to the whole appearance of a bust, missing limbs, damaged costumes and disfigured faces will alter the whole look of a classical statue.

• **Restoration** Damaged pieces would need to be undertaken by a skillful expert and the cost of this would be worth bearing in mind when making a purchase.

• **Stains** These could be a build up of dirt and can be removed with tepid water and the gentle use of a toothbrush. More permanent stains require expert advice before treating as Parian is slightly porous and is affected by some chemicals.

Market information

• The majority of busts and figures range from £80 / €115 / $140 to £300 / €430 / $520 but later examples from the 1890s, such as 'Princess Alexandra' and 'Lord Roberts' fetch between £30 / €45 / $50 and £50 / €70 / $90.

• One of the most valuable productions is a 20½in (52cm) bust of Queen Victoria, which can cost over £2,000 / €2,900 / $3,500 at auction. Busts of famous figures such as Lord Byron, c1890, below, are priced in the mid-hundreds.

Marks

This impressed initial mark was found on the back of Parian and bone china figural groups from c1885. A circular printed mark was used 'Robinson & Leadbeater England' 'Leadless Glaze Victorian Porcelain', c1891–1905.

Worcester

The Worcester factory was founded in 1751 by a group of 15 gentlemen, merchants and craftsmen, all managed by Dr John Wall. The porcelain manufactured by Worcester contained soapstone which made it very stable and able to withstand boiling water.

As a result Worcester concentrated on vast amounts of tea sets and dinnerware and made very few figures.

The complex story of Worcester contains many changes of ownership and family names which can be very confusing to the collector.

WORCESTER NAMES

Worcester is classified according to the factory's owners:

- **1751–74** Dr Wall or First period (Dr John Wall, William Davis and other partners).
- **1774–83** Davis period (William Davis principal manager.)
- **1783–92** Flight period (John and Joseph Flight.)
- **1792–1804** Flight & Barr period (Martin Barr senior, Joseph Flight and Martin Barr senior.)
- **1804–13** Barr, Flight & Barr period (Martin Barr senior, Joseph Flight and Martin Barr junior.)
- **1813–40** Flight, Barr & Barr period (Joseph Flight, Martin Barr junior and George Barr.)
- **1840–52** Chamberlain & Co period (The Chamberlain family and Flight, Barr & Barr amalgamated.) Figure production begins in earnest with models of animals and people.

Market information

- Kerr & Binns Worcester produced Parian figures and busts. The best examples, such as a busts of 'Bacchante' and 'Prince Albert' c1853, sell for between £450 / €650 / $790 and £500 / €720 / $880 respectively.
- Decorative pairs of figures such as the Egyptian musicians c1886, shown top right p.30, sell up to £2,500 / €3,600 / $4,400.
- Of the Victorian candle extinguishers the entry level example is 'Granny Snow', c 1890, costing around £100 /€145 / $175, whereas a good example of 'Town Girl', illustrated bottom left p.30, can cost up to £1,850 /€2,700 / $3,250
- The Kate Greenaway-inspired candle extinguishers, such as 'Town Girl' are the most desirable among collectors.

- **1852–62** Kerr & Binns period (W.H. Kerr and R.W. Binns joint owners.)
- **1862 to present** Worcester Royal Porcelain Co (known as Royal Worcester) – see pages 67–68 for further information.
- **James Hadley** This is the name most synonymous with figure modelling at the Royal Worcester factory in the late 19th century. He produced models of figures and figural candelabra, vases and dishes which normally bear his facsimile signature to the bases. The majority of Hadley's models were produced with a blush ivory and gilt-highlighted finish, such as the The Irishman, shown bottom right p.30, or in pastel coloured and glazed Parian. Among his most celebrated pieces is an Aesthetic period figural teapot c1882, modelled with a caricature of Oscar Wilde to one side, which has previously sold for £4,500 / €6,500 / $7,900.

CANDLE EXTINGUISHERS

Among the Royal Worcester buyers there is a niche group who specialize in collecting figural candle extinguishers. These novelties were produced in varying forms from the late 19th century onwards, some depicting a full-length figure, others in the form of a head. Many of the designs were continued in production for a long period so that this collecting area crosses over into the 20th century, and some of the highly collectable models were first produced at this time.

- **Marks** Examples are often unmarked, perhaps because they may originally have been produced with a small base which, over the years, has become lost or broken
- **Subject matter** Monks and nuns are the most common presentation.
- **Royal Worcester** In 1862 the company became the Worcester Royal Porcelain Company – Royal

Marks

- Early Worcester figures are rare and most are unmarked.
- From 1862 the Royal Worcester factory used a printed or impressed mark of a crowned circle enclosing interlaced Ws around a C encircling the number 51.
- A date code system was used from 1867 wherein a series of dots were added to the mark, with one dot added for each successive year. See p.67 for details of later marks.
- The words 'Royal Worcester England' were added in 1891.

Worcester – and the production of extinguishers continued with an extensive range of humourous and finely observed subjects.

• **Production** Some examples which had been manufactured by the Kerr & Binns factory continued to be produced by Royal Worcester, but many new models were added over the years.

• **Pattern Books** Most Worcester figures are listed in pattern books or price lists, but occasionally an unrecorded example arises.

• **Production period** It appears that the models were produced on a rotation system, sometimes with a gap of a few years, although the two most popular characters, 'The Monk' and 'The Abbess', were never out of production, even during the two World Wars.

• **Decoration** It is noticeable that the decoration on early

extinguishers is finer than on later examples, because latterly the artists were allowed less time to spend on their work.

PEGGING
All Worcester products have a narrow, unglazed margin around the interior of the footrim. This was a process known as 'pegging', caused when a peg was used to wipe away the thick glaze around the edge of a piece. This stopped the glaze from running onto the shelf of the kiln and becoming burnt.

DESIGNERS
• **James Hadley** Figural wares, particularly those made by James Hadley, proved more popular than the sculptural pieces. They are usually functional, incorporating a vase, a bowl or a candlestick.

• **Kate Greenaway** Figures inspired by the drawings of children by Kate Greenaway were the most popular, both then and now.

For further information on
Worcester see pages 52–68

Continental 18th & 19thC

The earliest Continental European ceramic figures were of tin-glazed earthenware, made in Italy (maiolica) and Holland (Delft) in the 17th and 18th centuries. These pieces usually had a functional purpose, such as a figure holding an open basket that would have been used for salt or sweetmeats, or a figure formed as a jug or supporting candleholders. Animals appeared on the covers of Delft butter tubs and Delft models of cows were left hollow and used as cream jugs. Purely decorative figures did not generally appear in pottery until the mid-18th century, by which time the potters were taking their lead from Meissen, Europe's most important and prolific manufacturer of porcelain.

Proper hard-paste porcelain such as that imported from China did not exist in Europe until its invention at Meissen in the mid-1710s. As the newly invented wares were expensive to make and the failure rate was high, successful pieces commanded high prices. The first figures were made in the 1720s and production was in full swing by the mid-1730s. The formula for porcelain had been kept a secret, but it soon spread, first to Austria, then to other German principalities and across Europe. By 1760 many other factories were making porcelain figures.

Unlike pottery, porcelain was a precious commodity and the figures produced were treated as miniature sculptures, with designs inspired by contemporary engravings and also from first-hand observation. At the Sèvres factory in France figure production was also spurred on by the appearance of imported Meissen figures, but the factory's soft-paste, very white body lent itself more to biscuit porcelain than glazed and coloured figures. The Sèvres porcelain figures made for table decoration are therefore much closer in appearance to the sugar and confectionery figures they replaced on the banquet tables of the royal and rich.

By the second half of the 18th century figure production was underway throughout Europe and figures became cheaper and less exclusive. They were being purchased as decorative items, and many more single and pairs of figures were made, rather than large sets. During the 19th century much figure production, both pottery and porcelain, looked back to what had gone before, particularly at Meissen. The mechanization of production as a result of the industrial revolution meant that more and more factories were able to produce figures, many of poor quality, that were intended to be sold cheaply to adorn the mantelpieces of the middle classes. Not all 19th-century figures were derivative or of poor quality, however. Factories such as Royal Dux made slip-cast large-scale figures that were intended to be a more affordable alternative to bronze, ivory or marble sculptures.

Despite mechanization, figure production was still a complex process. Good quality, hand-painted porcelain figures remained relatively expensive – as are the porcelain figures still being made at factories such as Meissen and Nymphenburg today.

BERLIN

The first Berlin factory was in production from c1752 to 1757, managed by W. K. Wegely. Most surviving examples are white hard-paste porcelain figures based on Meissen models.

In 1761 J. E. Gotzkowsky built a second factory, which was bought by Frederick the Great in 1763, together with a large stock of unglazed wares. It is therefore not certain that all marked pieces (figures and table wares) with the Gotzkowsky mark were painted in this period. Many artists had worked at Meissen, including the Meyer brothers, Friedrich Elias and Wilhelm Christian, who produced a series of figures called 'The Cries of Berlin'. The factory went on to become highly influential and has remained state property to this day.

- **Early Berlin pieces** Porcelain of the 18th century is extremely rare. You are far more likely to come across exquisitely decorated 19th-century pieces (see below, dated c1875), although these are easily confused with porcelain made around the same time in both Vienna and Paris.
- **Characteristics** Figures modelled by F. F. Meyer characteristically had disproportionately small heads and elongated bodies. By c1775 the bases had become more architectural

Berlin marks

Berlin marks include a sceptre on early pieces; from 1832 an orb appears. The mark, below left, was used between 1837 and 1844 Towards the end of WWII the models, library and porcelain collection were moved to Selb to escape destruction. The mark on the right was used on pieces made at Selb.

in design, notably with oval and square pedestals (see p149).

DOCCIA

The Doccia factory was founded by the Marchese Carlo Ginori, near Florence, Italy, in 1735 and is still operating today.

Doccia marks

The mark, introduced after Carlo Ginori's death in 1757, is a star, either impressed or painted in red, blue or gold.

- **Characteristics** The early porcelain at Doccia was a type of greyish hard paste with a rough texture. The characteristically thin glaze of Doccia porcelain emphasizes the underlying greyness, making it easy to recognize. However, the tone can be confused with Vezzi porcelain, notably on pieces made during the first years when Doccia had no mark.
- **Subjects** Doccia made numerous slip-cast figures, such as the Eastern Gentleman below, dated 1750–1800. Many represent Classical subjects with well-defined musculature, and have usually been left in the white.

- **Bases** Those made during the rococo period are quite vigorously modelled, and these were also used on miniature busts that were quite popular at Doccia.

DUTCH DELFT

Dutch potters began to copy Oriental products in the 1500s, using local clay instead of porcelain, which they were then unable to produce. There were two main centres of production, Rotterdam and Delft, with about 40 factories between them. Many types of Delft wares were produced, often reflecting the nature of society at the time and were largely functional. Decorative items are rare but tend to have survived in better condition, as they were not subjected to the rigours of daily use.

- **Look For** Early Dutch Delft is rarely marked, but by the end of the 17th century the well established factories began to use and register their own pottery marks. They usually comprise a group of initials representing the owner of the factory or a device, such as an axe for Het Bijltje (The Hatchet factory) or bells for De 3 Klokken (The Three Bells factory).
- **Fakes** Collectors of Delft animal figures such as the Delft cow above, dated c1750, should be aware that reproductions were made in the late 19th century and these often included fake marks such as the 'AK', or 'PAK' device of De Grieksche A factory.

ERNST BOHNE

From 1854 Bohne made hard-paste porcelain at Thuringia in Germany (see Hawk below, c1890). It was marked with an anchor bearing the initials 'E. B.', or simply 'B'.

FRANKENTHAL

Paul A. Hannong began porcelain production at the Frankenthal factory in 1755 under the patronage of Elector Carl Theodor. The company produced a wide range of figures and domestic wares in hard-paste porcelain, decorated with colours that tended to soak into the

glaze and lacked brilliance.

Frankenthal figures are among the best made in Germany. They are invariably stiffly modelled, but have an undeniable, doll-like charm with small, innocent features, big eyes, rouged cheeks and oversized hands. The plasticity of the porcelain allowed for quite detailed modelling, and the thin, opaque glaze does not obscure it.

• **Key modellers** were Johann Friedrich Lück and Johann Wilhelm Lanz. Lück's cousin Karl Gottlieb joined the factory in 1756 and made a wide range of rococo figures, such as the Young Woman and Old Man, above, and some amusing but not

Frankenthal marks

From 1755 to 1756 the mark was 'PH' for Paul Hannong, sometimes followed by a lion rampant and the quartered chequered shield of the Palatinate in blue. From 1759 to 62 the letters 'JAH' were used, for Joseph-Adam Hannong. Throughout the history of the factory the initials 'CT' in underglaze blue beneath a crown were used. Sometimes the last two numerals of the date were added to the monogram, generally below it.

very convincing Oriental musicians. Conrad Linck was appointed chief modeller in 1762 and introduced the first hints of neo-classicism to the factory's style. He modified the traditional factory base, retaining the undulation and the rococo scrolls, but making it more of a simple brown

Identifying marks

• Ceramic manufacturers began to mark their wares as early as the 16th century.
• There were no rules or standards for marking until the late 19th century.
• Marks of successful factories such as Meissen or Sèvres were extensively copied by smaller makers hoping to sell more of their products by association. Collectors should be aware of this, and treat marks on ceramics with caution.
• Many 18th-century factories did not mark their wares at all – which inevitably leads to further confusion.
When checking marks, look for the following:
• Appearance, i.e. is it printed or painted, underglaze or overglaze, incised or raised? What colour is it? If the mark that appears on the item does not tally with the description then you probably don't have the right mark.

• Are there incised or impressed letters or numbers? Sometimes impressed numbers can indicate the year of manufacture, but more often they are factory shape or pattern numbers, especially on figures.
• Is the piece pottery or porcelain and does the style of the object match what the date should be?
• The country of origin usually does not appear on a piece until after 1891. 'Germany' does not usually appear until after 1918 and 'Bohemia' only appears until 1918.
• Some marks are outright fakes, usually put on pieces in the late 19th or 20th century with the intent to deceive. Usually the quality of these pieces will be the giveaway.
• Figures are usually less well marked than tablewares, so don't despair – an unmarked figure could well be an interesting piece.

mound and adding little tufts of green moss. J. P. Melchior also joined the factory in 1779 and, now influenced by neo-classicism, he turned children into putti. Many of his figures were so flawless that they were sold unpainted in marble-like biscuit.

• **Look for** Melchior's figures which have a rather severe appearance.

The factory closed in 1799, but the moulds continued to be used by many other 19th-century German companies.

CLOSTER VEILSDORF

Closter Veilsdorf was established in 1760 in Thuringia, Germany, by Prince Friedrich Wilhelm Eugen von Hildburghausen. After his death in 1795 it was sold to the sons of Gotthelf Greiner of Limbach, and Friedrich Greiner of Rauenstein, and remained in the hands of their family until 1822.

• **Characteristics** Closter Veilsdorf figures are usually small, with little definition – for example, the fingers are not separate – and the faces, which are quite highly coloured, lack character. However, the final result is usually charming. The bases for the figures are simple mounds sometimes lightly carved with scrolls.

LIMBACH

Second in importance to Closter Veilsdorf, Limbach was founded in 1772 by Gotthelf Greiner, and was also in Thuringia, Germany.

The early porcelain is slightly yellow, but the later glaze has a lighter, more delicate quality.

The most successful products were stiff, charmingly naïve figures that mostly represented peasants and citizens, such as the Fruit Seller, c1780, above and imaginary royalty in unlikely, theatrical robes.

LUDWIGSBURG

The Ludwigsburg factory in Germany originally produced faïence, but was converted to manufacture porcelain by Carl Eugen, Duke of Wurtemberg.

The company came under the direction of J. J. Ringler, who was accompanied by Gottlieb Friedrich Riedel.

• **Figures** Riedel was responsible for the creation of the rococo-style figures which were the finest of Ludwigsburg's products. Occasionally naïve, they were crisply modelled and precisely decorated in pastel colours which blend with the smoky tone of the glaze. See pp146–48 for more Ludwigsburg figures.

• **Other modellers** at the factory were Johann Christian Wilhem Beyer, who was overseer of the modelling workshop c1764–67 and Johann Beyer and Johann Heinrich von Dannecker, both in the 1790s. The factory closed in 1824.

• **Figural subject matter** Ballets

Ludwigsburg marks

• The standard mark between 1758 and 1793 is a ducal crown above a pair of interlaced Cs – the cipher of Carl Eugen. This can be confused with the mark of Niderviller, but that is usually more loosely executed. Other, rarer, marks include:

• A royal crown over the initials FR or WR, for kings Frederick and William respectively.

• Stag's antlers from the arms of Würtemberg, either as a single set or in a group of three.

• Most marks are in underglaze blue, but a few were gilded or drawn in iron-red or black.

• On a very small number of pieces the mark has been impressed into the body.

and masques were the height of fashion in the mid-18th century, but miniature groups are among the most famous of all the Ludwigsburg figures. Most desirable are the figures designed by Jean-Jacob Louis such as the Butcher figure, 1762–72, bottom right, p.34, that represented scenes from the Venetian fair which was held annually by the Duke of Würtemberg. This was followed by groups modelled by Wilhelm Beyer, representing daily life, such as tavern scenes and cobblers' shops. Although less than 3½in (9cm) in height, these groups are much more animated than the larger figures. Later figures, after 1793, were of a much poorer quality.

MONTELUPO
Production of majolica began at Montelupo in northern Italy in the second half of the 13th century, and its golden age of production was possibly between 1450 and 1530. The Montelupo factory was famous for its brilliant blood red pigment, also known as 'Montelupo red', usually applied during the third firing, and its blue pigment made from cobalt and lead oxides.
• **Figural subject matter** In the first half of the 17th century potters produced high-quality single figures, mostly squires and knights

NEVERS
The Italian Conrade family first brought artistic earthenware to Nevers, central France, in the 16th century, and the city became the

most prominent manufacturing centre in France during the 17th century. The Italian style was eventually dismissed in favour of a new native style.
• **Figural subject matter** The style of the figures produced was mainly drawn from pastoral romances.

NIDERVILLER
Founded in 1735, this French factory originally produced both porcelain and faïence. In 1748 the factory was sponsored by the aristocrat Jean-Louis Beyerlé, who encouraged the production of porcelain. The figure of the Apple Seller, below, was produced c1775. By the beginning of the

Niderviller marks
The black N mark has been used on pieces from the start of production. The town name also appears, either impressed in full, or as the abbreviation 'Nider' in black.

1800s figures were again being made in both faïence and porcelain.

NYMPHENBURG
Nymphenburg was among the main German porcelain-producing centres of the 18th century, founded at Nymphenburg by Ignaz Niedermeyer with the sponsorship of Elector Max III Joseph of Bavaria and the help of porcelain painter Joseph Jakob

Ringler. The early high-quality porcelain was used to produce a wide range of domestic wares.
The modeller Franz Anton Bustelli, whose work was second only to J. J. Kändler at Meissen, modelled characters from the Commedia dell 'Arte as well as allegorical figures, Chinese characters, Turks, Moors, ladies and gentlemen, merchants, street vendors, shepherds and shepherdesses, religious subjects and dogs and cats. In 1770 the factory passed to Karl Theodor of the Palatinate, who already had interests in the factory at Frankenthal. The biscuit porcelain figure of a woman, above, was made c1800. The Nymphenburg factory took second place until the Frankenthal

Nevers marks
With a very few exceptions, early wares were unmarked, but this mark is attributed to Denis Lefebvre (c1629–49).

works closed in 1799.

The company remained in State possession until 1862, and was then leased into private ownership. The factory still exists today.

• **Look for** The essential elements in Bustelli's unique style are obvious, even in the simplest models. The graceful figures are detached and ethereal, with the lower parts a little elongated, in the traditional Bavarian style. Bustelli often modelled his figures as interacting pairs that were made to be displayed together. Unlike other makers, Bustelli's figures seem to grow out of their bases, which are usually flat with scrolled edges.

SÈVRES

The Sèvres porcelain manufactory was founded at Vincennes, France, by local craftsmen in 1740. It acquired Royal patronage in 1745 before moving to Sèvres in 1756. Although some figures were produced in the early period, the factory is most noted for its white biscuit porcelain figures, produced to a consistently high standard from moulds made after designs by the artist François Boucher. Figure production continued after the revolution, by which time the factory was state owned, and throughout the 19th century.

• **Characteristics** Early Vincennes

and Sèvres biscuit has a white, coarse, sugary appearance. Later pieces have a finer, smoother surface.

VIENNA

After Meissen, Vienna was the second European factory to begin producing hard-paste porcelain. The factory was founded by Claudius Innocentius du Paquier, who bribed and cajoled the secret of porcelain manufacture from various disgruntled Meissen employees. Until the 1780s Vienna produced a similar range of wares to those made by Meissen, but figures were rarer and more stiffly modelled, with slightly awkward stances, mostly depicting Chinese or Commedia dell'Arte characters. In 1744 the company was taken over by the State and the hitherto limited production increased in quantity. In 1784 a new director was appointed and the factory began producing wares in the neo-classical style. The Vienna factory closed in 1864 but many imitations of its more elaborate wares were produced in the late 19th century.

Porcelain from the du Paquier period (1719–44) is rarer than Meissen and few pieces have survived. It is similar in composition to early Meissen and often has a greenish tone; the glaze in general is much thinner and less glassy and dominant colours are puce, iron-red and monochromes. Compared with Meissen the manner of painting is naïve.

• **First state period (1744-1841)** The greatest innovation of this period was the wide variety of figures, particularly those modelled by Johann Josef Niedermeyer (d1784), who was chief modeller from 1747. A series of dwarves copied from engravings by the French printmaker Jacques Callot (1592–1635) is particularly notable.

Many were left in the white, while others were painted in very pale colours, such as lilac and lemon-yellow. The bases are usually a simple pad shape as in the Mother and Daughter figure, c1765, above, and are frequently embellished with a wavy gilt border around the bottom edge.

• **Sorgenthal Period (1784–c1830)** Figures were made on a limited scale at the end of the 18th century. Generally in biscuit porcelain, they were based on Classical sculptures and Pompeian paintings, or were busts of the imperial family and such luminaries as the composer Haydn.

Marks

The characteristic interlaced L's mark rarely, if ever, appears on figures.

Figures and groups marked with incised interlaced L's are usually poor quality 19th-century copies made by other French factories.

Vienna marks

During the 19th century the Vienna shield mark was much used by other factories that copied the Vienna style. The use of inverted commas, ie 'Vienna' is widely used to denote the origin of such pieces when cataloguing.

Dresden

The name Dresden does not refer to a single maker, but a combination of at least 40 porcelain workshops or decorators in and around the city of Dresden in Germany, which became a major centre of porcelain production. Numerous factories produced wares in the style of Meissen and Sèvres, and many of these makers used copies of old Meissen marks. The best pieces may be mistaken for Meissen, but the hard-paste porcelain used by most workshops is less white and refined than Meissen porcelain, and the decoration was not always carefully applied. Dresden workshops included Adolph Hammann (est mid-1860s), Richard Klemm (est late 1860s), Donath & Co (est c1872) and Oswald Lorenz (est 1880).

One of the best was the factory of Helena Wolfsohn (est 1843) who copied Meissen wares of the 1740s, and even added the Augustus Rex mark until Meissen obtained an injunction forcing her to change the mark to a crown above the word 'Dresden'.

Among the most common products are modelled or cast mythological, allegorical and pastoral figures and groups, birds and animals. Figures usually wear 18th-century costume but are larger and far more elaborate than Meissen originals. Groups may include several heavily decorated figures crammed onto one base. Dresden pieces are not in the same league as Meissen originals but, at a lower price, they offer good value for money.

CONTINENTAL

PRODUCTION
Although there was a tradition in Dresden, stretching back to the 18th century, of producing fine porcelain figures, less expensive figures by Dresden manufacturers also found a ready market. Very inexpensive figures would be made in a single two-piece mould, while more elaborate examples, often pleasing and of reasonable quality, were assembled from many pieces.

WHAT TO LOOK FOR
• **Marks** Dresden figures are often not marked except by impressed numbers (usually factory shape codes not dates) and buyers should not dwell on the maker of the piece but on the quality.
• **Quality** The piece should be well made, with crisp details, see the 19th-century candlesticks, left.
• **Colours** The colours should make sense and look realistic and not be too garish, such as the budgerigar, c1890, right. Many late 19th-century Dresden figures have a distinctive pale turquoise and pink colouration.

Market Information
• Figures made by the various Dresden and other German factories often copy Meissen but are generally of poorer quality, and prices reflect this.
• Single figures would probably start at under £100 / €145 / $175 increasing to several hundred for figural candelabra and large groups.
• Condition is important – small losses should be acceptable, but a restuck arm or head will probably reduce the value to as little as a quarter of the 'good condition' price.

Fairings

Fairings, small figural groups that were made from porcelain and often brightly coloured, derive their name from the English fairs where they were sold or given as prizes between 1850 and 1914. Cheap, cheerful and aimed at the popular end of the market, fairings anticipated the saucy humour of the seaside postcard, complete with punning captions.

Although English in theme and caption, fairings were in fact made in Germany for export. The principal manufacturer from c1880–1900 was Conta & Boehme of Possnek. Demand for these German-made items came to an end with the outbreak of WWI. The value of any fairing depends upon the rarity of the subject and the quality of the modelling.

WHAT TO LOOK FOR
• **Figural Subjects** Favourite subjects included marital scenes, courting couples, animals and children. Events from everyday life, such as a visit to the dentist, are featured and the Crimea and the Franco-Prussian Wars also inspired models. Some pieces were in the form of match strikers or spill vases, such as the Welsh Tea Party, 1880, right.
• **Quality** had declined by the end of the 19th century and new products such as the crested china made by Goss provided increasing competition in the souvenir market.

The Welsh Tea party

Conta & Boehme marks
Though Conta & Boehme's early fairings were unmarked, from the late 1870s some models were stamped on the base with a crooked arm holding a dagger, and the pieces were also given an impressed serial number. After 1891 the words 'Made in Germany' were sometimes added.

Gebrüder Heubach

The company was founded by the Heubach brothers in Thuringia, Germany, originally to make porcelain, including figures and bisque dolls' heads. The factory was established in 1840 and by 1905 the firm was registered as making entire dolls. Gebrüder Heubach is famous above all for the variety of its bisque-headed character dolls. Among the firm's other products were bonnet dolls (with bonnet hats), small bisque figures known as piano babies and mantelpiece figures. The factory continued production until c1945.

PIANO BABIES
Gebrüder Heubach made all-bisque figures of crawling or seated babies or children with a variety of expressions, see the girls, c1900, right. These figures were intended for display on pianos and hence became known as 'piano babies' by collectors.
• **Marks** It is important that both these figures and the larger 'mantelpiece figures' bear the Heubach marks, as similar unmarked pieces that were reproduced by other firms are not as valuable. Most dolls are marked with the rising sun mark or 'Heubach' incorporated into a square. These marks should not be confused with the horseshoe mark generally used by Ernst Heubach, who was also a doll maker.

Meissen

From the early 1720s, beautifully modelled and painted figures were produced at the Meissen porcelain factory in Germany, establishing its reputation as the pre-eminent porcelain factory in Europe. The extensive range of figures and wares are characterized by an extraordinary virtuosity of modelling; the expressions and sense of movement remain a testament to the skills of the painters, modellers and other artisans employed. The factory dominated the mid-18th century style of porcelain, and Meissen wares and figures were imitated by craftsmen at other factories throughout Europe.

Small figures used to decorate the dining tables of the wealthy were originally modelled in sugar, wax, or gum by cooks and confectioners. Demand for more permanent material led to the production of the first porcelain figures at Meissen in 1727, when Johann Gottlieb Kirchner was appointed the first chief modeller. Kirchner initially produced figures of saints and animals in strong baroque style. In the same year, Frederick Augustus I, Elector of Saxony, commissioned Kirchner to create 910 monumental models of animals and birds to decorate his Japanese-style palace in Dresden. However, the thick porcelain body required to make large items meant that pieces tended to crack or even completely collapse in the kiln. The most famous modeller, Johann Kändler, joined the factory in 1731 to assist Kirchner, but he too could not solve the technical problems. The difficulties and the high cost of producing such works encouraged Kändler to experiment with the production of small-scale figures. He then went on to produce some of the finest individual figures and groups ever made at the factory. His early figures have a wonderful sense of liveliness and movement that other manufacturers were unable to

imitate. They are vigorously modelled, dramatic and sculptural, with flamboyant or theatrical gestures. Among the range of subjects were exotic birds, figures from distant lands, romantic couples and court jesters. By the mid-18th century the fashion for baroque style was declining, to be replaced by the delicate, light-hearted rococo style. Figures of lovers in idyllic pastoral settings, as well as allegorical and mythological figures representing the seasons, the months, Classical gods and goddesses were produced. From 1750 the factory made smaller scale figures that were painted with pastel colours. The simple, flower-encrusted bases of previous years were abandoned in favour of more elaborately scrolled bases. Other wares became influenced by these Meissen figures and it was not unusual to find knops on the covers of teapots and larger vessels in the form of small figures.

By the beginning of the 19th century the Meissen factory was in decline, due to competition from other European factories and the effects of the Napoleonic Wars (1799–1815). However, by the 1820s production had increased four-fold as a result of using round kilns and the introduction of gloss gilding (a cheaper method of decoration using gold mixed in a solution). Fortunes were further revived when, in the early 1830s, rococo styles became fashionable again and the company began to reuse their 18th-century figure moulds. These figures, produced under the supervision of chief modeller Ernst August Leuteritz, were in great demand and formed the bulk of the output during the second half of the 19th century. Carefully moulded and painted to the highest standards, they represent typical 18th-century subjects such as shepherds and shepherdesses, the aristocracy and allegorical figures of the Seasons and the four Continents.

CONTINENTAL

WHAT TO LOOK FOR

- **Faces** on Kändler's figures are usually a bit severe, but the colouring is very subtle.
- **Figures** in groups are always separate and very detailed.
- **Hair** is usually very finely executed with black or dark brown brush strokes.
- **Modelling** has so much twisting movement that figures often look as if they are about to topple over.
- **Weight** Meissen porcelain is very dense and figures feel heavy compared to similar figures from other factories.

FIGURAL SUBJECTS

- **Ladies and gentlemen** of the court.
- **Characters** from the Italian Commedia dell'Arte.
- **Harlequins** – most popular of all Kändler figures, modelled between 1738 and 1744.
- **Other** sets of figures include: soldiers such as the bandleader, 1765, below, peasants in national costume, shepherds and shepherdesses, The Cries of Paris, The Cries of London, Chinese and Middle Eastern figures, and animals and birds, particularly parrots.

KÄNDLER MARKS

The earliest Kändler figures were often glazed and marked on the underside. However, by 1740 the bases were usually unglazed and

Marcolini marks

The crossed swords of the Marcolini period (1774–1814) are larger and longer than on earlier products. They have a star between the hilts, and sometimes the Roman numerals I or II have been added below.

After Marcolini the star was no longer used and from the early 19th century onwards, the bases of figures are incised with large cursive numbers and stamped with small serif numbers.

their marks were ground away when flattened. As a result it became the custom to paint a very small mark on the back or side of a figure during the next ten years.

EARLY FIGURES

- **Colour palette** was dominated by vivid colours – strong red, yellow and black – applied in broad washes.
- **Bases** were a simple pad shape with applied flowers and leaves, often turquoise at first but naturalistic green by the 1740s; religious figures had sculptural bases.
- **Important modellers** include Kirchner and Kändler.

- **Important designers** include Johann Friedrich Eberlain (1695–1749), Friedrich Elias Meyer (1723–85) and Peter Reinicke (1715–68).

LATER FIGURES

- **Colour palette** often included pastel-green, mauve, and pale yellow.
- **Bases** were unglazed with marks on back and side of figure; rococo scrolls around the edges, heightened with gilding and enamelled colours, and sometimes pierced.
- **Subjects** include lovers in pastoral settings, representations of the seasons, the months, classical gods and goddesses.

Market Information

In almost 300 years of production, the Meissen factory has produced a greater range of figures in larger quantities than any other European porcelain factory.

- The highest prices have been for the large bird and animal figures made in the 1730s, with a pair of birds recently sold in Paris for a seven-figure sum. A good 1740s Meissen Commedia dell'Arte figure group could cost anywhere between £50,000–100,000 / €72,000–144,000 / $87,500–175,000. These prices have risen rapidly over the last ten years as their rarity and quality has become appreciated.
- Groups of lovers and Cupid figures made between 1750 and 1775 can be found at reasonable prices (see p.160). Interestingly, it is not all about the date, as some 19th-century figures can make almost as much as their 18th-century counterparts, due to their good quality.
- Prices for 19th-century Meissen figures were very strong in the late 1980s and early '90s but the market has been quieter recently. There are definitely bargains to be had now. Some late 19th-century figures – those designed at that time, not copies of 18th-century models – can make relatively high prices. Such figures tend to be rarer than the traditional groups of lovers and cupids as less of them were sold at the time of production and, as a consequence, they can be hard to find today, which inevitably leads to higher prices.

Royal Dux

Royal Dux, based in Duchcov in Czechoslovakia, was the most prolific Bohemian factory. Production began in 1853 and concentrated on animals and classically inspired maidens. A small number of pieces were more risqué in appearance and these were more popular in America and Europe.

Many of the factory's records have been lost over the years as a result of various upheavals in Czecholslovakia's political history and, therefore, much of its history and product details are vague. After the collapse of the Communist government in 1990 the company was privatized and is now concentrating on regaining the success that it achieved during the period between the two World Wars.

WHAT TO LOOK FOR

• **Colouring** This is sometimes inspired by traditional Viennese bronze and ivory sculptures.

• **Marks** These include an applied salmon pink triangle impressed with 'Royal Dux' in arch form.

The word 'Bohemia' appears on wares made before 1918, after which the country became Czechoslovakia. Pieces made after that date bear the word 'Czech.'

Some wares carry both marks and were probably made c1918 or held, undecorated, in stock.

For examples of Royal Dux figures made in the 20th century please see pp199–202.

Samson

Edmé Samson and his son Emile originally worked as decorators in Paris in 1845 where they specialized in china matching. This venture was very successful and the company expanded into reproducing other porcelain wares such as figures. These sold for a fraction of the price of genuine Meissen or Chinese wares and, although Samson always stated that it made honest reproductions, many pieces were sold as genuine articles by unscrupulous dealers. The Samson mark – a conjoined SS – rarely appeared and fake marks from all the great factories were consequently used in its place. As a result, today many pieces are still undiscovered Samson reproductions. The irony continues as Samson porcelain has become respected in its own right, due to its good quality and attractive decoration, and now many fakes are being mistaken for Samson pieces.

WHAT TO LOOK FOR

• **Style** Samson figures are often slightly over-elaborate, and the use of colour is largely insensitive compared to the originals they were copying.

• **Unglazed areas** reveal the smooth, greyish colour of the hard-paste porcelain that is often very different from that of the originals they were copying.

• **Colours** Samson bases are a different colour green to original

Meissen and are subtly rounded rather than sharp-edged.

• **Fine kiln grit** This is often found on the perimeter of the base.

• **Most collectable** These are Sampson copies of Meissen figures by Eberlein or Kändler. Their famous version of Eberlein's Tyrolean dancers is accurately modelled and coloured, although early Meissen is more meticulously decorated. The Turkish Girl, c1900, right, is a copy of a Bloor Derby figure.

CONTINENTAL

Decorative Arts

The term Decorative Arts covers a range of movements in the field of design between 1850 and c1940. Broadly speaking these are Arts & Crafts, the Aesthetic Movement, Art Nouveau and Art Deco.

By 1850 there was a concern that the industrial age was beginning to remove the concept of hand crafting. The Arts & Crafts movement was a real attempt by some of the leading designers of the day, such as William Morris and A. W. N. Pugin, to reintroduce a style of craftsmanship whereby hand-applied decoration and naturalistic form would be harmonized together to form a room setting of great simplicity and beauty. The Aesthetic Movement of the 1870s and early 1880s followed very closely on the heels of Arts & Crafts. At this time new opportunities existed for travel to exotic destinations such as Japan, and artists and merchants saw a growing demand for Japanese works of art. Japanese lacquer ware in particular became much imitated with its use of delicate natural imagery which soon found its way onto British ceramics and furniture. Minton Art Pottery owed a great debt to Japanese imagery as did many Worcester pieces. By the 1880s there was more demand than ever before for good quality design and the end of the decade saw an exciting style begin to evolve throughout Europe and the United States – Art Nouveau. The term itself was coined by the merchant Samuel Bing, who chose it as the name of his shop in Paris where he gathered together all manner of objects and furnishings that exuded this new style. As a style Art Nouveau owed a debt to Arts & Crafts and the Aesthetic Movement. It too grew out of a desire to bring harmony and natural imagery to bear on a diverse range of hand-crafted objects.

As the new century approached, the worldwide love for Art Nouveau began to shape the look of the modern world. Art Nouveau was becoming much more mass-produced than the earlier Arts & Crafts style

had ever been, and this was partly in response to the huge worldwide demand it fostered. Many leading artists saw the female form as ideally suited to this style, and hence one of the chief expressions of Art Nouveau is the maiden with long flowing hair, often rising out of a seashell or a wooded glade. The woman of 1900 was not seen as an emancipated free spirit but as an image of purity and natural beauty.

As the world moved towards war in 1914, the Art Nouveau style was beginning to lose its universal appeal. The horrors of war meant that young people wanted a lifestyle that would help them forget what they had been exposed to, and by 1920 a new and more streamlined style began to emerge. This was a style that captured the spirit of the `Jazz Age' and it was known as Art Deco. Yet again, it's true origins were to be found in Paris. Many of the French designers who had been successful in producing Art Nouveau pieces now turned their attentions to Art Deco. Gone were the demure maidens of 1900 and in their place came the 1920s flapper girl, a free-thinking spirit whose main concerns were career and partying till dawn. She was depicted in short skirts or trouser suits, often walking her two borzoi dogs. The finest examples are the beautifully carved and painted works of Ferdinand Preiss and Demêtre Chiparus. Both artists used bronze and ivory to depict the young girl of the day expressing herself in dance. Much of the architecture of the era also reflected the new Art Deco style, particularly in the US where the Manhattan skyline featured such marvels as the Empire States Building and the Chrysler Building. Hollywood, too, had its impact on designers, as more and more people became exposed to the glamour of movie sets. Ceramic artists such as Clarice Cliff and Susie Cooper made teawares that captured the bold freedoms of Art Deco style and allowed dreary suburban houses to radiate colour. Art Deco was all about streamlining and doing away with the ornamental and fussy.

Market information

Today, the market for Decorative Arts is polarized in a way that reflects the entire antiques trade. Buyers are looking for key examples by known names, paying great attention to both the scarcity and condition of a piece.

• This is an excellent time to find bargains in the field of Decorative Arts because there is much less competition for 'style' items that don't have an important maker's name behind them. Hence collectors can buy some Arts & Crafts, Art Nouveau or Art Deco pieces more cheaply than they could 20 years ago.

• Top designer names are more popular than ever although average examples of their work will warrant very little attention, whereas the best examples will be fought over.

• A flawed example may only be worth a third of what collectors will pay for the same model but in excellent condition.

Ashtead Pottery

Ashtead Potters Ltd was founded by Sir Lawrence Weaver in 1923. The factory operated at the Victoria Works in Ashtead, Surrey and employed disabled ex-servicemen who worked alongside many prominent designers. At its peak, 40 servicemen were creating a wide range of wares from figures and commemoratives to everyday crockery.

During 1924 and 1925 the Ashtead potters showed their skills and wares to the public at working stands at the Wembley British Empire Exhibitions. The factory continued for another ten years until increased competition, the Depression, and the death of Lawrence Weaver forced it to close in January 1935.

Artists

Prominent artists who were involved with the Ashtead Potters were:

• Phoebe Stabler, also associated with Poole Pottery (see page 50)

• Anne Acheson, also associated with Royal Worcester (see page 67)

• Percy Metcalfe, also associated with the design of coins, medals and seals

• Donald Gilbert, a sculptor who exhibited at the Royal Academy

MARKS

All Ashtead Pottery has very precise marks which coded every stage of manufacture. These include:

• A stylized tree stamp which includes the words 'Ashtead Potters' and was the general mark of the factory (see left).

• An early postcode

• A date code which was in the form of a symbol e.g. a star or triangle

• Artist's hand-drawn mark in the form of another symbol.

• Three digit number which was used when the blank was brought in from another factory. The number was their dating system but the piece could have been sitting on the Ashtead Potters shelf for years, hence the frequent date difference.

• Model number in the form of a 'P' for plate and a number.

• Glaze code in the form of a letter e.g. 'm' for orange.

• Two letters referring to the decoration e.g. 'cn' for a sailing ship.

• Hand-thrown mark in the form of 'HT', this was used when the piece was not made in the usual slipware.

Market information

Ashtead's output was surprisingly large when one considers that they were in production for only 12 years. As with most ceramics, value depends largely on rarity and condition.

• Robert Kay of Bumbles in Ashtead reports that most figures by Phoebe Stabler and Percy Metcalfe will sell for £350–400 / €500–570 / $600–700.

• A rarer figure, such as 'Shy' by Phoebe Stabler, has been known to command £1,000 / €1,450 / $1,750.

Bovey Pottery

The Bovey Tracey Pottery Co began in 1842 at the Folly Pottery in Bovey Tracey. Bought by Messrs Thomas Wentworth Buller and John Divett, the factory produced Staffordshire-type tableware, figures, commemoratives and souvenirs. In 1894 the company changed its name to Bovey Pottery Co; The factory closed in 1957.

Marks
The shield mark, left, was used between 1949–56 whilst the shield mark on the right appeared from 1954–57.

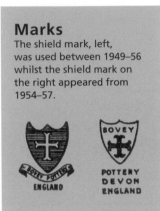

WHAT TO LOOK FOR
• **Designers** The figures designed by Gwyneth Holt and Fenton Wyness during the 1940s.
• **Characters** The cream-glazed figures designed by Gwyneth Holt were in the form of wartime, or political characters and were often known as 'Our Gang' or 'On Parade' and included 'The Pilot', 'Stalin', and 'The Sargeant Major' (see right, dated c1945).
• **Rarities** Figures representing Hitler and Mussolini are very rare.

Burmantofts

The Burmantofts Pottery factory was originally founded in 1858 in the Burmantofts district of Leeds to produce salt-glazed architectural wares such as pipes. The company began making art pottery in the 1880, using earthenware mined from the factory site and covered with feldspathic glazes that were then fired to high temperatures to make the body extremely hard. Items produced ranged from vases and jardinières to vessels in the form of grotesque frogs or dragons, and mantel clocks with a variety of naturalistic or grotesque animals resting on top. The new ranges sold well and the company opened its own showroom in London and, in 1888, changed its name to The Burmantofts Company. However, the following year the firm merged with five other Yorkshire companies to form the Leeds Fireclay Co.

Market information
The market for Burmantofts Pottery has grown considerably in the last five years as collectors of William De Morgan and Doulton Lambeth wares have found themselves being priced out of the market.
• Highly popular are the grotesque animal spoon warmers, such as that shown right, c1890. These are reminiscent of the work carried out by the Martin Brothers, in that they present weird and wonderful creatures with scaly skins and big gaping mouths. Expect to pay £300–400 / €430–570 / $520–700 each at auction.
• Prices for the mantel clocks surmounted by grotesque animals range from £500–1,000 / €720–1,450 / $880–1,750.

Denby

The Denby Pottery was established in 1809 by William Bourne and became famous for its salt-glazed stoneware, which included figural cordial flasks. However, in the 1920s, due to changes in fashion and a need to establish a new identity, the company expanded its range of ornamental wares. A new decorating department was established in 1923 under the management of pottery decorator Albert Colledge. Its output, which experimented with new glazes, was successful and included the new Danesby stoneware ranges.

Although Denby suffered from a slump in trade following the Wall Street crash of 1929, the works were modernized by Norman Wood in 1931 and the company changed its emphasis from industrial ware to more domestic lines. The addition in 1934 of sculptor Donald Gilbert from the Royal College of Art encouraged a new series of ornamental wares that included animal models. Despite the break in production during WWII the next decades were influenced by highly skilled designers. In 1976 the company was renamed Denby Tableware and it is still in production today.

DONALD GILBERT

Gilbert designed Animal Ware, a range of animals and birds that were either freestanding models or sculpted onto pots. His animals had a simplicity of line but also captured the essence of the creature and reflected the Art Deco and Modernist styles of the period.

- **Animal Ware** Pieces include bookends, love birds, flying fish, a sea lion, a group of three geese, a Scottie dog and a hot-water bottle called Wilfred the Hot Water Rabbit, which was modelled as a freestanding stylized rabbit together with a squirrel and a penguin. Other warmers included one embossed with a cat eyeing a

mouse and one with a pair of curled dormice.

COLLEDGE AND TEICHTNER

Albert Colledge and Alice Teichtner were two other key designers of the factory's figures and thy expanded many of the novelties.

- **Novelties** These included Marmaduke rabbit; Byngo the bulldog (shown below, dated c1937); five terriers, Fido, produced in four sizes; Dachshunds; hounds; a flock of Lambs; a giraffe; a teddy bear; an elephant; an ARP dog and Denby rabbits in a variety of glazes (see right, dated c1935).
- **Figures** These included a footballer, a golfer and a skier.
- **Sizes** These ranged from tiny to 'doorstop' and the items were often used to form hot-water bottles, bookends, containers, bowls and vases.

DECORATIVE ARTS

Marks

The word 'Denby' or 'Bourne Denby', is incorporated in the mark, sometimes with pattern or a designers name

Gallé

Emile Gallé (1846–1904) was born into a ceramic and glassmaking family in Nancy, France. He established a glassmaking business in 1874, producing enamelled glasswares in a variety of styles and techniques. Gallé's work received great acclaim at the Paris exhibition of 1878 and he became a leading force in the French Art Nouveau movement. His designs were used in glass, ceramics and marquetry, and as a botanist, he was greatly influenced by nature, insects, flowers and dragonflies. At the turn of the 20th century he produced a series of faïence cats with glass eyes, decorated with brightly coloured glazes.

Marks

• Gallé faïence pottery is typically marked 'E. Gallé, Nancy' and with the Cross of Lorraine.
• Collectors should be aware that faïence cats were produced in the style of Gallé, but these will not have the signature. Without a signature the value could be halved.

GALLE CATS.
Collectors look for the following:
• **Red clay body** This is typical of the clay in the Nancy region.
• **Decoration** Bands of ribbon and flora on the cat's body and with a painted medallion featuring a dog portrait (see p.182)
• **Mark** A Gallé signature to the cat's paws.
• **Condition** Signs of restoration to ears and paws will knock value.

Market information

Good examples of cats in good condition can regularly realize £3,000 / €4,300 / $5,200 at auction, which is around double the price of an example without a medallion and that may just have heart-shape motifs painted on its body.

Goldscheider

Goldscheider was founded in Vienna, Austria in 1885. By 1892 Goldscheider had set up a branch in Paris and exhibited at many exhibitions and fairs. The factory also employed leading designers of the day who created pieces in porcelain, faïence and terracotta, as well as metal.

During the 1920s, under the direction of Marcel and Walter Goldscheider, the company made the brightly coloured figures for which they are now famous. African-inspired face masks were also produced.

In the late 1930s the Staffordshire firm of Myott, Son & Co acquired the rights to produce Goldscheider figures. Marcel Goldscheider went on to establish his own pottery in Hanley, Staffordshire, where he produced new models in earthenware and china until 1959. Pieces made there bear a signature mark.

Market information

• The market is very good for painted face masks. 'Tragedy', which features a girl holding a theatrical mask, can fetch up to £1,000 / €1,450 / $1,750 at auction.
• On average, face masks are priced in the mid-hundreds; collectors prefer examples without restoration to the curls in the hair.
• Most popular Goldscheider figures depict glamorous Art Deco dancers, with the most desirable often designed by Josef Lorenzl. Prices can be in excess of £2,500 / €3,600 $4,400 for a good figure such as the Butterfly Girl, c1935, shown on page p.47, left.

WHAT TO LOOK FOR
• **Figures** These were classically inspired, such as the earthenware maiden, c1900, shown top right p.47, some featured sea nymphs, a traditional Art Nouveau motif and later Art Deco figures that encapsulate the spirit of the 'Jazz' age are extremely popular.
• **1930s costume** The most

DECORATIVE ARTS

Key designers

Influential designers involved with the Goldscheider factory include:
Josef Lorenzl
Stefan Dakon
Ida Meisinger
Michael Powolny
Vally Wieselthier

collectable and sought-after figures are those wearing 1930s costume (see p.186) and these will achieve good prices.

• **Good condition** This is essential. Check carefully for restoration; tell-tale signs include subtle changes in skins tones and the glaze.

MARK
Pieces after 1918 have a transfer-printed mark 'Goldscheider Wien. Made in Austria', which superseded the earlier, pre-war mark of an

Marks

The printed signature of Marcel Goldsceider may be found on figures.

Goldscheider

Often the impressed mark 'Reproduction Reservée' will also be seen.

embossed rectangular pad of a kneeling figure from Greek pottery. Commissioned wares sometimes carry the name of the designer as well as a serial

• **Myott** Pieces are clearly marked and are not as sought after as the Goldscheider figures made in Austria.

Hutschenreuther

Hutschenreuther was founded by Carolus Magnus Hutschenreuther in 1814 in Hohenberg, Germany and made artistic and utility wares. His son, Lorenze opened another porcelain factory in 1857 in the German city of Selb. It was completely independent from his father's business, and he went on to purchase factories at Altrohlau, Arzburg and Tirschenreuth. Both companies were in competition until 1969, when they merged to become Hutschenreuther A.G. which is still in production today.

OUTPUT
Figure production began at the Selb factory in 1917. Here the sculptors and skilled labourers excelled at natural representations of animals, birds and figures that have a great sense of movement and realism, as illustrated by the dancer, c1925, shown right. By 1926 Hutschenreuther had won wide acclaim and their porcelain figures were highly sought after.

MARKS
Output can be dated according to the different periods of management by the following marks.

• **C. M. Hutschenreuther** The mark for this period incorporates a shield surmounted by a crown and the initials 'CMHR'.

• **L. Hutschenreuther** The mark for this period incorporates a lion, the initials 'LHS' and the words 'Hutschenreuther Selb'.

Katzhütte

The German firm of Hertwig & Co in Katzhütte was established in 1762 and was one of the largest manufacturers of dolls, many of which were exported. However, it is known mainly for its animals and Art Deco figures with finely modelled and well-painted faces that were produced under the trademark Katzhütte. These pieces are now prized by many Art Deco collectors. Summing up the spirit of the 'Jazz Age', they came in many different poses with a variety of accessories and sometimes with a pet. Most were made with a white base and all carry the Katzhütte mark.

Lenci

The Italian firm Lenci was established in Turin in 1919 by Enrico di Scavini, but it was not until the 1920s that they began to produce their earthenware and porcelain figures. Mainly in the form of women, the figures were modelled both in the nude and decorated in brightly coloured contemporary dress with intricately worked details. They are also distinguished by elongated limbs, bright yellow hair and both matt and glossy glazes.

LENCI FIGURES

Lenci figures can command high prices and this is because they really reflect the spirit of the Art Deco period. Artistic license was used in their portrayal of the human form by exaggerating the arms and legs. Women were shown in leisurely poses, often wearing chic clothing see left, dated 1930.

MARKS

Lenci figures sometimes come with paper labels identifying the factory; individual designers usually remained anonymous. There were various marks for the Lenci workshops.
• 'Lenci' The single word is sometimes painted on the figure.
• 'Lenci made in Italy Torino'
• **Be aware** On some signed pieces the word 'Lenci' reads backwards – which is the result of having been set in positive rather than reverse in the mould.

Market information

Lenci figures are becoming increasingly hard to source; prices have therefore risen in the last two years.
• The most desirable is the outlandish, rather saucy Art Deco woman and some of the rarer examples have commanded in excess of £10,000 / €14,400 / $17,500. In general the more stylish and Deco the example, the higher the price.

Condition is important but will matter less the better the subject matter.
• Less desirable, and therefore lower in value, are the standard figures with little Art Deco style, (see above right, dated c1930).
• When buying at auction collectors must expect competition from wealthy Italian collectors bidding by phone, so a bargain could be hard to find.

Martin Brothers

The Martin Brothers Pottery was founded by Robert Wallace Martin, the eldest of four brothers, in the late 1860s. In 1874 he set up a new pottery with his brothers, Charles, Walter and Edwin Martin in Fulham, London. In 1877 they moved to Southall, where they made salt-glazed stoneware with Gothic revival influences. The Martin Brothers became famous for their eccentric, grotesquely modelled 'Wally Birds' – named after their creator Robert Wallace – and wheel-thrown sculpted face jugs, vases and other items inspired by the art and architecture of the Middle Ages. In addition to the Wally birds they also produced a line of more functional pottery, painted with relief decoration. After various difficulties, including a serious fire in 1910 and deaths in the family, the company closed in 1915 and interest in Martin Brothers pieces declined. However, in the 1970s the brothers' work was promoted at auction and interest was rekindled, particularly in the 'Wally Birds'.

CHARACTERISTICS
Martin Brothers pieces can be identified by the following:
• **Faces** These often have exagerated human characteristics.

• **Feet and beaks** These are well modelled and very detailed.
• **Glazes** Subdued salt glazes in creams, greens and browns.
• **Detachable heads** enabled the models to be marketed as jars.

WHAT TO LOOK FOR
Prospective purchasers should observe the following:
• Check carefully for restoration. Ask for a condition report and to have the bird placed under an ultra violet light – this will highlight any restored areas.
• Always confirm that the bird's head is correct for the body – both should have the same date and the head should fit snugly and match the body in character and glazing.
• Take your time to read up on the subject and get a feel for the product, as this is a very costly area in which to make a mistake.

Marks
All Martin wares are hand-incised on the underside with the name and address of the maker and the date of production. The most sought-after pieces, made before 1863, are marked 'Fulham'. Later pieces are marked 'London & Southall'. The words 'Bros' or 'Brothers' were added in 1882. A number of fakes are in circulation so always consult a specialist dealer or auction house.

R W Martin
Fulham

Market information
Martin ware has gone from strength to strength in the last two years.
• Most popular are the tobacco jars and lids in the form of grotesque birds such as that shown above, 1900. At a recent auction of an important private collection of British Decorative Arts in New York an extensive collection of Martin birds set new world records. The largest bird, 25½in (65cm) high, went on to make £46,300 / €67,000 / $81,000.

• Today, any Martin bird coming up for sale at auction will have numerous 'condition report' requests. Collectors are looking for birds modelled with great character, so in many ways the rule of thumb is the uglier the bird, the more it is likely to make.
• Among other wares, the double-sided face jugs are popular, with prices around £1,000–3,000 / €1,450–4,300 / $1,750–5,300, while spoon warmers, owls and any form of grotesque creature will always be fought over.

Poole Pottery

Poole pottery began in Poole, Dorset as Carter & Co in 1873, producing a variety of lustre-glazed useful wares. In 1921 the company expanded and changed its name to Carter, Stabler & Co after taking the surnames of the partners Charles Carter, Harold and Phoebe Stabler and John Adams. Under their influence a range of sculptural pieces was introduced and figures include 'The Bull', 'Picardy Peasants' (see p.197). The 1920s and 1930s saw the development of elegant and decorative designs of the Modernism movement and a variety of designers were invited to create works for the pottery. Along with tableware, vases and other items, Phoebe Stabler developed a series of pottery figures. These were to be reproduced in later years. Owing to government restrictions during the 1940s production concentrated on utility wares. However, a number of earthenware models were made in the form of rabbits, bears, gazelles and lambs, and these were often decorated in Picotee, Vellum and Sylvan-type glazes. In the 1950s, design director Alfred Read and senior thrower Guy Sydenham created a series of innovative vases with abstract decoration which propelled the company into the fashion-influenced 1960s. In 1963 the company began using the name Poole Pottery and they successfully combined art pottery and commercial wares. The 1970s saw the development of models such as owls, ducks, deer, cats, squirrels, otters, guinea pigs, dogs, toads, rabbits and other animals. Poole Pottery is still producing brightly-coloured studio ware to this day.

Marks

The firm used a variety of marks and if the piece is unmarked it is almost certainly not Poole.
• The base is usually impressed 'Carter Stabler & Adams Ltd' or 'C.S.A', and includes the decorator's monogram. Some pieces have pattern codes – usually of two letters. If three letters are shown, the third usually indicates the dominant colour.
• Few pieces are dated and those that are may have been made as commemorative pieces for specific organizations. After 1963, only the Poole mark was used. No fakes have been identified.

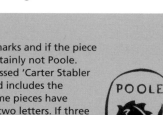

Market information

• **Most desirable** are early Carter Stabler Adams figures (see right, prototype figure by Phoebe Stabler, dated c1935). Particularly well-modelled groups such as 'Europa and the Bull' can command over £2,500 / €3,600 / $4,400.
• **Less desirable** are the later floral and bird subjects of the 1950s and '60s; demand for these pieces is currently slow.
• During the 1990s some of the London auction rooms were holding annual sales of Poole pottery, but since then interest in Poole has cooled somewhat.
• The novice collector can enter the Poole market with a budget of under £50 / €70 / $90 and find some pleasing examples.

Zsolnay Pêcs

Established at Pêcs, Hungary in 1853, the factory was initially started by the father of Ignaz Zsolnay to produce creamware. However, in 1862, the business was passed to his brother Vilmos whose enthusiasm and talent marked the beginning of success for the Zsolnay factory. The company developed a material called pyroganite, a form of moulded stoneware that was resistant to freezing. This material became widely used in their manufacture of decorative roof tiles and cobbles. Influenced by the French potter Clément Massier who had been instrumental in developing metallic lustre, the company developed its own iridescent glaze known as Eosin, and it was this that won Zsolnay many prizes at world exhibitions. During the Art Nouveau movement Vilmos and his principal designer Tade Sikorski used the newly-developed glaze to create a whole range of decorative wares that had a world-wide appeal. The designs, which were very varied, were often inspired by forms in nature or other cultures. However, the process was time-consuming and expensive and involved many artists and chemists. In the 1950s, with the new political and cultural freedom in Hungary, the factory encouraged designers to experiment with abstract pieces that revived earlier Zsolnay ornamental wares, architectural pieces and metallic glazes. The factory is still in production today, celebrating its historic achievement and style. All pieces are marked with variations of a medallion depicting the five church towers of Pêcs.

The market for Zsolnay is very much split between the early Zsolnay Pêcs lustre wares and the mid-20th-century decorative wares.
• **Marks** Collectors should be familiar with the wide range of marks used by the factory over the years. This will allow them to date pieces correctly and in turn pay the right price for the period of production.

ART NOUVEAU PERIOD
There are some stunning examples dating from the Art Nouveau period (broadly 1890–1915) and it is these pieces that collectors get most excited about.
• **Characteristics** All are produced in a shiny iridescent lustre glaze.

The pieces themselves often have an organic shape such as a shell or plant form, and may be embellished with marine creatures or foliage and then glazed in vivid iridescent colours.
• **Designers** The designer Lajos Mack who worked at Zsolnay at the beginning of the 20th century is particularly sought after because his pieces really capture the essence of Art Nouveau. The exotic bird dated 1914 and shown left is an example of his work

Designers
Influential designers inlvolved with the Zsolnay factory include:
• Miklos Zsolnay (1800–1880)
• Vilmos Zsolnay (1828–1900)
• Tade Sikorski (1852–1940)
• Jozsef Rippl-Ronai (1861–1927)
• Walter Crane (1845–1915)
• Sandor Apati-Apt (1870–1916)
• Lajos Mack (1876–1963)
• Mihály Kapás Nagy
• Henrik Darielek
• Julia Zsolnay (1856–1950)

Market information
The market for Zsolnay is clearly divided in terms of taste and price so there is much scope for collectors of all budgets.
• Early pieces such as those by Lajos Mack are particularly sought after and prices for his work can be in excess of £5,000 / €7,200 / $8,800.

20th Century

The key feature of collecting 20th-century ceramics is that the age of mass production brought collecting to a wider audience than had ever been possible before. Leading the way in this field were visionary men such as John Beswick, Henry Doulton and George Wade. All three operated with profitable factories in Stoke-on-Trent where good-quality imaginative ceramics could be produced to satisfy a growing demand for collectable wares. Part of their success formula was to employ good designers and painters who were in touch with what the average collector wanted to see in a ceramic figure or jug. Some of the great names from the early 20th century were Leslie Harradine, Charles Noke and Harry Fenton working at Doulton Burslem, and Arthur Gredington and Albert Hallam working at Beswick. Between them they designed and produced thousands of different models which have stood the test of time. The Wade company also enjoyed a prolific output between 1930 and 1980 and

it is really only in the last 25 years that the potteries have seen troubled times with mass redundancies and outsourcing abroad. There have been a number of peaks and troughs in the sale of figures in recent years, none more so than the Doulton Bunnykins market which was very profitable in the mid-1990s, both on the internet, at auctions and at fairs, but today is very much subdued. Growth in early rarer figures has been more sustained, such as those produced by Shelley in the 1930s or where there is a niche market of devoted collectors such as for Ken Allen's range of Winstanley cats. In the 1970s manufacturers introduced the concept of the limited edition piece. The popularity of this grew and grew but with growing demand came increased edition sizes, and editions of 5,000 were soon produced, which made nonsense of the word limited. Collectors nowadays require genuinely small edition sizes, and manufacturers are more likely to offer editions of 250 or under.

BRITAIN

Many manufacturers were influenced by the Chelsea pottery figures of the 18th century.

• **Royal Worcester** A whole range of figural studies were produced that brought a sense of the elegant 18th-century drawing room to mass production. They were manufactured from moulds and then additional hand-modelled features, such as flowers, were added. Lastly they

were hand-painted by girls who were trained to paint and model. These figures would then be sold in gift shops and department stores throughout the country, and by the 1950s many were also being exported for sale abroad.

ANIMALS

Undoubtedly one of the biggest themes in 20th-century ceramic production was the manufacture of animal models. Collectors have always responded well to models that remind them of the innocent days of childhood.

• **Beswick** This firm combined some of the finest modelling and painting skills to produce animal studies of outstanding accuracy and precision, such as the cockerel made c1968, shown left.

• **Royal Crown Derby**

manufactured more expensive and serious animal studies and to this day they still excel in producing their own highly ornate animal studies, often in a slightly abstract form that really captures the inate nature of the animal concerned.

• **Royal Doulton** A range of animals was designed that were glazed in an impressive flambé technique based on ancient Chinese glazes.

• **Wade** Not wanting to fall behind the times, the Wade company (see p.64) also forged ahead in the mass-production of animal models, including their famous selection of Whimsie models that could be collected for just a few pence each.

• **SylvaC** This key Staffordshire firm (see p.63) realized that nostalgia had great commercial possibilities and prooduced a whole range of appealing animal studies. Again, some of the glazing techniques used by the factory were rather outrageous when compared to those being used on the Continent.

EUROPE
• **Germany** The Rosenthal Studio (see p.58) was also very much in tune with the different collecting tastes and produced some wonderful figures that presented a modern twist to images from German folklore. For example, fauns were depicted cavorting with Art Nouveau-style maidens or Bacchanalian figures.
• **Denmark** The Royal Copenhagen Studio (see p.59) also looked to their folklore for inspiration. In addition they produced figures depicting the different national costumes of the world. The style of these pieces was quite different to the style of ceramic models being produced in Britain. The glazing techniques also differed in that there was more use of subtle greys and blues rather than the vivid colours that were characteristic of a Royal Doulton or Wade Art figure.

INTERNET AUCTIONS
Today, internet auction sites offer the biggest trading markets for 20th-century ceramic figures. Collectors find it easy and quick to trade this way, but auction houses are still seen as important outlets for pieces priced at over £250 / €360 / $440. This is because it is preferable to examine and handle examples above this value in order to avoid possible disappointment. However, some collecting areas, such as Goss and Crested wares, are generally appreciated by an older generation who can be less comfortable with the internet, and hence these also tend to be traded through auction rooms.

Beswick

Robert Beswick, who in 1830 moved with his family from Lancashire to Stoke-on-Trent, began potting with his partner John Leese. In the late 19th century James Beswick and his son founded the Beswick pottery in Longton, Staffordshire, eventually opening two more factories. They produced tablewares, figures and other domestic wares, and by 1930 the factories employed 400 workers. In 1964 they were bought by Royal Doulton.

COLLECTABILITY
There is a large range of Beswick animal studies to collect including models of dogs, birds, farm animals and horses along with a good range of novelty wares (such as Laurel and Hardy salt and pepper shakers) and commemorative and brewery-related items. It is very important to understand the different glazes with which Beswick painted their animals because there is often a big difference in the value of a model which is determined by the colour of the glaze. For example, a `rocking horse grey' model is usually priced higher than one in black or tan. Arthur Gredington's range of Connoisseur Horse studies have never been bettered in their attention to detail, and such was the popularity of Beswick's animal models, that hundreds of different studies were put into production and their famous range of five graduated flying ducks became a symbol of mid-20th century suburban living as they were placed over the fireplaces of many homes.
• **Affordability** Prices for much of the Beswick range remain tempting to the novice collector and many items are available to choose from at under £70 / €100 / $120.
• **Beatrix Potter** In the '90s there was a huge interest among collectors for the Beswick range of Beatrix Potter figures, such as the mouse Anna Maria, made 1963–72, shown below. Some 110 figures were available to choose from, each with a choice of at least five different backstamps.
• **Backstamps** These held great importance to the collector in that they determined the value of the piece, with an early gold circular Beswick mark being the most desirable

Market information
• The market for Beswick has increased dramatically since the closure of the Beswick factory in 2001.
• Collectors speculating that Beswick wares would become increasingly difficult to find caused many secondary market prices to more than double.
• As of 2005 the brand name has been sold to new owners, so production of Beswick wares will resume.

Bing & Grøndahl

Bing & Grøndahl was the second most important producer of ceramics in Denmark, after Royal Copenhagen. The company was founded in 1853 by Frederick Vilhelm Grøndahl, a former Royal Copenhagen employee, together with Jacob Herman and Meyer Herman Bing. The factory is known for its high-quality table and artistic wares in both porcelain and stoneware. The firm is still in production today and pieces are marked with the initials 'B. & G.'. See p.227 for illustrations of their figures.

Carlton Ware

Carlton Ware was founded by J. F. Wiltshaw and J. Robinson in 1890, based at the Carlton Works in Stoke-on-Trent and by the mid-1890s the Carlton Ware trademark was being used. The pottery became very successful during the 1920s and '30s, when it produced a huge range of decorative items including animal models, Toby jugs, female figures and tablewares. They also produced a very successful line of lustre wares inspired by Oriental designs and these were often decorated with fruit, vegetables, and flowers. Production continued throughout WWII and the company emerged into the post-war years with contemporary designs, new patterns and an impressive list of modellers and designers. The business was bought by Arthur Wood & Sons in 1967 and continued to produce their range of novelty wares, such as Walking Ware and the models of political and royal personalities that are now synonymous with Carlton Ware. The factory closed in 1992 but in 1998 the business was relaunched and today various manufacturers are making, under licence, limited edition collectors' pieces, some from original moulds and styles, under the Carlton Ware name.

If he can say as you can Guinness is good for you

Carlton Ware is a very diverse market encompassing a wide range of patterns, shapes and glazes. Collectors are advised to choose a section of production that appeals the most to them as it would be difficult to collect examples of the various factories' output since 1890. A recent example is the John Prescott character jug shown on p.55, top right, which was produced in 2002.

GUINNESS
In the 1950s, Guinness commissioned the Carlton Ware pottery to produce a range of promotional items.
• **Toucan** These were mainly inspired by the 1960s Guinness toucan, shown left, which was

developed by the artist John Gilroy and the copywriter Dorothy Sayers.
• **Fakes** Guinness memorabilia is popular with collectors today but this popularity, and the high prices achieved by the Toucan series, has recently led to the production of fakes, some cast from original moulds and bearing a backstamp.

Marks
• Some early marks dating from the 1920s have the script mark of Wiltshaw & Robinson as well as the name Carlton Ware.
• The word 'handpainted' was dropped by the company's new owners, Arthur Wood & Son, from 1967.
• Designers are not generally named.

Crown Devon

Crown Devon was the trade name used by the family firm of S. Fielding & Co, founded in Stoke-on-Trent in 1873 by Simon Fielding, producing majolica and black, brown and green-glazed ware, hand-painted ware and a wide range of domestic earthenware. A period of expansion followed when Fielding's son Abraham joined the firm five years later. Under his directorship the company developed a prolific, highly collectable range of moulded earthenware tableware, salad ware, novelties and figures. Other production included figure models, some extremely realistic, in Devon Ivrine and Bronzine glazes. Abraham's son Arthur Ross Fielding took over the business in 1932 and by 1934 Crown Devon was producing well modelled contemporary-style figures with titles such as 'A Windy Day' and 'Rio Rita', some created by the freelance designer Kathleen Parsons. The pottery also introduced a cheaper range of smaller figures, known as Sutherland Figures, which were fired, painted and sprayed with cellulose. The company continued production throughout WWII, and after the war, under the management of Reginald Ross Fielding who succeeded his father in 1947, underwent a period of development until 1966, when it was sold. After being sold again in 1976, the factory closed in 1982 and the premises and moulds were bought by Caverswall China early in 1983 and then sold to the retailers Thomas Goode & Co in 1984. After being sold again in 1987, the pottery was demolished.

COLLECTABILITY
Prices in the mid- to high hundreds can be paid for stylish Art Deco Crown Devon figural studies such as the lady and a dog, c1935, shown right, particularly those with a lustre glaze. Some models rank with Lenci and Goldscheider in terms of style, but are usually more affordable.
    Often a more affordable alternative to Carlton Ware, Crown Devon offers the same variety of

Marks
The company traded under the names Crown Devon and Royal Devon. The marks incorporate a crown and 'Fielding's' or the company's initials. From 1913 the words 'Crown Devon' were included.

20TH CENTURY

collecting possibilities. The range of
Art Deco wares, such as wall
pockets, represent good value.
• **Wall pockets** These were often
finished with a monotone matt
glaze which made them easy for
the factory to produce. Today many
models sell at under £75 / €100
/ $130, with animal studies being
particularly popular.
• **Novelty items** A popular
collecting area, examples with a
sporting theme such as the golfer
ashtray c1930, right, or Tennis are
particularly sought after.
• **Condition** Collectors should
check for restoration, as this will
reduce value.

Goebel

The west German porcelain factory Oeslau &
Wilhelmsfeld was founded in 1871 by Franz
Detleff Goebel, and taken over by his son
William Goebel from 1879. Ornaments in
porcelain, fine earthenware and terracotta
were produced, along with bisque dolls'
heads and half-dolls.

Although better known for its novelty
range, the Goebel factory also produced
sinuous, elegant, stylized figures that were
generally better modelled and painted
than those of their English counterparts,
whose figures are often in rather
stilted poses.

Maria Innocenta Hummel trained as
an artist before joining the

Franciscan Convent of Siessen in
1931. She continued to draw
pictures of country children and
these were turned into ceramic
figures such as 'Meditation', 1980,
right and 'Spring Cheer', which was
discontinued in 1984, left, with the
help of Franz Goebel at the Goebel
porcelain factory. Launched at the
Leipzig Spring Fair in 1935, these
figures were instantly successful and
despite Sister Hummel's death in
1946, production continued. An
artistic panel was established at the
convent to oversee the production
which continues today, based on
Hummel's original drawings.
• **Other items** As well as figures,
in 1971 the company introduced the
first annual M. I. Hummel plate.

• **Collectors' Club** 1977 saw the
introduction of the Goebel
Collectors' Club.

Goss & Crested China

The late 19th century saw the development of Britain's railways and the boom of seaside tourism. This lead to an increase in 'souvenir' trinkets which were an affordable memento of the day out. W. H. Goss, along with his son, Adolphus, lead the way with small pieces of china decorated with heraldic crests. The company sent out agents to seek permission to use crests from towns around the country and there are 7,000 different heraldic devices on Goss ceramics. Goss porcelain was high quality and intended for the middle classes. Pieces started as monuments, buildings, classical works of art or war-related items, and progressed to less serious subjects such as animals, domestic wares and cottages. It was not long before the strong market for such items became obvious and other potteries such as Arcadian, Carlton, Shelley and Willow Art began to produce similar pieces in lesser-quality porcelain. This added to the diverse range of novelty designs that were very popular with the public. The craze reached its peak during the Edwardian period when the vast majority of homes contained at least one piece of crested china. However, WWI and the Depression in the early 1930s caused demand for such frivolous items to drop significantly and, by WWII, demand was nonexistent.

COLLECTING

Modern collectors often concentrate on a particular aspect of crested china.
• **Most popular subjects** These include animals and military and comic novelty items, such as the Willow Art model of a fat lady on scales, c1920, shown right.
• **Crests** Some people prefer to collect the crests of particular towns or cities.
• **Other items** As well as heraldic ceramics and model buildings Goss, alongside Robinson & Leadbeater, produced a keenly collected range of decorative figures and busts,

some based on famous sculptures.
• **Goss** Despite competition from other manufacturers, Goss items remain the most popular.

Marks
• Genuine Goss china should have a printed mark with a hawk.
• Some crested pieces which were produced in Germany are marked 'Gemma'.
• Beware of fake cottages produced with spurious hand-painted Goss marks

CARE

When storing your crested china be sure not to wrap it in newspaper – the ink can oxidize the paint, resulting in faded colours.

Lladro

Three brothers from a farming family, Juan, José and Vincente Lladro, founded a workshop at their parents' home in Almácera, near Valencia, Spain in 1953. A small ceramic workshop followed, and from these humble beginnings the first Lladro factory was opened in 1958, producing plates, jugs, vases and classically-inspired sculptures. In 1969, the company moved to larger premises in the nearby town of Tavernes Blanques and, in the 1970s the Lladro porcelain company began to expand its export of wares, many of them costing half what a similar model by Doulton or Worcester might cost. Some collectors felt that they would be just as happy with a Lladro model than a more expensive Stoke-on-Trent example, and the effect of this was to hit the home market and demand started to decrease. Over 4,000 different items have been created since the company originated and the factory is still in production today.

MANUFACTURE

Each sculpture designed by Lladro artists is made up of several individual pieces, from which separate alabaster moulds are created. The parts are joined with liquid porcelain, which acts as a fixing agent. Some of the figures, especially the large group sculptures, are assembled from more than 200 separate pieces which are then hand painted, glazed and fired. 'The Jester's Serenade', c1994, is shown right.

Marks

The blue Lladro mark was created in 1974 from an ancient chemical symbol and a stylized bellflower (a popular flower in the Valencia region). It is usually stamped on the base of the piece.

Rosenthal

The German firm of Rosenthal was established in 1879 in Selb, and made fine-quality ceramic figures and tableware porcelain. Rosenthal pieces use inventive shapes and tend to be ornate in form and pattern; the art department were noted for their responsiveness to contemporary tastes.

Rosenthal figures have an individual, sculptural quality, which gradually became more stylized through the 1920s and 1930s, being very different in style; pieces modelled by the artist Gerhard Schliepstein depict svelte, sculptural, elongated and stylized women and greyhounds in pure white porcelain, their sculptural qualities enhanced by the fact that they have been left unpainted.

Rosenthal also produced a range of cabinet objects, including animals and fine-quality, detailed, naturalistic porcelain figures of dancers, often wearing colourful, exotic or futuristic costumes, together with women in modern dress.

Rosenthal work is relatively under-rated; it is probably the nearest equivalent to Meissen (see p. 39), but is far more affordable. Rosenthal figures are undoubtedly of a very fine quality and the factory employed a number of highly talented modellers in the early to mid-20th century. The figure of the bathing girl made in the late 1920s, shown right, is one such example. The superb quality porcelain is hand-painted in flesh tones and the blue of the towel is a colour often associated with Rosenthal.

• **Early Figures** The works of Otto Hintze and Ferdinand Liebermann characterize the early period of production and are very detailed and imaginative, often representing fauns, maidens, dragonflies and children.

• **Gerhard Schliepstein**

His Rosenthal figures with their modern abstract style are particularly popular with the younger collector. The majority of his works are glazed in white and have a modernist style that blends in well with contemporary interiors. Many are affordable being typically in the mid hundreds.

CONDITION

Collectors should be wary of restored areas, particularly any features that may have been broken off and repaired. Collectors today tend to regard the unpainted, white pieces as unfinished and unexciting and, as a result, some wonderful pieces can be surprisingly inexpensive.

MARKS

All Rosenthal figures are marked on the base with the company mark and an impressed number.

Royal Albert

Royal Albert was founded in 1896. Initially branded Albert Crown China, they first produced Royal commemoratives as early as 1897 to celebrate Queen Victoria's Diamond Jubilee; the word 'Royal' was added in 1904, but the full name was soon shortened to 'Royal Albert'. By 1910 the factory was exporting its porcelain floral tea and breakfast sets around the world. In 1964 the company was bought by Pearson & Co and became part of Allied English Potteries, merging with Royal Doulton in 1972. Beatrix Potter figures and fancies are among Royal Albert's more recent collectable products.

COMMEMORATIVE WARE
Some of the early Royal Albert commemorative wares are popular with collectors. The manufacturing frenzy prompted by Queen Victoria's Diamond Jubilee has resulted in a wealth of items being produced. These are now freely available to collectors at fairs and antique shops for under £100 / €140 / $175.

BACKSTAMPS
There was a storm of controversy in the late 1980s when Royal Albert took over the Beswick backstamp for their famous range of Beatrix Potter figures, only to see the backstamp revert back to Beswick by the middle of the 1990s.

• **Collectability** Collectors now like to seek out the Royal Albert back-stamps because these were only in production for a few years. Most are available at under £50 / €70 / $85.

Royal Copenhagen

The Royal Copenhagen Porcelain Manufactory was founded 1775 by F. H. Müller in Copenhagen, Denmark. In 1883, the ceramic artist Arnold Krog introduced innovative glazing and decorative techniques; in 1890 the company opened shops in Paris and London's Bond Street, and the Copenhagen shop received custom from the Russian Tsar, Alexander III. The factory came into its own during the Art Nouveau period and was very successful with its figures of children, dancers, and satyrs. By the 20th century the figures and groups were well-modelled and painted in detail with subtle shades. These traditional-style models were hugely successful and are among the company's most popular pieces. Favourite themes include figures clothed in historical and regional dress. Shown below is a figure of a girl with a doll, made c1961.

Marks
Marks have changed over the years and can offer a clue to dating.
• The 'wave' mark was adopted by the factory in 1775, and appears in underglaze blue. The mark shown on the right was used from 1889.
• A vertical wave mark is found on figures.
• Parian wares are marked 'ENERET', meaning copyright.

Royal Crown Derby

Several factories were established in the Derby area at the end of the 19th century. The Derby Crown Porcelain Company, which later became Royal Crown Derby, was established in Osmaston Road in 1876, specializing in Imari wares. These were very successful and reached a peak between 1890 and 1915.

Figure production was increased from the 1930s, 'Marjorie', below right, was made c1933, and included reissued models from the 1880s, such as Don Quixote, Robin Hood and characters from Dickens. In 1935 Royal Crown Derby acquired the King Street works, headed by Samson Hancock. The factory was originally a rival and made similar pieces based on the patterns and shapes produced by the first Derby company in the early 19th century.

During WWII output was largely restricted to useful wares, although by 1946 animal models, fancies, figures and statues were included in the catalogue. After the war production deteriorated and later pieces from the two factories are far less sought after today. In 1964 Royal Crown Derby was acquired by the Lawley Group.

LATER PIECES
• **Robert Jefferson** Employed during the 1960s as a sculptor, Jefferson later modelled a series of animal and bird paperweights, six of which were launched in 1981.
• **Other popular Jefferson models** These include Les Saisons, a group of figures inspired by Alphonse Mucha, and The Great Lovers, depicting Antony and Cleopatra, Romeo and Juliet, Lancelot and Guinevere and Robin Hood and Maid Marian.
• **The Classic Collection** Was created by Jo Ledger and modelled by Jefferson was launched in 1986. The first figures represented Persephone, Dione, Penelope and Athena.
• **Later models** These include the aristocratic cats, brought out in

Marks
• Derby pieces are nearly always clearly marked, usually in red, with a printed crown and cipher and normally a year code; these marks are rarely faked.
• The King Street factory used the original Derby painted mark with the initials 'SH' on each side. Sometimes these initials have been ground away in an attempt to make the piece look older than it really is.

1987. These, each wearing royal headgear, symbolize the crowned heads of Abyssinia, Siam, Persia, Egypt, Russia and Burma.
• **Paperweights** These are among the greatest successes in the firm's recent history and are avidly collected. The cat paperweight shown below left was produced c1990.
• **Decoration** has continued with the tradition of adapting old Oriental colours and motifs, and gold is used lavishly.
• **New editions** Designs by John Ablitt and some of Jefferson's earlier models, such as Cat, Rabbit, Duck, Badger and Hedgehog have recently been remodelled.

Market information
• Derby wares were traditionally considered the poor relation of Worcester and Minton, and until recently, items have been be undervalued.
• Price increases have been seen in the last few years, particularly for fine cabinet pieces with signed decoration.

Royal Doulton

The first Doulton factory was founded in London in 1815 and Burslem, Staffordshire, c1880. By 1900 the production of Doulton, which became Royal Doulton in 1902, spanned the whole world of pottery and porcelain. Figure-making was introduced to Doulton by Charles J. Noke as art director during WWI. Initially these figures could not compete with the cheaper models being imported from Germany, but during the 1920s production was streamlined and new styles were introduced to reflect popular fashion. Models were made by leading sculptors such as Albert Toft, Phoebe Stabler, Charles Vyse and Leslie Harradine, who created a large number of successful figures for Doulton in the 1920s and 1930s, including crinoline ladies and other costume and character figures. These were hugely successful and vast numbers were exported to the US. To date, thousands of different figures have been produced, and new models are added in most years while others are deleted, thus encouraging the collector.

BUNNYKINS

Bunnykins were conceived by Barbara Vernon Bailey, a nun and daughter of Doulton's managing director, Cuthbert Bailey, who submitted her designs from the convent. The characters, inspired by many bedtime stories that her father had told her as a child, were launched in 1934, and the Bunnykins design remains a popular nursery ware pattern today.

• **Early models** The first Bunnykins models were produced in 1939, although manufacture was halted by the war, making these early models extremely rare. Early models such as Freddie, Reggie, Mother and Billy are still making good money – £600 / €860 / $1,700 up to £1,200 / €1,700 / $2,100 each according to rarity – but the value will be halved with damage.

• **Later models** In the 1970s, Albert Hallam modelled a new series of Bunnykins figures and in the 1980s designs were created by Harry Sales.

• **Diamond Jubilee** To coincide with Bunnykins Diamond Jubilee in 1984, eight new figures were released such as the drummer, right.

• **Market** The bunnykins market is very subdued compared to five years ago. Many collectors have either moved out of the market, having realized that buying every new bunny is a costly business, or are just concentrating on the small limited edition figures which can sell out immediately.

CHARACTER JUGS

Charles Noke was responsible for the revival of character jugs, also made with collectors in mind, beginning with John Barleycorn, produced in 1934.

• **Collectability** There is a good market for prototype character jugs.

Market information
• There is an enormous collectors' market for Royal Doulton, with a following in the UK, US, Canada and South Africa, but the market for figures has re-evaluated itself in the last three years.
• Today the lower- to middle-range studies that would once have commanded enthusiastic bidding at auction are sometimes selling for half what they might have made five years ago.
• Collectors are now concentrating on the early figures from 1913–30 and Art Deco studies such as 'Sunshine Girl' can make upwards of £2,500 / €3,600 / $4,350. Early studies such as 'Upon Her Cheeks She Wept' can make £3,500 / €5,000 / $6,100 and more.

A good example could be worth up to £10,000 / €14,400 / $17,500, although a mass-produced jug such as John Barleycorn may only be worth £60 / €85 / $100.

DOULTON LAMBETH

Doulton Lambeth wares remain popular, with leading artists such as Hannah Barlow, George Tinworth and Frank Butler selling at a premium. Tinworth in particular is currently doing very well at auction with some of his rarer mice groups hitting the £10,000 / €14,400 / $17,500 mark.

ORIENTAL-INSPIRED PIECES

Technicians Charles Noke and Harry Fenton were able to reinvent a 20th-century equivalent of ancient Chinese glazes at the Royal Doulton Factory which they called `flambé' `sung' and `chang' ware.

20TH CENTURY

• **Animal studies** A small number of animal studies available in naturalistic colourways were also produced in these exciting and dramatic Oriental-style glazes. At the time they would have been more expensive than the naturalistic models because of the difficulties involved in controlling the glaze. The models needed to be heated to high temperatures and this caused many to break up in the kiln and the glaze would need to be controlled very carefully to prevent discolouration. These factors added considerably to the cost of each piece.

• **Collectability** Today, collectors have realized how scarce the Oriental-glazed models are. Certain examples can now make in excess of £2,500 / €3,600 / $4,400 at auction.

Figures backstamp
• Many Doulton figures carry the Royal Doulton lion and crown backstamp.
• Most figures carry a registration number prefixed by HN, the initials of Harry Nixon the chief colourist at Doulton in 1913, and the figure's name. These extra marks provides useful hints for the precise dating of figures, starting with HN1 for the figure 'Darling' c1913, right, up to HN registration numbers of 4,000 plus today.

Shelley

The factory was first known as Wileman & Co when it was established in 1872, then as Foley and as Shelley from 1925, becoming Shelley Potteries Ltd in 1929, and finally Shelley China Ltd in 1965.

The firm's art director, Frederick A. Rhead produced a number of hand-painted earthenware miniature grotesques, animals and Toby jugs in the 1890s which were deliberately made to look ugly, but it was not until the 1920s and '30s that Shelley pieces achieved their ultimate success. Their high-quality Art Deco-style tableware became famous with the help of a national advertizing campaign.

The later years saw Shelley producing a popular range of figures of fairies and other characters, as well as nursery wares based on the illustrations of Mabel Lucie Attwell. These pieces are now keenly sought after, along with versions made by the firm Enesco.

FIGURES
Shelley pieces are always popular and the two main collecting areas are the Art Deco teawares and Mabel Lucie Attwell figures, which can represent little children, as in 'Our Pets' c1937, right, golfers or clergy. These can easily be expected to make around £600 / €860 / $1,050 each and Shelley figures are among the strangest ever produced.

BOO-BOOS
High prices are reserved for the chubby-cheeked child studies accompanied by fairy folk known as Boo-Boos. Many of these were modelled riding a variety of animals and birds, or standing by toadstalls or in groups, sometimes with the addition of rabbits. Prices start at approximately £450 / €640 / $830 but can rise to £2,000 / €2,900 / $3,500 for a good double group.

COPIES
No Shelley fakes are known, although there are many contemporary copies, as the firm set a standard for porcelain in the 1920s and 1930s.

SylvaC

SylvaC began as the Staffordshire firm of Shaw & Copestake (1894–1982). The company began making small animal figures in the late 1920s. The trade name SylvaC was used from 1936 and was taken from the firm's Sylvan works factory, with the final 'C' added for Copestake. At this time the company was producing tableware as well as the animal figures and ornaments for which it is best known today.

Famous lines included rabbits (produced for over 40 years in different colours and sizes), dogs of various breeds (over 200 different designs in various colours) and a wide range of other creatures from squirrels, hump-backed cats, lambs, frogs and hares, to bears. All are well-modelled, with close attention paid to such detail as hand-painted eyes and noses, in muted colours including beige, blue, green and brown. As well as animals, popular subjects included pixies and natural and floral themes.

SylvaC is becoming increasingly popular among collectors.
• **Animals** Keenly sought after, especially dogs, these appeal greatly to collectors of dog novelties. This is

illustrated by the model of the Scottie dog, left, made in the 1930s. Rabbits are also popular; the example shown right was also made in the 1930s. For more examples of SylvaC animals see pages 262–63.
• **Jugs** A range made with handles moulded in the shape of animals are also keenly collected.

MARKS
Most pieces are impressed on the base with the model number, the company name, and 'England'.

Volkstedt

The Thuringian factory Volkstedt was founded in 1760 by a clergyman, Georg Heinrich Macheleid, who had an interest in natural sciences. The company's survival was due to the patronage of the princes of Schwarzburg-Rudolstadt, who became the proprietors. Many of the firm's wares were crude copies of Meissen pieces, but Volkstedt's hard-paste porcelain was well suited to modelling. The Volkstedt factory produced a wide variety of wares ranging from dinnerware, vases, candlesticks, basins and boxes. Some of its finest products are bright and ingeniously animated rural figures.

DRESDEN LACE
By the mid-19th century the Volkstedt factory had begun producing their famous figures wearing lace clothing. The effect, also known as 'DRESDEN lace', was accomplished when real cotton lace was dipped in soft-paste porcelain and then fired. The fabric burned away, leaving the fragile porcelain 'lace' shell.
• **Early pieces** Early Volkstedt hard-paste porcelain was heavy and grey, with an unclear glaze.

• **Firing faults** Painters used scattered flowers to hide the many bubbles and fire-cracks; the later porcelain, although better, is still flawed but on many items the flaws are camouflaged by the rococo modelling.

20TH CENTURY

Wade

The Wade group of potteries was founded in 1922 in Burslem, Staffordshire, by George Wade. The firm consisted of three potteries in England – A. J. Wade Ltd, George Wade & Son Ltd, and Wade Heath & Co – and a factory in Ireland, established in the 1940s, where it made porcelain for the tourist industry and export market.

Wade concentrated on mainly utilitarian pottery before WWII, and produced a comparatively small amount of gift ware which included a range of moderately priced pottery figures with a patented finish known as Scintillite. In 1934 the factory's show at the British Industries Fair consisted almost entirely of pottery 'sculpturesque figures'. Models varied from those with restrained, Victorian-style poses such as 'Dolly Varden' in a crinoline dress, to Art Deco-influenced models such as 'Sunshine'. At the same time George Wade & Son also produced a range of animals that varied in size.

Many of the larger animals and birds were made from wood carvings by Faust Lang, while some of the figures were modelled by Jessie van Hallen. Some figures were advertized in 1948, including 'Wynken', 'Blinken', 'Nod' and 'Curtsey', the first range of costume figures on which appliqué hand-made-flowers formed an important decorative feature. These were only available for the export market.

It was not until after the 1950s, however, when wartime restrictions were lifted, that the company launched its most famous decorative ornamental and novelty lines. In 1953 its range of 21 Nursery Rhyme figures was heavily promoted, and other small decorative subjects were produced including models of Pearly Kings and Queens. A successful series of small animal models known as Whimsies was introduced in 1954. When the demand for decorative items slumped in 1965, most giftware production was stopped, although George Wade & Son carried on making a small number of such items. Wade, Heath & Co had its own design and marketing company, Wade PDM. This was taken over by Beauford Plc and named Wade Ceramics in 1989, it is currently still in operation.

DISNEY FIGURES

A range of inexpensive cellulose figures was produced by Wade in the 1930s. These are especially vulnerable to flaking paint, and prices are lower than ceramic figures from other factories.

• **Boxed sets** In 1934 the firm secured the rights to reproduce earthenware Mickey Mouse figures. Mickey, Minnie, Pluto and Horsecollar were brought out as boxed sets with an attractive label.

• **Snow White and the Seven Dwarfs** Walt Disney figures such as 'Thumper', c1961, right, were soon included in the Wade, Heath & Co catalogue. Snow White and the Seven Dwarfs were early examples, produced in 1938 to coincide with the launch of Walt Disney's film, *Snow White and the Seven Dwarfs.* These were reissued in 1981 and can now fetch up to £500 / €740 / $920.

• **Collectability** Investment pieces include Disney-related Wade as the interest in Disney is likely to be sustained for many years to come. Value depends on rarity. The more commonplace examples can still be purchased for pocket-money prices while rarer figures are more costly.

• **Boxes** If a model still has its original box, its value can be increased by as much as 50 per cent.

• **Condition** This does affect value, so be aware of small chips and imperfections which will reduce the price quite significantly.

FIGURES

The Wade figures from the 1930s are now becoming increasingly hard to find, particularly without damage or overpainting. Many of them were designed by Jessie van Hallen and were produced in a very fragile cellulose material.

- **Art Deco** Figures such as `Curtsey', `Romance',`Pompadour' and 'Dawn' (below) really sum up the spirit of the Art Deco era, but cellulose will fade with sunlight over time and is also very brittle, so collectors should ensure that they pay the right price for the item.

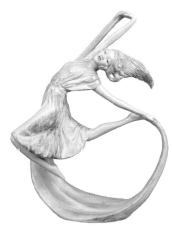

- **Marks** Figures are not always marked and do not have serial numbers.

WADE WHIMSIES

Wade Whimsies were introduced at the British Industries Fair in 1954.

- **Early animal models** These were sold in boxed sets consisting of a fawn, a horse, a poodle, a squirrel, a spaniel and an Alsatian, c1957, (above right) and, to the pottery industry's surprise, were an immediate success with children and their parents.
- **Hat Box Series** These featured characters from Walt Disney's film *Lady and the Tramp*, and Wade Minikins, a series of 48 miniature models. The Hat Box series is very popular but the little cardboard boxes need to be in excellent condition to make top price.

- **Limited Edition** Sets were produced in order to stimulate demand and encourage buyers to purchase new designs.
- **Promotional Whimsies** These free gifts appeared with everything from Christmas crackers, to tea and crisps and are extremely popular.
- **Collectability** Wade is an easy and affordable collecting area. Not only do many people have Wade Whimsies left over from their childhood that they can trade, but Wade is also freely available at most car boot sales as well as collector fairs and auctions. However, those who decide to start a Whimsie collection should be aware that

c100,000 copies of any given Whimsie were able to be made from a single die without any detail being lost. This allowed the company to make millions of Whimsies at very little cost and hence prices today are still at boot sale rather than collectors' fair level.

WADE PIGS

In 1983, the National Westminster Bank in the UK created an incentive scheme in the form of ceramic pigs. These encouraged children to bank increasing values into a new account over a two-year period.

- **Models** These were different according to savings reached and ranged from Baby Woody for £3 / €4 / $5, Annabel for £25 / €35 / $45, Maxwell for £50 / €75 / $90, Lady Hilary for £75 / €110 / $140

Irish Wade

- Some of Wade's Irish pieces were marked 'Shamrock Pottery'.
- From 1953 earthenwares with the trade name 'Irish Porcelain' have been made at the Ulster Pottery in Portadown.
- Many marks featuring the clover were used by this firm.
- A printed or impressed mark was used from 1953; 'Made in Ireland' was added from 1954.
- 'Wade & Co. Armagh' was added later. The mark appears with or without a painter's initial, such as the letter 'E'.

and finally, after two years and if at least £100 / €145 / $185 had been saved, Sir Nathaniel Westminster.
• **Rarities** The offer ended in 1988 and comparatively few children collected the full set, thus making Sir Nathaniel the rarest figure.
• **Maxwell pigs** Named after tycoon Robert Maxwell, these were made in fewer numbers and are more collectable today than other family members. Shown right are Maxwell, Annabel and Baby Woody.
• **Cousin Wesley** Introduced in 1999 to promote a £1,000 / €1,450 / $1,850 savings bond, Cousin Wesley was not successful, making them sought after by collectors.

• **Fakes** There are National Westminster Pigs on the market that were made by another pottery and these are not as desirable as Wade examples. Look for the incised Wade logo on the base.

Winstanley

Ken Allen has been making Winstanley hard-fired earthenware model cats for the last 50 years and these are still in production today, based in north Norfolk.
The company is named after Jenny Winstanley, who joined the pottery as an artist in 1959 and later married Ken Allen in the 1960s. Guest cat designers include Maisie Senechal, Robert Green and Veronica Walker.

DESIGNS
The Winstanley cat models come in more than 80 varieties including Persian, Siamese and Manx. Other animals include rabbits, dogs and mice and they are all painted by a team of artists.

because they are hand-potted no two are painted the same. The cat below was made in 2001.
• **Sought-after pieces** These include articulated and clothed cat dolls of which only 20 were made;

the Millennium Cat which was made in a limited edition of only 200.

IDENTIFICATION
• **Sizes** All Winstanley cats have size codes: small cats A–D and

COLLECTABILITY
• **Animals** Winstanley animals are unique and highly collectable;

Marks
• **Jenny Winstanley** This designer's early work has a back-sloping signature.
• **Sachs Cats** In the 1960s Sachs Fifth Avenue sold Winstanley cats, and these should be marked with a printed gold store label.

half-sized cats 1–12. These codes have changed over time and dating can be difficult, although the cats' eyes can hold a clue to the date.

• **Eyes** Early cat models may have misted eyes, as they were made by painting the iris slit in the pottery eye socket. A few years later Ken

Allen solved this problem by painting the iris slit on the back of a cathedral glass eye which was inserted later.

Worcester

Worcester figures were rare before the late 19th century, but in the 1930s Royal Worcester played a significant part in the production of ceramic figures.

Freda Doughty modelled children, and charming animals were modelled by Doris Lindner. These were very popular in America in the 1950s.

In the 1960s and 1970s Worcester made larger-scale limited edition animal, bird, equestrian and figural subjects.

As investments, the fortunes of these items have been mixed, but they are now enjoying renewed interest as it is understood that workmanship of this quality is unlikely to be repeated.

WHAT TO LOOK FOR
• **Fred Doughty figures** These figures, such as 'February', c1965, shown right, have a universal collecting appeal but, rather like their Royal Doulton equivalent, they are less popular today than with previous generations. This has meant that prices have stagnated somewhat in the past ten years; collectors should familiarize themeselves with auction and

collectors' fair prices.
• **Children of the Nations** This series of studies produced between 1934 and 1940 is particularly desirable, but again collectors need to be aware of price differences: the figure of 'India' for example is only worth a quarter of what the figure of 'Japan' would sell for.
• **Variations** Early figures like 'The Duchess's Dress' was made in two

very similar versions, but the version where the Duchess has her hand to the side of the rose is worth £100 / €140 / $175 or so less than the version where she has her hand beneath the rose.

Marks
From the late 19th century Worcester pieces were marked with a cypher that incorporated a crown, interlinked 'Ws' in a circle and the words 'Royal Worcester England'. A series of dots were added to this mark, starting with one dot in 1892 and so on, until by 1927 there were 11 dots and a star. The mark below is therefore attributed to 1926.
• 1928 the dots and star were replaced by a small square
• 1929 the square was replaced by a small diamond
• 1930 the mark was a '÷'
• 1931 the mark was two interlinked circles
• 1932 three interlinked circles
• 1933 one dot to three circles
• 1934 two dots added to three circles
and so on, until 1941 when there were nine dots
• 1949 a 'V' placed under the mark
• 1950 – 1963 a 'W' placed under mark alongside a series of dots, until the 'W' was replaced with 'R'
• 1963 onwards saw the end of the complicated dating system and pieces were marked with pattern names and the date that the pattern was first introduced.

• **Colourways** Some figures are available in various colour combinations so collectors need to be aware that when building a collection of Worcester figures there are numerous variations to consider.

• **Marks** There is often a difference in the value of figures and this is determined by the backstamp. The early puce mark which was in the 1930s and '40s will generally be more desirable than the backstamp used later.

CANDLE EXTINGUISHERS

Due to the change in living conditions in the 20th century there was a large decline in the manufacture of candle extinguishers.

However, despite the switch to electricity, the public continued to purchase candle extinguishers for decorative purposes. Favourite Worcester models included 'Nun', 'Monk', 1913, (shown right) and 'Cook'; by the 1930s these had been joined by vast quantities of the newcomers: 'Witch', 'Mandarin' and 'Hush'. The 1970s and '80s saw the reproduction of earlier extinguishers including 'Nun', 'Monk', 'Hush', 'Old Woman', 'Young Woman', 'Mr & Mrs Caudle', 'Mr Punch', 'Budge', 'Toddy', 'Owl', 'Cook', 'Girl with Feathered Hat' and the 'Girl with Mob Cap'. These were issued in Bone China and used a soft colour palette.

what to pay

British Pottery 18th & 19thC

A cow creamer, with running manganese glaze, restored, 18thC, 7½in (19cm) wide.
£550–660 / €790–950
$960–1,150 ⚒ WW

An agate salt-glazed stoneware model of a pug dog, with an impressed studded collar, c1750, 2¾in (7cm) high.
£3,100–3,700 / €4,450–5,300
$5,400–6,500 ⚒ WW

▶ **A salt-glazed stoneware jug and cover,** in the form of a bear, with applied clay chippings, c1760, 9½in (24cm) long.
£3,200–3,800 / €4,600–5,500
$5,600–6,700 ⚒ WW

A model of a pug dog, with coloured glazes, c1780, 3in (7.5cm) high.
£540–600 / €780–860
$950–1,050 ⊞ TYE

A creamware model of a recumbent lion, with coloured glazes, c1790, 3in (7.5cm) high.
£400–450 / €580–650
$700–790 ⊞ TYE

◄ **A pearlware Yorkshire Toby jug,** smoking a pipe, c1790, 10in (25.5cm) high.
£1,900–2,200 / €2,750–3,150
$3,350–3,850 ⊞ JBL
A Toby smoking a pipe is particularly rare.

A pearlware model of a recumbent lion, c1790, 4in (10cm) wide.
£390–440 / €560–630
$680–770 ⊞ TYE

A creamware model of a bear, with coloured glazes, c1790, 3in (7.5cm) high.
£1,050–1,200 / €1,500–1,700
$1,850–2,100 ⊞ TYE

► **A salt-glazed stoneware inkwell,** in the form of Mr Punch, impressed mark 'Gardner's Ink Works, Lower White Cross St, London', impressed registration mark, 19thC, 5in (12.5cm) high.
£270–320 / €390–460
$470–560 ⚲ BBR

A Perry & Co lustre inkwell, in the form of a dolphin, marked, 19thC, 4½in (11.5cm) high.
£80–95 / €115–135
$140–165 ✗ **BBR**

▶ **A pair of pottery figures,** 19thC, 8in (20.5cm) high.
£120–135 / €175–195
$210–240 ⊞ **ACAC**

A glazed terracotta model of a polar bear, 19thC, 22½in (57cm) high.
£450–540 / €650–780
$790–950 ✗ **S(Am)**

▶ **A model of a cockerel,** decorated in Pratt colours, with a removable cover, c1800, 9in (23cm) high.
£3,600–4,000 / €5,200–5,800
$6,300–7,000 ⊞ **HOW**

A pearlware Toby jug, c1800, 10in (25.5cm) high.
£1,800–2,000 / €2,600–2,900
$3,150–3,500 ⊞ JBL

A cow creamer, with coloured glazes, North Yorkshire, c1800, 5¼in (13.5cm) high.
£990–1,100 / €1,400–1,600
$1,750–1,950 ⊞ JHo

A pearlware model of a cow and milkmaid, decorated with Pratt colours, c1800, 6in (15cm) high.
£1,100–1,250 / €1,600–1,800
$1,900–2,200 ⊞ HOW

◀ **A Toby jug,** North Country, 19thC, 9¾in (25cm) high.
£280–330 / €410–490
$530–630 ⚷ SJH

▶ **A pearlware figural group of the Virgin and Child,** slight damage, 1800–10, 13¾in (35cm) high.
£420–500 / €600–720
$740–880 ⚷ DN

◀ **A Wood-style figural group of St George and the Dragon,** damaged, early 19thC, 13¼in (33.5cm) high.
£750–900 / €1,100–1,300
$1,300–1,550 ⚒ SWO

A pair of pearlware figures of the Welsh Tailor and Wife, after Derby, both modelled riding a goat, damaged, early 19thC, 5½in (14cm) high.
£170–200 / €240–290
$300–360 ⚒ PF

A cow creamer, North Yorkshire, early 19thC, 5½in (14cm) wide.
£1,200–1,350 / €1,750–1,950
$2,100–2,350 ⊞ JHo

◀ **A model of a dog,** on a pearlware plinth, slight damage, restored, c1820, 5¼in (13.5cm) high.
£210–250 / €300–360
$370–440 ⚒ SWO

A salt-glazed stoneware inkwell, in the form of a grotesque woman's head, with two quill holes to the shoulders, c1820, 2½in (6.5cm) high.
£520–620 / €750–890
$910–1,100 ✗ BBR

▶ **A pearlware figural group,** in the form of birds in a tree flanked by a man and a woman, both holding a bird, above a hat with chicks, losses, c1820, 10¼in (26cm) high.
£590–700 / €850–1,000
$1,050–1,250 ✗ DN(BR)

A model of a horse, Scottish, c1820, 6in (15cm) high.
£2,950–3,300 / €4,250–4,750
$5,200–5,800 ⊞ HOW

A Wood-style model of a cockerel, c1820, 9¾in (25cm) high.
£1,500–1,800 / €2,150–2,600
$2,650–3,150 ✗ G(L)

◀ **A pearlware model of a dog,** c1820, 4in (10cm) high.
£450–500 / €650–720
$790–880 ⊞ AUC

A **pearlware stirrup cup,** in the form of a hound's head, c1830, 5in (12.5cm) long.
£1,250–1,400 / €1,800–2,000
$2,200–2,450 ⊞ HOW

◀ **A John Walton model of a sheep beside a tree,** slight damage, impressed mark, c1825, 7in (18cm) high.
£500–600 / €720–860
$880–1,050 ⚒ G(L)

A **spill vase,** with a pig, Scottish, c1830, 6in (15cm) high.
£1,550–1,750 / €2,250–2,500
$2,700–3,050 ⊞ HOW

◀ **A Don Pottery Hearty Goodfellow Toby jug,** with pearlware glaze, maker's mark, dated 1830, 10in (25.5cm) high.
£810–900 / €1,150–1,300
$1,400–1,600 ⊞ JBL

A model of a goat, possibly Kirkaldy Pottery, Scottish, c1835, 7in (18cm) high.
£1,250–1,400 / €1,800–2,000
$2,200–2,450 ⊞ HOW

A Swansea Pottery cow creamer, Welsh, c1835, 7in (18cm) wide.
£300–340 / €430–490
$530–600 ⊞ WeW

A model of a cat, Scottish, c1840, 7in (18cm) high.
£2,250–2,500 / €3,250–3,600
$3,950–4,350 ⊞ HOW

A Copeland and Garrett earthenware model of a dog, damaged, impressed maker's mark, c1840, 11¾in (30cm) high.
£360–430 / €520–620
$630–760 ⚶ SWO

▶ **A model of a spaniel,** Scottish, c1845, (10in 25.5cm) high.
£2,000–2,250 / €2,900–3,250
$3,500–3,950 ⊞ HOW

A graduated set of Toby jugs, complete with measures, c1855, largest 10in (25.5cm) high.
£900–1,000 / €1,300–1,450
$1,550–1,750 ⊞ JBL

◀ **A Victorian terracotta figure of a female tennis player,** by W. C. Lawton, No. 186, impressed signature, 8½in (21.5cm) high.
£45–50 / €65–75
$80–90 🔨 G(L)

A W. H. Goss figure of an angel holding a stoup, a copy of the font at St John's church, Barmouth, 1862–86, 6in (15cm) high.
£400–450 / €580–650
$700–790 ⊞ G&CC

A model of a cat, decorated with flowers, c1870, 9in (23cm) high.
£810–900 / €1,150–1,300
$1,400–1,600 ⊞ RdeR

A majolica model of a frog, c1875, 4¼in (11cm) wide.
£380–450 / €550–650
$670–790 🔨 **WW**

A pottery tureen, in the form of a hen and a chick, base missing, c1875, 7in (18cm) wide.
£75–85 / €110–125
$130–145 ⊞ **SER**

A pair of models of cats, with gilt decoration, Scottish, c1880, 13in (33cm) high.
£1,800–2,000 / €2,600–2,900
$3,150–3,500 ⊞ **HOW**

A Beswick figure of a Welsh lady, impressed mark, 1878, 5½in (14cm) high.
£145–165 / €210–240
$250–280 ⊞ **ACAC**

A Llanelli Pottery cow creamer, Welsh, c1880, 7in (18cm) wide.
£360–400 / €520–580
$630–700 ⊞ **WeW**

A pair of jugs, in the form of begging King Charles spaniels, c1880, 10in (25.5cm) high.
£900–1,000 / €1,300–1,450
$1,600–1,800 ⊞ RdeR

A Doulton Lambeth group, by George Tinworth, entitled 'Play Goers', in the form of mice watching a Punch and Judy show, c1886, 5¼in (13.5cm) high.
£5,700–6,400 / €8,200–9,200
$10,000–11,200 ⊞ POW

A pair of models of pug dogs, with glass eyes, Scottish, c1900, 12in (30.5cm) high.
£500–550 / €720–800
$870–960 ⊞ HOW

► A Yorkshire Toby jug, c1900, 10in (25.5cm) high.
£580–650 / €840–940
$1,000–1,100 ⊞ JBL

Minton

A Minton spill vase, entitled 'Babes in the Wood', c1835, 6in (15cm) high.
£680–760 / €980–1,100
$1,200–1,350 ⊞ DAN

▶ **A set of four Minton figures,** representing the seasons, c1840, 6in (15cm) high.
£3,600–4,000 / €5,200–5,800
$6,300–7,000 ⊞ HKW

◀ **A Minton candle snuffer,** entitled 'Lady Teazle', c1850, 4in (10cm) high.
£790–880 / €1,150–1,300
$1,400–1,550 ⊞ TH

A Victorian Minton majolica group of a fox and a crane, after Aesop's fable, damaged and repaired, 8¼in (21cm) high.
£6,200–7,400 / €8,900–10,700
$10,900–13,000 ⚒ G(L)

A Minton centrepiece, damaged and restored, c1851, 14¼in (36cm) high.
£1,750–1,950 / €2,500–2,800
$3,050–3,400 ⊞ MER

◄ **A Minton majolica leaf dish,** the bowl supported by two rabbits, c1860, 10in (25.5cm) wide.
£3,500–3,900
€5,000–5,600
$6,100–6,800 ⊞ BRT

A Minton majolica inkwell, c1860, 13in (33cm) wide.
£1,400–1,600 / €2,000–2,350
$2,400–2,850 ⊞ BRT

A Joseph Holdcroft dish, applied with a model of a squirrel holding a nut, c1870, 8in (20.5cm) diam.
£540–600 / €790–870
$950–1,050 ⊞ BRT

A Minton vase, by Joseph Holdcroft, in the form of an elephant, c1870, 8in (20.5cm) high.
£700–780 / €1,000–1,100
$1,200–1,350 ⊞ BRT

A late Victorian Minton model of a seated dog, moulded mark, 5½in (14cm) high.
£210–250 / €300–360
$370–440 ↗ G(L)

A pair of Minton majolica models of magpies, after Meissen, impressed marks and date code, c1870, 21in (53.5cm) high.
£580–690 / €840–990
$1,000–1,200 ↗ SWO

▶ **A Minton porcelain figure of Whistler's mother,** after his painting 'Study in Black', 1872, 11in (28cm) high.
£630–700
€900–1,000
$1,100–1,250
⊞ JAK

▶ **A Minton majolica model of a grey heron,** modelled by Paul Comolera, slight damage, impressed marks, date cypher for 1876, 39½in (100.5cm) high.
£7,800–9,300 / €11,200–13,400
$13,700–16,300 ↗ WW

Prattware

◄ **A Prattware figure of a woman,** c1780, 5in (12.5cm) high.
£155–175 / €220–250
$270–310 ⊞ SER

A Prattware figure of Apollo, c1790, 5in (12.5cm) high.
£135–150 / €195–220
$240–270 ⊞ SER

A Prattware figural group of a man and a dog, c1790, 10in (25.5cm) high.
£760–850 / €1,100–1,250
$1,350–1,500 ⊞ AUC

◄ **A Prattware Martha Gunn Toby jug,** c1790, 10in (25.5cm) high.
£1,150–1,300 / €1,650–1,850
$2,000–2,200 ⊞ JBL

► **A Prattware model of a cockerel,** c1790, 4in (10cm) high.
£390–440 / €560–630
$680–770 ⊞ DAN

◄ **Two Prattware models of birds,** c1795, 3¼in (8.5cm) high.
£1,900–2,200
€2,750–3,150
$3,350–3,850
⊞ JRe

A Prattware model of a chicken, c1800, 3¼in (8.5cm) high.
£290–330 / €420–480
$510–580 ⊞ AUC

◀ **A Prattware plaque,** in the form of a female term wearing robes and a laurel wreath, c1800, 7¾in (19.5cm) high.
£150–180 / €220–260
$260–310 ➚ WW

A Prattware figure of a fiddler, c1800, 7½in (19cm) high.
£1,650–1,850 / €2,400–2,650
$2,900–3,250 ⊞ JHo

A Prattware model of a reclining horse, c1800, 3½in (9cm) high.
£1,050–1,200 / €1,500–1,700
$1,850–2,100 ⊞ JHo

A Prattware jug, in the form of Bacchus, early 19thC, 11in (28cm) high.
£340–400 / €490–580
$600–710 ➚ G(L)

A Prattware figural group, depicting St George and the Dragon, early 19thC, 11¼in (28.5cm) high.
£1,300–1,550 / €1,850–2,200
$2,300–2,700 ✗ **WW**

A Prattware group of a ram and shepherd with lambs, Yorkshire, c1810, 7in (18cm) high.
£1,600–1,800 / €2,300–2,600
$2,800–3,150 ⊞ **HOW**

A Prattware pipe, in the form of a sailor sitting astride a barrel, slight damage, c1805, 6in (15cm) high.
£950–1,100 / €1,350–1,600
$1,650–1,950 ✗ **Bri**

A Prattware snuff box, in the form of a hand, with detachable screw base, possibly Scottish, c1810, 3in (7.5cm) high.
£1,450–1,650
€2,100–2,400
$2,550–2,900 ⊞ **GAU**

A Prattware pipe, entitled 'The Farmer', in the form of a seated man smoking a pipe, c1810, 5½in (14cm) high.
£580–680 / €840–990
$1,000–1,200 ✗ **DN(Bri)**

◄ **A Prattware model of a camel,** 1810–20, 2¾in (7cm) high.
£620–740 / €890–1,050
$1,100–1,300 ✗ **WW**

Staffordshire

A pair of Staffordshire earthenware models of animals, c1760, 2in (5cm) high.
£2,700–3,000 / €3,900–4,300
$4,750–5,300 ⊞ JRe

A Staffordshire Wood family creamware Toby jug, with measure, damaged and restored, late 18thC, 9½in (24cm) high.
£1,300–1,500 / €1,850–2,200
$2,300–2,700 ⅄ S
The Wood family of Burslem were important potters in the late 18th and early 19th centuries.

▶ **A Staffordshire model of a recumbent lion,** slight damage, c1780, 3in (7.5cm) long.
£310–350
€450–500
$540–610
⊞ G&G

A Staffordshire model of a deer, with bocage, late 18thC, 5¾in (14.5cm) high.
£190–220 / €270–320
$330–390 ⅄ G(L)

◀ **A Staffordshire creamware cow creamer,** c1790, 7in (18cm) long.
£850–950 / €1,200–1,350
$1,500–1,650 ⊞ DAN

A Staffordshire Toby jug, damaged, 19thC, 10¼in (26cm) high.
£300–360 / €430–520
$560–670 ↗ **WW**

A pair of Staffordshire models of lions, with a treacle glaze, 19thC, 12in (30.5cm) wide.
£620–740 / €890–1,050
$1,100–1,300 ↗ **AH**

A pair of Staffordshire models of pigeons, early 19thC, 3in (7.5cm) high.
£790–880 / €1,150–1,300
$1,400–1,550 ⊞ **JHo**

A Staffordshire Toby jug, 19thC, 9¾in (25cm) high.
£270–300 / €400–440
$500–560 ↗ **SJH**

A Staffordshire Toby jug, early 19thC, 10in (25.5cm) high.
£300–360 / €440–530
$560–670 ⚲ **SJH**

A pair of Staffordshire figures of a man and a woman, entitled 'Old Age', 1810–15, 9in (23cm) high.
£670–750 / €960–1,100
$1,150–1,300 ⊞ **DAN**

A Staffordshire figure of a putto, holding a basket of flowers, slight damage, c1810, 5¼in (13.5cm) high.
£135–150 / €195–220
$240–270 ⊞ **G&G**

◄ **A Staffordshire pearlware group of a stag and birds,** c1810, 6in (15cm) high.
£1,350–1,500
€1,950–2,150
$2,350–2,650
⊞ **HOW**

A Staffordshire figure, by Walton, entitled 'the Widow of Zarephath', 1810–20, 11in (28cm) high.
£440–490 / €630–700
$780–870 ⊞ TYE

A Staffordshire model of a recumbent leopard, c1815, 8in (20.5cm) long.
£4,000–4,500 / €5,800–6,500
$7,000–7,900 ⊞ HOW

A Staffordshire group of three sheep beneath a tree, No. 2299, c1815, 4¾in (12cm) high.
£250–290 / €360–400
$440–500 ⊞ SER

A Staffordshire spill vase, with a sheep and a lamb standing before bocage, No. 2298, c1815, 5¼in (13.5cm) high.
£250–290 / €360–400
$440–500 ⊞ SER

A pair of Staffordshire pearlware models of lions, slight damage, c1820, 6in (15cm) wide.
£1,750–2,100 / €2,500–3,000
$3,100–3,700 ⚒ BWL

A Staffordshire model of a recumbent deer, before bocage, 1820, 4½in (11.5cm) high.
£140–165 / €200–240
$250–300 🔨 SJH

A Staffordshire pearlware model of a cow, before bocage, c1820, 7in (18cm) high.
£1,800–2,000 / €2,600–2,900
$3,150–3,500 ⊞ HOW

A Staffordshire model of a pug dog, c1820, 3¾in (9.5cm) high.
£490–550 / €710–790
$860–960 ⊞ JHo

A Staffordshire spill vase, with a bull, c1820, 8in (20.5cm) high.
£1,750–1,950 / €2,500–2,800
$3,050–3,400 ⊞ HOW

◀ A Staffordshire pearlware model of a doe, before bocage, 1820, 6in (15cm) high.
£320–360 / €460–520
$560–630 ⊞ TYE

A Staffordshire pearlware group of Abraham, Isaac and the Angel, restored, c1820, 7½in (19cm) high.
£420–500 / €600–720
$740–880 ✗ WW

A Staffordshire group of a ewe and a lamb, before bocage, c1820, 6in (15cm) high.
£310–350 / €450–500
$540–610 ⊞ TYE

A Staffordshire pottery model of a pug dog, c1825, 4in (10cm) high.
£390–440 / €560–630
$680–770 ⊞ DAN

A Staffordshire pearlware group of Vicar and Moses, c1830, 10¼in (26cm) high.
£200–240 / €290–350
$350–420 ✗ SWO

A Staffordshire Toby jug, handle repaired, c1830, 9¾in (25cm) high.
£220–260 / €320–380
$390–460 ⚒ SWO

A Staffordshire model of a poodle, by Samuel Alcock, c1835, 3in (7.5cm) high.
£230–260 / €330–370
$400–450 ⊞ DAN

A Staffordshire Wellington Toby jug, with a treacle glaze, c1835, 7in (18cm) high.
£115–130 / €165–185
$200–230 ⊞ DHA

A Staffordshire porcellaneous model of a poodle, 1835–40, 4in (10cm) high.
£340–380 / €490–550
$600–670 ⊞ DAN

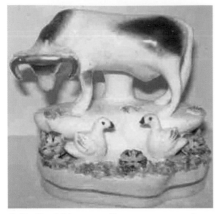

A Staffordshire porcellaneous group of a cow and two ducks, c1840.
£160–190 / €230–270
$280–330 ➢ SJH

A Staffordshire stoneware model of a lop-eared rabbit, 1840, 3in (7.5cm) high.
£450–500 / €650–720
$790–880 ⊞ HOW

▶ A pair of Staffordshire models of spaniels, by Alcock & Co, c1840, 5in (12.5cm) high.
£1,250–1,400
€1,800–2,000
$2,200–2,450
⊞ HOW

Two Victorian Staffordshire Toby jugs, smaller jug cracked, larger 10in (25.5cm) high.
£90–100 / €130–145
$160–175 ➢ G(L)

A Staffordshire model of a spaniel, c1845, 7in (18cm) high.
£670–750 / €960–1,100
$1,100–1,300 ⊞ HOW

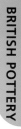

◀ **A pair of Staffordshire models of spaniels,** c1845, 6in (15cm) high.
£850–950
€1,250–1,400
$1,500–1,650
⊞ HOW

A pair of Staffordshire models of spaniels, each with a puppy, c1850, 7¾in (19.5cm) high.
£240–280 / €350–410
$420–500 ⚒ G(L)

A pair of Staffordshire models of seated Dalmatians, c1850, 5in (12.5cm) high.
£320–380 / €460–550
$560–670 ⚒ G(L)

A Staffordshire group of a princess and a goat, c1850, 6in (15cm) high.
£210–240 / €300–330
$370–420 ⊞ DHA

A Staffordshire model of a dog smoking a pipe, c1850, 10in (25.5cm) high.
£1,800–2,000 / €2,600–2,900
$3,150–3,500 ⊞ HOW

A pair of Staffordshire models of ponies, c1850, 5in (12.5cm) high.
£750–850 / €1,100–1,250
$1,300–1,500 ⊞ HOW

A pair of Staffordshire models of spaniels, c1850, 5in (12.5cm) high.
£1,550–1,750 / €2,250–2,500
£2,700–3,050 ⊞ HOW

A Staffordshire Toby jug, slight damage,
c1850, 9in (23cm) high.
£105–120 / €150–165
$185–210 ⊞ F&F

A Staffordshire group of three dogs, c1850, 7½in (19cm) high.
£1,750–1,950 / €2,500–2,800
$3,050–3,400 ⊞ HOW

**A Staffordshire model of a dog smoking a
pipe,** c1850, 9in (23cm) high.
£1,250–1,400 / €1,800–2,000
$2,200–2,450 ⊞ HOW

A pair of Staffordshire models of spaniels, with separated front legs, c1850, 6in (15cm) high.
£580–650 / €840–940
$1,000–1,150 ⊞ HOW

A Staffordshire Wellington Toby jug, No. 2236, c1850, 7in (18cm) high.
£310–350 / €450–500
$540–610 ⊞ SER

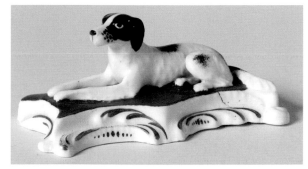

A Staffordshire model of a recumbent dog, c1850, 4½in (11.5cm) wide.
£135–150 / €195–220
$240–270 ⊞ SER

A pair of Staffordshire models of exotic birds, c1850, 9in (23cm) high.
£990–1,100 / €1,450–1,600
$1,750–1,950 ⊞ HOW

◄ **A Staffordshire spill vase,** with a whippet before a tree trunk, c1850, 7in (18cm) high.
£990–1,100 / €1,450–1,600
$1,750–1,950 ⊞ HOW

A pair of Staffordshire models of spaniels, c1850, 6in (15cm) high.
£810–900 / €1,150–1,300
$1,400–1,600 ⊞ DAN

A Staffordshire spill vase, with a leopard and cubs, c1850, 10in (25.5cm) high.
£880–980 / €1,250–1,400
$1,500–1,700 ⊞ HOW

A pair of Staffordshire models of poodles, c1850, 8in (20.5cm) high.
£310–350 / €450–500
$540–610 ⊞ NAW

A pair of Staffordshire porcelain models of poodles, both holding a basket, mid-19thC, 3¼in (8.5cm) high.
£170–200 / €240–290
$300–360 ✦ WW

A Staffordshire figural group of Jenny Marston as 'Perdita' and Fredrick Robinson as 'Florizel', entitled '*Winter's Tale*', c1850, 11¾in (30cm) high.
£75–85 / €110–125
$145–165 ✦ DA

A **Staffordshire group of a horse and lion,**
c1850, 12in (30.5cm) high.
£760–850 / €1,100–1,250
$1,350–1,500 ⊞ HOW

A pair of **Staffordshire models of
greyhounds,** with inkwell bases,
1850–1900, 6in (15cm) long
£180–210 / €260–310
$320–380 ⚒ WW

◄ A **Staffordshire Crimean War
figural group of a French soldier
and an English sailor,** minor
damage, c1854,
13½in (34.5cm) high.
£700–840 / €1,000–1,200
$1,250–1,500 ⚒ DN

A **Staffordshire model of a bird,** perched
upon branches, c1855, 8½in (21.5cm) high.
£320–380 / €460–550
$560–670 ⚒ G(L)

A pair of **Staffordshire flatback spill vases,** with peacocks,
c1855, 8¼in (21cm) high.
£290–340 / €420–500
$510–600 ⚒ G(B)

A Staffordshire model of a horse, c1855,
5in (12.5cm) high.
£340–380 / €490–550
$600–670 ⊞ HOW

A pair of Staffordshire models of spaniels, both holding a basket
of flowers, c1855, 8in (20.5cm) high.
£1,400–1,600 / €2,000–2,250
$2,450–2,800 ⊞ HOW

**A pair of Staffordshire models of St Bernards with royal
children,** c1855, 9in (23cm) high.
£2,250–2,500 / €3,250–3,600
$3,950–4,400 ⊞ HOW

A Staffordshire model of a parrot, c1855,
9in (23cm) high.
£520–580 / €750–840
$900–1,000 ⊞ DAN

A Staffordshire model of a Welsh springer spaniel, c1855,
8in (20.5cm) wide.
£1,750–1,950 / €2,500–2,800
$3,050–3,400 ⊞ HOW

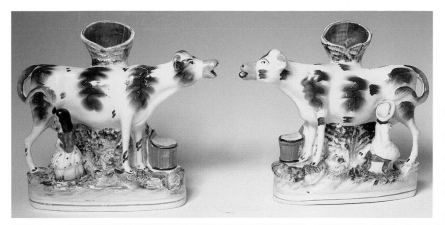

◄ A pair of Staffordshire spill vases, in the form of cows before tree trunks, c1855, 9in (23cm) high.
£720–800
€1,050–1,200
$1,250–1,400
⊞ HOW

A pair of Staffordshire models of spaniels, both holding a basket, c1855, 8in (20.5cm) high.
£1,400–1,600 / €2,000–2,300
$2,450–2,800 ⊞ HOW

A Staffordshire model of a spaniel, c1855, 9½in (24cm) high.
£980–1,150 / €1,400–1,650
$1,700–2,000 ↗ SWO

► A pair of Staffordshire models of spaniels, both with a puppy, c1855, 6in (15cm) high.
£1,400–1,600
€2,000–2,250
$2,450–2,800
⊞ HOW

A Staffordshire model, entitled 'Billy the Rat Catcher',
c1855, 6in (15cm) high.
£900–1,000 / €1,300–1,450
$1,600–1,800 ⊞ **HOW**

A Staffordshire spill vase, with two foxes and their
quarry, c1855, 9in (23cm) high.
£720–800 / €1,000–1,150
$1,250–1,400 ⊞ **HOW**

◄ **A pair of Staffordshire models of lion dogs,** c1855,
8in (20.5cm) high.
£870–980 / €1,250–1,400
$1,500–1,700 ⊞ **HOW**

► **A pair of
Staffordshire
models of sheep,**
both with a flag,
c1855, 3in
(7.5cm) high.
£340–380
€490–550
$600–670
⊞ **HOW**

A **Staffordshire tureen**, in the form of a hen on a nest, with chicks, c1855, 7in (18cm) high.
£720–800 / €1,050–1,200
$1,250–1,400 ⊞ HOW

A **Staffordshire group of a dog and a child**, the dog holding a basket, c1855, 10in (25.5cm) high.
£1,000–1,150 / €1,450–1,650
$1,750–2,000 ⊞ HOW

◄ A **pair of Staffordshire figures**, with dogs and kennels, c1855, 9in (23cm) high.
£720–800 / €1,050–1,200
$1,250–1,400 ⊞ HOW

A **pair of Staffordshire spill vases**, each with a doe and fawn, one fawn restored, c1860, 6¾in (17cm) high.
£240–280 / €350–400
$420–500 ↗ SWO

A **Staffordshire model of a greyhound**, holding a dead hare, neck repaired, c1860, 9¾in (25cm) high.
£60–70 / €85–100
$105–125 ↗ G(L)

A Staffordshire group of a huntsman with fox and hounds, restored, c1860, 9¾in (25cm) high.
£380–450 / €550–650
$670–790 ✂ SWO

A Staffordshire spill vase, with a lion, c1860, 5in (12.5cm) high.
£310–350 / €450–500
$540–610 ⊞ HOW

A Staffordshire group of a seated Afghan hound and a girl, c1860, 13in (33cm) high.
£850–950 / €1,200–1,350
$1,500–1,650 ⊞ ML

▶ **A Staffordshire Landlord Toby jug,** with original stopper, c1860, 13in (33cm) high.
£850–950 / €1,200–1,350
$1,500–1,650 ⊞ JBL

A pair of Staffordshire miniature models of roosters,
c1860, 4in (10cm) high.
£430–480 / €620–690
$750–840 ⊞ HOW

A pair of Staffordshire Jackfield-style models of cats,
c1860, 8in (20.5cm) high.
£750–840 / €1,100–1,250
$1,300–1,450 ⊞ HOW

A Staffordshire spill vase, with a fox before a wheat-
sheaf, c1860, 5in (12.5cm) high.
£350–390 / €500–560
$610–680 ⊞ HOW

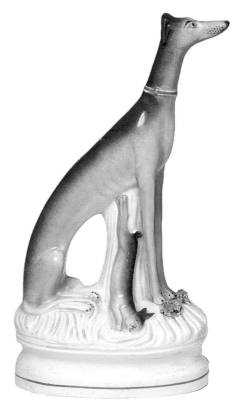

A pair of Staffordshire models of greyhounds,
entitled 'High' and 'Mighty', c1860, 13in (33cm) high.
£1,250–1,400 / €1,800–2,000
$2,200–2,450 ⊞ HOW

◄ **A pair of Staffordshire models of sporting dogs
with game,** c1860, 9in (23cm) high.
£1,050–1,200 / €1,500–1,700
$1,850–2,100 ⊞ HOW

A pair of Staffordshire spill vases, both with a fox and a lamb, c1860, 8in (20.5cm) high.
£1,050–1,200 / €1,500–1,700
$1,850–2,100 ⊞ HOW

A Staffordshire spill vase, with a cow before a tree trunk, c1860, 13in (33cm) high.
£1,600–1,800 / €2,300–2,600
$2,800–3,150 ⊞ HOW

A Staffordshire spill vase, with an elephant before a tree trunk, c1860, 7in (18cm) high.
£720–800 / €1,050–1,200
$1,250–1,400 ⊞ HOW

▶ **A Staffordshire jug,** in the form of a begging spaniel, c1860, 10in (25.5cm) high.
£450–500 / €650–720
$790–880 ⊞ HOW

◄ A pair of **Staffordshire spill vases,** both with a poodle and kennel, c1860, 8in (20.5cm) high.
£1,050–1,200 / €1,500–1,700 / $1,850–2,100 ⊞ HOW

A pair of **Staffordshire models of zebras,** by Thomas Parr, c1860, 5in (12.5cm) high
£720–800 / €1,050–1,200 / $1,250–1,400 ⊞ HOW

A pair of **Staffordshire models of spaniels,** both with a puppy, c1860, 8in (20.5cm) high.
£720–800 / €1,050–1,200 / $1,250–1,400 ⊞ HOW

A pair of **Staffordshire models of spaniels,** No. 1, c1860, 13in (33cm) high.
£630–700 / €900–1,000 / $1,100–1,250 ⊞ HOW

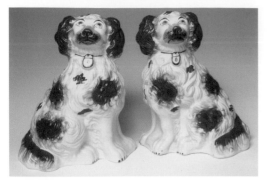

A pair of Staffordshire models of spaniels, c1860, 13in (33cm) high.
£900–1,000 / €1,300–1,450
$1,550–1,750 ⊞ HOW

A pair of Staffordshire models of spaniels, both with a puppy, c1860, 7in (18cm) high.
£670–750 / €960–1,100
$1,150–1,300 ⊞ DAN

A pair of Staffordshire models of poodles, c1860, 7in (18cm) high.
£370–420 / €530–600
$650–740 ⊞ DAN

A Staffordshire model of a cow, c1860, 5in (12.5cm) high.
£320–360 / €460–520
$560–630 ⊞ DAN

A pair of Staffordshire models of zebras, c1860, 8in (20.5cm) high.
£540–600 / €780–860
$940–1,050 ⊞ HOW

A pair of Staffordshire models of zebras, c1860, 6in (15cm) high.
£490–550 / €710–790
$860–960 ⊞ HOW

A Staffordshire Toby jug, 1860, 8½in (21.5cm) high.
£330–370 / €480–530
$580–650 ⊞ RAN

A pair of Staffordshire models of sporting dogs, c1860, 10in (25.5cm) high.
£1,250–1,400 / €1,800–2,000
$2,200–2,450 ⊞ HOW

A pair of Staffordshire tureens and covers, each in the form of a pigeon on a nest, beaks chipped, damaged, c1860, 8¾in (22cm) high.
£660–790 / €960–1,150
$1,200–1,400 ⚒ SWO

◄ **A Staffordshire Toby jug,** 1860, 8¾in (21.5cm) high.
£350–390 / €500–560
$610–680 ⊞ RAN

A pair of Staffordshire spill vases, both with a horse and foal, c1860, 13in (33cm) high.
£1,750–1,950 / €2,500–2,800
$3,050–3,400 ⊞ RGa

A pair of Staffordshire copper lustre models of spaniels, with separated ront legs, 1860–65, 10in (25.5cm) high.
£350–400 / €500–560
$610–700 ⊞ ML

A pair of Staffordshire earthenware models of spaniels, c1865, 12½in (32cm) high.
£300–360 / €430–520
$530–630 ⚒ G(L)

A Staffordshire Mr Punch Toby jug, damaged, 1860, 12in (30.5cm) high.
£420–470 / €600–680
$740–820 ⊞ RAN

A Staffordshire model of a cow, before a fence, No. 2297, c1870, 4in (10cm) high.
£290–330 / €420–470
$510–580 ⊞ SER

A pair of Staffordshire models of spaniels, c1870, 9in (23cm) high.
£100–120 / €145–170
$200–240 ⚒ SWO

A pair of Staffordshire models of seated spaniels, each holding a basket of flowers, c1870, 7½in (19cm) high.
£450–540 / €650–780
$790–950 ⚒ TMA

A Staffordshire tureen, in the form of a hen on a nest, c1870, 9½in (24cm) long.
£170–190 / €240–270
$300–330 ⊞ BWL

◄ **A Staffordshire spill vase,** with a horse and foal, c1870, 13in (33cm) high.
£490–550 / €710–790
$860–960 ⊞ HOW

▶ **A pair of Staffordshire models of whippets,** each holding a rabbit, c1870, 7½in (19cm) high.
£130–150
€185–220
$230–270 ⚒ G(L)

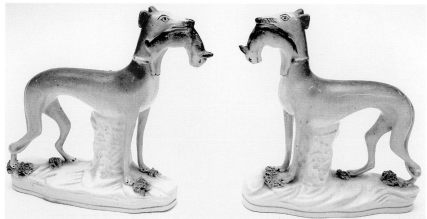

A Staffordshire Snuff Taker Toby jug, with a treacle glaze, c1870, 10in (25.5cm) high.
£70–80 / €100–115
$135–155 ⊞ IW

A Staffordshire model of a dog, with gilt collar, incised initials 'WM' and 'NT', c1870, 10¾in (27.5cm) high.
£130–155 / €185–220
$230–270 ⚒ SWO

A pair of Staffordshire models of spaniels, c1870, 14in (35.5cm) high.
£850–950 / €1,200–1,350
$1,500–1,650 ⊞ HOW

A pair of Staffordshire copper lustre models of dogs, No. SF780 T15, c1870, 8in (20.5cm) high.
£110–125 / €160–180
$195–220 ⊞ CHAC

A pair of Staffordshire models of zebras, No. 2313, c1870, 9in (23cm) high.
£430–480 / €620–690
$750–840 ⊞ SER

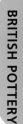

A Staffordshire model of a hen on a nest, c1870, 13in (33cm) high.
£340–380 / €490–550
$600–670 ⊞ HOW

A Staffordshire model of a cow, entitled 'Milk Sold Here', c1870, 15in (38cm) high.
£1,350–1,500 / €1,950–2,150
$2,350–2,650 ⊞ HOW

A Staffordshire spill vase, with Macoma and the Lion, c1870, 8¼in (21cm) high.
£800–960 / €1,200–1,400
$1,400–1,650 ✗ SJH

A pair of Staffordshire majolica guggle jugs, both in the form of a fish, c1870, 8in (20.5cm) high.
£180–200 / €260–290
$310–350 ⊞ BRT

▶ A Staffordshire Brownfield model of a begging terrier, seated on a cushion with a basket in its mouth, c1870, 7¾in (19.5cm) high.
£130–155 / €185–220
$230–270 ✗ L&E

A Staffordshire Toby jug, his tricorn hat with a measuring cup, restored, c1870, 9¾in (25cm) high.
£100–120 / €145–175
$190–230 🔨 SWO

A Staffordshire Squire Toby jug, pipe missing, c1875, 10in (25.5cm) high.
£580–650 / €850–960
$1,100–1,250 ⊞ JBL

A pair of Staffordshire models of dogs, No. SF488 T45, c1870, 9½in (24cm) high.
£350–400 / €500–560
$610–700 ⊞ CHAC

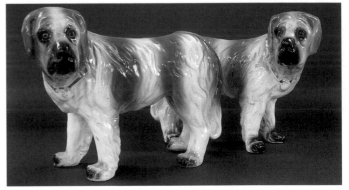

A pair of Staffordshire models of St Bernards, with glass eyes, one leg damaged, late 19thC, 10in (25.5cm) high.
£250–280 / €360–400
$440–490 ⊞ BWL

A pair of Staffordshire copper lustre models of spaniels, No. 755 T25, c1875, 12½in (32cm) high.
£220–250 / €320–360
$390–440 ⊞ CHAC

A Staffordshire model of a hen on a nest, c1875, 7in (18cm) high.
£430–480 / €620–690
$750–840 ⊞ HOW

A Staffordshire model of a horse, ears and neck restored, late 19thC, 11¾in (30cm) long.
£480–570 / €690–820
$840–1,000 ↗ SWO

A Staffordshire model of a zebra, c1875, 6¼in (16cm) high.
£45–50 / €65–75
$85–95 ↗ G(L)

◄ **A pair of Staffordshire models of spaniels,** No. SF T25, c1875, 9½in (24cm) high.
£220–250 / €320–360
$390–440 ⊞ CHAC

► **A pair of Staffordshire models of dogs,** No. SF492 T25, c1880, 7½in (19cm) high.
£240–270
€350–390
$420–470
⊞ CHAC

A Staffordshire Mr Pickwick Toby jug, late 19thC, 8in (20.5cm) high.
£55–65 / €80–95
$105–125 ⚒ G(L)

A Staffordshire spill vase, in the form of a goat before a tree trunk, c1880, 4in (10cm) high.
£165–185 / €230–270
$280–320 ⊞ SER

A Staffordshire model of a recumbent dog, 1880, 5in (10cm) wide.
£175–195 / €250–280
$300–340 ⊞ TYE

A pair of Staffordshire models of pug dogs, c1880, 7in (18cm) high.
£630–700 / €900–1,000
$1,100–1,250 ⊞ HOW

A pair of Staffordshire models of pug dogs, c1880, 11in (28cm) high.
£1,000–1,150 / €1,450–1,650
$1,750–2,000 ⊞ HOW

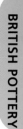

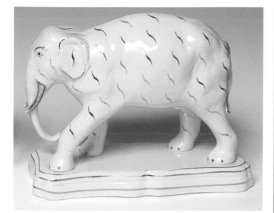

A pair of Staffordshire models of elephants, c1880, 8in (20.5cm) high.
£2,300–2,600 / €3,300–3,750
$4,050–4,550 ⊞ HOW

A pair of Staffordshire models of pug dogs, c1880, 12in (30.5cm) high.
£540–600 / €780–860
$950–1,050 ⊞ ML

A Staffordshire model of a dog, c1880, 4in (10cm) high.
£310–350 / €450–500
$540–610 ⊞ SER

A Staffordshire Squire Toby jug, 1875–1925, 9½in (24cm) high.
£180–210 / €260–310
$340–400 ➶ SJH

A Staffordshire Squire Toby jug, 1875–1925, 10¾in (27.5cm) high.
£90–100 / €130–145
$170–190 ⚒ WW

A pair of Staffordshire copper lustre models of dogs, c1890, 8in (20.5cm) high.
£50–60 / €75–85
$100–115 ⚒ G(L)

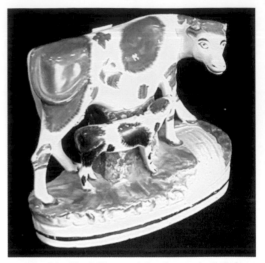

A pair of Staffordshire models of cows, both with a calf, damaged, c1880, 9in (23cm) high.
£400–480 / €580–690
$700–840 ⚒ SWO

A pair of Staffordshire models of dogs, damaged and repaired, c1890, 11¾in (30cm) long.
£200–240 / €290–350
$350–420 ⚒ SWO

A Staffordshire model of a horse, c1890, 12in (30.5cm) wide.
£2,450–2,750 / €3,550–3,950
$4,300–4,800 ⊞ RGa

A pair of Staffordshire models of cats, c1890, 8in (20.5cm) high.
£350–400 / €500–560
$610–700 ⊞ ML

A Staffordshire tureen and cover, in the form of a hen on a nest, c1895, 9in (23cm) long.
£180–210 / €260–310
$320–380 ⚘ SJH

A Staffordshire cow creamer and cover, transfer-printed with Willow pattern, slight damage, c1900, 6¼in (16cm) high.
£90–100 / €130–145
$170–190 ⚘ WW

A pair of Staffordshire models of camels, c1900, 6in (15cm) high.
£1,800–2,000 / €2,600–2,900
$3,150–3,500 ⊞ HOW

◀ **A Staffordshire Snuff-Taker Toby jug,** by Allertons, c1900, 7in (18cm) high.
£75–85 / €110–125
$145–165 ⊞ DHA

Wemyss

A Wemyss model of a pig, with black glaze, Scottish, c1885, 7in (18cm) long.
£1,050–1,200 / €1,600–1,800
$2,000–2,200 ⊞ GLB

A Wemyss model of a pig, c1895, 6¼in (16cm) long.
£1,250–1,400 / €1,800–2,000
$2,200–2,450 ⊞ GLB

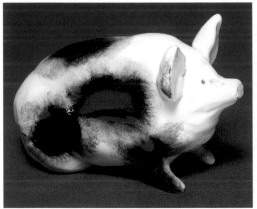

A Wemyss model of a pig, Scottish, c1895, 7in (18cm) long.
£780–880 / €1,100–1,250
$1,350–1,550 ⊞ GLB

A Wemyss model of a pig, c1900, 7in (18cm) long.
£900–1,000 / €1,300–1,450
$1,600–1,800 ⊞ GLB

▶ **A Wemyss model of a pig,** c1900, 7in (18cm) long.
£650–730 / €940–1,050
$1,150–1,300 ⊞ GLB

A Wemyss model of a pig, c1900, 17in (43cm) long.
**£2,250–2,500 / €3,250–3,650
$3,950–4,450** ⊞ RdeR

A Wemyss model of a pig, c1900,
16½in (42cm) long.
**£1,850–2,100 / €2,650–3,000
$3,250–3,700** ⊞ GLB

► **A Wemyss model of a
pig,** c1900, 7in (18cm) long.
**£670–750 / €960–1,100
$1,150–1,300** ⊞ GLB

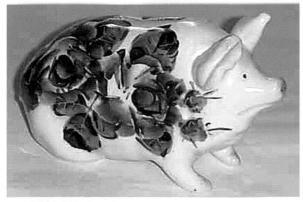

A Wemyss model of a pig, c1900, 6¼in (16cm) long.
**£1,250–1,400 / €1,800–2,000
$2,200–2,450** ⊞ GLB

A Wemyss model of a pig, impressed mark,
Scottish, c1900.
**£800–890 / €1,150–1,300
$1,400–1,550** ⊞ RdeR

Ralph Wood

A Ralph Wood model of a goat, 1775–85, 6½in (16.5cm) high.
£2,400–2,850 / €3,450–4,100
$4,200–5,000 ➴ G(L)

A Ralph Wood figure of a shepherd carrying a sheep, late 18thC, 8½in (21.5cm) high.
£180–210 / €260–310
$320–380 ➴ BWL

A Ralph Wood pearlware figure of a shepherd, the base decorated with sheep and birds, c1785, 8½in (21.5cm) high.
£450–500 / €650–720
$790–880 ⊞ JRe

A Ralph Wood figure of a woman holding two vases, stamped '67', c1785, 9in (23cm) high.
£1,400–1,600 / €2,000–2,200
$2,500–2,800 ⊞ JRe

A **Ralph Wood model of a ram,** c1790, 7in (18cm) long.
£2,050–2,300 / €3,000–3,300
$3,700–4,100 ⊞ HOW

A **Ralph Wood pearlware figure of a woman holding a tambourine,** c1790,
11½in (29cm) high.
£1,100–1,250 / €1,600–1,800
$1,950–2,200 ⊞ AUC

A **Ralph Wood figural group of a man and woman with a bird cage,** restored, marked 'Wood No. 89', c1790,
10½in (26.5cm) high.
£900–1,000 / €1,300–1,450
$1,550–1,750 ⊞ JRe

◄ A **Ralph Wood-style figure of Chaucer,** impressed and
inscribed marks, c1800, 12in (30.5cm) high.
£250–300 / €360–430
$440–530 ⚹ SWO

British Porcelain 18th & 19thC

A scent bottle, in the form of a young lady, 18thC, 3in (7.5cm) high.
£400–450 / €580–650 $700–790 ⊞ LBr

A pair of Longton Hall figures, entitled 'Harlequin' and 'Columbine', 1754–57, 5in (12.5cm) high.
£4,000–4,450 / €5,800–6,400 $7,000–7,800 ⊞ DMa

A pair of Wedgwood black basalt models of griffins, one with impressed mark, c1780, 9¾in (25cm) high.
£9,800–11,800 / €14,100–17,000 $17,200–20,700 ⚒ S

A Parian figural group of a knight and a maiden, 19thC, 16in (40.5cm) high.
£160–190 / €230–270 $280–330 ⚒ G(L)

A figural group, probably Samson, after Meissen, slight damage, 19thC, 6in (15cm) high.
£260–310 / €370–440 $460–540 ⚒ BWL

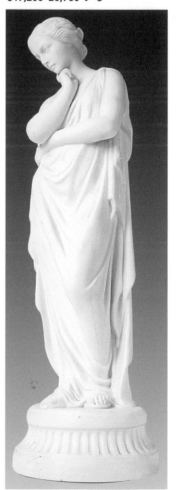

A Parian figure of a muse, 19thC, 14¼in (36cm) high.
£70–80 / €100–115 $125–140 ⚒ SWO

► **A Staffordshire model of a spaniel,** 19thC, 3½in (9cm) high.
£130–150 / €185–220 $230–270 ⚒ WW

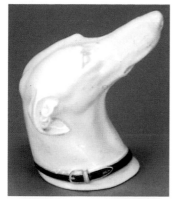

◄ **A porcellaneous stirrup cup,** in the form of a greyhound's head, slight damage, 19thC, 6¾in (17cm) high.
£220–260 / €320–380
$390–460 ⚒ **DN**

► **A Samuel Alcock model of a wolf,** impressed '192', c1840, 7in (18cm) high.
£600–680 / €860–980
$1,050–1,200 ⊞ **TYE**

◄ **A Staffordshire model of a begging poodle,** c1850, 4in (10cm) high.
£360–400 / €520–580
$630–700 ⊞ **DAN**

A pair of Victorian Parian figures of Shakespeare and Milton, slight damage, 14in (35.5cm) high.
£160–190 / €230–270
$280–330 ⚒ **FHF**
These are copies of the monuments in Westminster Abbey, London.

A Victorian biscuit figure of Ceres, 13in (33cm) high.
£150–180 / €220–260
$260–310 ⚒ **G(L)**

◄ **A Staffordshire model of a dog,** c1845, 4in (10cm) wide.
£240–280
€350–400
$420–480
⊞ **DAN**

A J. & T. Bevington Parian model of a monkey, a dog and a rat, after Aesop's fable, c1865–77, 4in (10cm) high.
£100–120 / €145–175 $175–210 ⊞ JAK

A model of a cat, with printed retailer's mark for John Mortlock, London, mid-19thC, 11½in (29cm) high.
£1,500–1,800 / €2,150–2,600 $2,650–3,150 ⚒ S(O)

A J. & T. Bevington Parian figure, entitled 'The Reading Girl', c1865, 12in (30.5cm) high.
£400–450 / €580–650 $700–790 ⊞ JAK

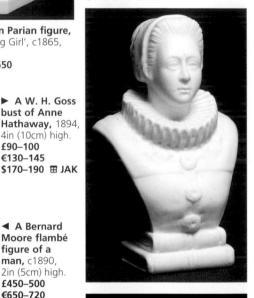

► **A W. H. Goss bust of Anne Hathaway,** 1894, 4in (10cm) high.
£90–100 €130–145 $170–190 ⊞ JAK

◄ **A Bernard Moore flambé figure of a man,** c1890, 2in (5cm) high.
£450–500 €650–720 $790–880 ⊞ BWDA

► **A Moore Brothers figural centrepiece,** in the form of two cherubs flanking a bowl encrusted with blackberries, wings restored, printed and impressed marks, late 19thC, 9in (23cm) high.
£320–380 €460–550 $560–670 ⚒ SWO

A porcelain model of a chicken, with a spill holder, restored, late 19thC, 10½in (26.5cm) high.
£150–180 / €220–260 $260–310 ⚒ SWO

Belleek

A pair of Belleek figural candlesticks, each carrying a basket, Irish, First Period, 1863–90, 9in (23cm) high.
£900–1,000 / €1,300–1,450
$1,600–1,800 ⊞ MLa

A Belleek Parian group of greyhounds, Irish, First Period, 1863–90, 8in (20.5cm) high.
£5,200–6,200 / €7,500–8,900
$9,100–10,900 ⚒ JAd

A pair of Belleek figures, entitled 'Affection' and 'Meditation', Irish, First Period, 1863–90, 14in (35.5cm) high.
£5,400–6,000 / €7,800–8,600
$9,500–10,500 ⊞ MLa

A pair of Belleek figural candlesticks, Irish, First Period 1863–90, 9in (23cm) high.
£3,550–3,950 / €5,100–5,800
$6,200–7,000 ⊞ DeA

A Belleek ram's head cornucopia spill vase, Irish, First Period, 1863–90, 4in (10cm) long.
£850–950 / €1,200–1,350
$1,500–1,650 ⊞ MLa

A Belleek model of a pig, Irish, Second Period, 1891–1926, 3in (7.5cm) long.
£195–220 / €280–320
$340–390 ⊞ WAA

Bow

A Bow figure of a cherub and a fruiting vine, restored, c1750, 7in (18cm) high.
£1,100–1,300 / €1,600–1,900
$1,950–2,300 ↗ WW

► **A Bow figure of Winter,** repaired, c1755, 5in (12.5cm) high.
£350–420 / €500–600
$610–730 ↗ WW

A Bow figure of a flautist, repaired, c1752, 4in (10cm) high.
£1,500–1,700 / €2,150–2,450
$2,650–3,000 ⊞ JUP

A Bow figure of Autumn, damaged, 1755–60, 5½in (14cm) high.
£900–1,050 / €1,300–1,550
$1,600–1,900 ↗ S

A pair of Bow figures of the New Dancers, 1758–60, 6in (15cm) high.
£1,600–1,800 / €2,300–2,600
$2,800–3,150 ⊞ DMa

A Bow figure of a flowergirl, after a Chelsea figure entitled 'Spring', with label inscribed 'English Ceramic Circle 1948 No. 189', 5¾in (14.5cm) high.
£1,100–1,300 / €1,600–1,900
$1,950–2,300 ↗ TEN

A Bow figure of a nun reading a bible, c1760, 5¾in (14.5cm) high.
£520–620 / €750–890
$910–1,100 ⚒ WW

A Bow figure of Faustina, c1760, 12in (30.5cm) high.
£1,050–1,200 / €1,500–1,700
$1,850–2,100 ⊞ DMa

A Bow figure of Minerva, with an owl and flowers, neck restored, slight damage, c1760, 14¼in (36cm) high.
£490–590 / €710–850
$860–1,000 ⚒ Bea

◄ A Bow figure of a Sight, in the form of a lady holding a mirror, slight damage, c1760, 7½in (19cm) high.
£2,400–2,700 / €3,450–3,900
$4,200–4,750 ⊞ JUP

A pair of Bow models of goldfinches, restored, 1760–70, 3½in (9cm) high.
£420–500 / €600–720
$740–880 ⚒ WW

A Bow figure of Air, in the form of Juno and the Eagle, after Etienne Le Hongre, restored, red anchor mark, c1765, 10in (25.5cm) high.
£400–480 / €580–690
$700–840 ⚒ WW

◀ **A Bow figure of Columbine,** c1765, 7½in (19cm) high.
£1,450–1,650 / €2,100–2,400
$2,500–2,800 ⊞ DMa

A Bow figure of Earth, in the form of a maiden and a lion, restored, anchor and dagger mark, c1765, 9½in (24cm) high.
£500–600 / €720–860
$880–1,050 ✗ WW

▶ **A Bow figure of Flora,** c1765, 10in (25.5cm) high.
£850–950 / €1,200–1,350
$1,500–1,650 ⊞ DMa

◀ **A Bow figure of Air,** from The Elements series, c1765, 8in (20.5cm) high.
£690–780 / €990–1,100
$1,200–1,350 ⊞ DMa

A Bow figural candlestick, restored, c1765, 7in (18cm) high.
£260–310 / €380–440
$460–540 ✗ WW

◀ **A pair of Bow figures of the New Dancers,** with bocage, c1765, 9in (23cm) high.
£2,100–2,350 / €3,000–3,400
$3,700–4,100 ⊞ DMa

Chelsea

A pair of Chelsea models of pheasants, probably decorated in the workshop of William Duesbury, damaged and repaired, raised red anchor marks, 1750–52, 8¼in (21cm) high.
£16,500–19,800 / €23,700–28,500 $29,000–34,700 ⚒ Bea
Although one of these pheasants was extensively damaged, they were keenly contested because pairs are scarce and these are very well decorated, probably in the workshop of William Duesbury. As the pheasant was quite crudely repaired, it would be relatively simple to take it apart and restore it to professional standards.

A Chelsea model of a parakeet, repaired, raised red anchor mark, 1751–53, 4¾in (12cm) high.
£7,800–9,300 / €11,200–13,400 $13,700–16,300 ⚒ S(NY)

A Chelsea model of a pheasant, raised red anchor mark, repaired, c1752, 6in (15cm) high.
£3,150–3,500 / €4,500–5,000 $5,500–6,100 ⊞ JUP

▶ **A Chelsea figure of a carter,** by Joseph Willems, red anchor mark, 1754–5, 5in (12.5cm) high.
£4,800–5,300 €6,900–7,600 $8,400–9,300 ⊞ DMa

A Chelsea figural flower holder, after a Saint Cloud original, in the form of a fish seller, slight damage, red anchor mark, c1755, 9in (23cm) high.
£800–950 / €1,150–1,350 $1,400–1,650 ⚒ LFA

A Chelsea figure of Pierrot,
c1755, 6in (15cm) high.
£5,400–6,000 / €7,800–8,600
$9,500–10,500 ⊞ DMa

▶ **A set of four Derby figures,**
by N. J. F. Fauron, after Tournai,
c1760, 9in (23cm) high.
£2,250–2,500 / €3,250–3,600
$4,000–4,400 ⊞ DMa

A pair of Chelsea figural sweetmeat dishes, in the form of Turkish
harvesters, c1755, 6in (15cm) high.
£3,350–3,800 / €4,800–5,500
$5,900–6,700 ⊞ DMa

A Chelsea sweetmeat dish, in the
form of a Turkish harvester,
5in (12.5cm) high.
£2,150–2,400 / €3,100–3,450
$3,750–4,200 ⊞ DMa

▶ **A Chelsea masquerade figure,**
c1760, 8½in (21.5cm) high.
£2,250–2,500 / €3,150–3,600
$3,850–4,400 ⊞ DMa

A Chelsea, candlestick, decorated
with foxes and fruiting vines,
restored, 1760–65,
12½in (32cm) high.
£900–1,050 / €1,300–1,550
$1,600–1,900 ⋏ WW

◀ **A Chelsea figure of Flora,** with a lion, slight damage, gold anchor mark, c1765, 8¼in (21cm) high.
£920–1,100 / €1,300–1,550
$1,600–1,900 ➚ WW

A pair of Chelsea figures, restored, c1765, 11in (28cm) high.
£2,250–2,500 / €3,150–3,600
$3,850–4,400 ⊞ AUC

◀ **A pair of Chelsea figures of harvesters,** gold anchor mark, c1765, 5in (12.5cm) high.
£2,400–2,700 / €3,450–3,900
$4,200–4,750 ⊞ DMa

A pair of Chelsea figural candlesticks, entitled 'The Four Seasons', c1765, 11in (28cm) high.
£5,300–5,900 / €7,600–8,500
$9,300–10,300 ⊞ DMa

A pair of Chelsea figures holding bakets of flowers, 1770, 6in (15cm) high.
£590–660 / €850–950
$1,000–1,100 ⊞ DeA

Copeland

A Copeland bust, entitled 'Purity', 1860, 13in (33cm) high.
£450–500 / €650–720
$790–880 ⊞ JAK

A Copeland Parian figure of Night, after Raphael Monti, in the form of a woman standing above a child, slight damage, impressed and incised marks, c1862, 26in (66cm) high.
£1,400–1,600 / €2,000–2,400
$2,400–2,850 ⚒ DN

A Copeland figure, entitled 'Innocence', c1847, 17in (43cm) high.
£670–750 / €960–1,100
$1,150–1,300 ⊞ JAK

◀ **A pair of Copeland busts of Edward Prince of Wales and Princess Alexandra,** 1863, 12in (30.5cm) high.
£850–950
€1,200–1,350
$1,500–1,650
⊞ JAK

▶ **A Copeland figural group of Ino and Bacchus,** by J. H. Foley, grapes restored, 1884, 21in (53.5cm) wide.
£2,150–2,400
€3,100–3,450
$3,750–4,200
⊞ JAK

A Copeland bust of Lord Byron, 1880, 25in (63.5cm) high.
£1,400–1,600 / €2,000–2,200
$2,450–2,800 ⊞ JAK

Derby

A pair of Derby figures of a shepherd and a shepherdess, c1756, 6in (15cm) high.
£2,500–2,800 / €3,600–4,050 $4,400–4,900 ⊞ **DMa**

A Derby figure of a violinist, 1754–56, 6in (15cm) high.
£2,000–2,250 / €2,900–3,250 $3,500–3,950 ⊞ **DMa**

A Derby figural group of Leda and the Swan, c1755, 12in (30.5cm) high.
£2,700–3,000 / €3,900–4,300 $4,750–5,300 ⊞ **DMa**

A Derby figure of James Quinn as Falstaff, c1765, 9in (23cm) high.
£490–550 / €710–790 $860–960 ⊞ **DMa**

A Derby model of a leopard, c1756, 3in (7.5cm) wide.
£3,500–4,000 / €5,000–5,700 $6,100–7,000 ⊞ **JUP**

A Derby model of a ewe, standing before bocage, c1765, 7in (18cm) high.
£490–550 / €710–790 $860–960 ⊞ **TYE**

A Derby figure of Neptune, c1765, 10in (25.5cm) high.
£850–950 / €1,200–1,350
$1,500–1,650 ⊞ DMa

A Derby figure of Milton, slight damage, c1765, 11¼in (28.5cm) high.
£280–330 / €400–480
$490–580 ↗ WW

A Derby figure of a girl musician, c1770, 6in (15cm) high.
£380–430 / €550–620
$670–750 ⊞ TYE

◄ **A Derby figural group of Asia,** from the Four Quarters of the Globe series, c1770, 7in (18cm) high.
£400–480 / €580–690
$700–840 ↗ WW

A pair of Derby figures of a shepherd and a shepherdess, patch marks, c1770, 7in (18cm) high.
£750–840 / €1,050–1,200
$1,300–1,450 ⊞ TYE

◄ **A Derby figure of a harlequin,** c1770, 5in (12.5cm) high.
£1,400–1,550 / €2,000–2,250
$2,450–2,700 ⊞ DMa

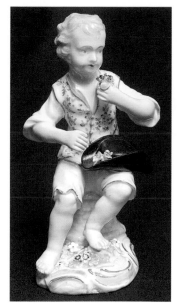

A pair of Derby models of sheep, seated before bocage, c1775, 3¼in (8.5cm) high.
£880–980 / €1,250–1,400
$1,500–1,700 ⊞ AUC

A Derby figure of a boy, patch marks, c1770, 5in (12.5cm) high.
£390–440 / €560–630
$680–770 ⊞ TYE

◄ **A pair of candlesticks,** decorated with rabbits and bocage, c1775, 8in (20.5cm) high.
£2,450–2,750
€3,500–4,000
$4,300–4,800
⊞ DMa

A Derby figure of Neptune, c1775, 9in (23cm) high.
£1,150–1,300 / €1,650–1,850
$2,000–2,250 ⊞ DMa

► **A Derby figure of a female musician,** c1780, 10½in (26.5cm) high.
£310–350 / €450–500
$540–610 ⊞ SER

A Derby Tithe Pig figural group, c1780, 5in (12.5cm) high.
£980–1,100 / €1,400–1,600
$1,700–1,900 ⊞ DMa

A Derby biscuit figural group,
entitled 'Two Virgins Awakening
Cupid', marked, late 18thC,
10in (25.5cm) high.
£600–720 / €860–1,000
$1,050–1,250 ⚲ TMA

A Derby figure of a flower seller,
marked, c1785, 5in (12.5cm) high.
£380–430 / €550–620
$670–750 ⊞ TYE

A Derby figure of female gardener,
incised 'No. 7', c1785,
5in (12.5cm) high.
£360–400 / €510–570
$630–700 ⊞ TYE

A pair of Derby figures of gardeners,
incised mark for Isaac Farnsworth, size
No. 2, incised '7', slight damage, late
18thC, 5½in (14cm) high.
£450–540 / €650–770
$780–940 ⚲ TMA

A pair of Derby figures of Shakespeare and Milton, slight damage, late
18thC, 12¼in (31cm) high.
£1,300–1,550 / €1,900–2,250
$2,250–2,700 ⚲ WW

► **A Derby model of a cow and a calf,** standing before bocage, c1800,
6in (15cm) high.
£700–780 / €1,000–1,100
$1,200–1,350 ⊞ TYE

◄ **A Derby figure of a lady,** c1805, 4in (10cm) high.
£670–750 / €960–1,100
$1,100–1,250 ⊞ CoS

A Derby figure of John Philip Kemble as Richard III, 1825, 11in (28cm) high.
£1,200–1,350 / €1,750–1,950
$2,100–2,350 ⊞ DMa

A Derby figural group, entitled 'The Hairdresser', c1800, 7in (18cm) high.
£580–650 / €840–940
$1,000–1,100 ⊞ DMa

► **A pair of Derby figures of a woodcutter and his wife,** c1820, 6in (15cm) high
£1,150–1,300
€1,650–1,900
$2,000–2,250
⊞ HKW

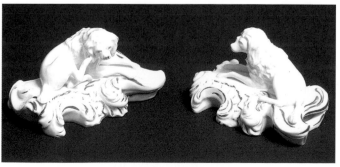

◄ **A Derby figure of a woman,** No. 369, restored, incised and painted mark, c1830, 10in (25.5cm) high.
£160–190
€230–270
$280–330 ⚒ WW

A pair of Derby models of poodles, c1845, 4in (10cm) wide.
£610–680 / €880–980
$1,050–1,200 ⊞ TYE

Minton

A Minton flatback figure of Don Quixote, restored, c1825, 6in (15cm) high.
£130–150 / €185–220
$230–270 ✗ WW

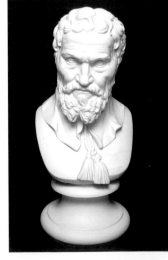

A Minton Parian model of a spaniel, c1840, 4in (10cm) long.
£250–280 / €360–400
$440–490 ⊞ TYE

◀ **Minton figure of Dorothea,** by John Bell, signed, c1847, 14in (35.5cm) high.
£700–780 / €1,000–1,100
$1,200–1,350 ⊞ GSA

A Minton Parian figure of Margaret of Anjou, date code for 1851, 17in (43cm) high.
£220–260 / €310–370
$380–450 ⊞ G(B)

◀ **A Minton Parian porcelain bust of Michelangelo,** 1851, 24½in (62cm) high.
£1,350–1,500 / €1,950–2,150
$2,350–2,650 ✗ JAK

A Minton Parian figural group of Una and the Lion, the base relief-moulded 'John Bell', damaged, moulded registration lozenge, impressed marks and date codes, c1860, 14¾in (37.5cm) high.
£380–450 / €550–650
$670–790 ➶ RTo

► A Minton bust of Albert, Prince of Wales, 1863, 13in (33cm) high.
£360–400 / €520–580
$630 700 ⊞ JAK

A Minton figure of Whistler's Mother, 1872, 11in (28cm) high.
£630–700 / €900–1,000
$1,100–1,250 ⊞ JAK

A Minton Parian porcelain figure of a boy holding a basket, 1870, 7½in (19cm) high.
£310–350 / €450–500
$540–610 ⊞ JAK

► A Minton figure of Miranda, 1880, 16in (40.5cm) high.
£450–500 / €650–720
$790–880 ⊞ JAK

Robinson & Leadbeater

A Robinson &
Leadbeater bust of
Charles Dickens, 1880,
9in (23cm) high.
£140–160 / €200–220
$250–280 ⊞ JAK

**A pair of Robinson & Leadbeater Parian
figures of young women,** c1880,
13in (33cm) high.
£530–600 / €760–860
$930–1,050 ⊞ MRA

**A Robinson & Leadbeater tinted
Parian figure of a young woman,**
c1880, 15in (38cm) high.
£450–500 / €650–720
$780–880 ⊞ MRA

A Robinson & Leadbeater
bust of Lord Byron, 1890,
14in (35.5cm) high.
£400–450 / €580–650
$700–790 ⊞ JAK

A Robinson & Leadbeater model of a dog, c1880, 8in (20.5cm) high.
£360–400 / €520–580
$630–700 ⊞ JAK

▶ **A Robinson & Leadbeater bust of General Buller,** 1899, 8in (20.5cm) high.
£160–180 / €230–260
$280–320 ⊞ JAK

Worcester

A Royal Worcester vase, in the form of an elephant, after James Hadley, restored, 19thC, 8in (20.5cm) high.
£100–120 / €145–170
$175–210 ROS

A Chamberlain's Worcester model of a poodle, marked, 1820–40, 4in (10cm) wide.
£400–450 / €580–650
$700–790 TYE

▶ A Worcester Kerr & Binns porcelain bust of General Havelock, by W. B. Kirk, 1858, 9in (23cm) high.
£310–350 / €450–500
$540–600 JAK

A pair of Royal Worcester figural candlesticks, in the form of putti holding cornucopia shells, repaired, impressed marks, 19thC, 6¾in (17cm) high.
£210–250 / €300–360
$370–440 FHF

A Worcester Kerr & Binns bust of Prince Albert, c1853, 15in (38cm) high.
£450–500 / €650–720
$780–880 JAK

A Worcester Parian figural group of Paul and Virginia, damaged and repaired, c1865, 13½in (34.5cm) high.
£320–380 / €460–550
$560–670 ↗ DN

A pair of Royal Worcester candle extinguishers, attributed to James Hadley, entitled 'Town Girl' and 'Country Girl', restored, c1880, 5½in (14cm) high.
£1,300–1,450 / €1,850–2,100
$2,250–2,550 each ⊞ TH

◀ **A Royal Worcester Parian candle extinguisher,** attributed to James Hadley, entitled 'Mob Cap', shape No. 766, c1880, 3½in (9cm) high.
£1,450–1,650 / €2,100–2,400
$2,550–2,900 ⊞ TH

A Royal Worcester candle extinguisher, attributed to James Hadley, entitled 'Feathered Hat', c1880, 4in (10cm) high.
£1,350–1,500 / €1,950–2,150
$2,350–2,600 ⊞ TH

A Royal Worcester candle extinguisher, entitled 'French Cook', c1880, 3in (7.5cm) high.
£390–440 / €560–630
$680–770 ⊞ TH

A Royal Worcester figure of John Bull, by James Hadley, printed and impressed marks, c1881, 7in (18cm) high.
£180–210 / €260–310
$320–380 ↗ WW

A Royal Worcester figure of a Chinese man, restored, impressed and printed marks, c1882, 6¾in (17cm) high.
£140–165 / €200–240
$250–300 ⚒ WW

A pair of Royal Worcester figures of Egyptian musicians, slight damage, 1886, 13in (33cm) high.
£2,000–2,250 / €2,900–3,250
$2,000–4,000 ⊞ MER

A Royal Worcester candle extinguisher, entitled 'Town Girl', 1881, 5in (12.5cm) high.
£1,650–1,850
€2,350–2,650
$2,900–3,250 ⊞ TH

A pair of Royal Worcester figural groups of schoolboys, with verses by Goldsmith printed in gold, one group repaired, c1888, 4¼in (11cm) high.
£400–480 / €580–690
$700–840 ⚒ G(L)

A Royal Worcester figure of a water carrier, No. 1250, 1888, 9½in (24cm) high.
£240–280 / €340–400
$420–490 ⚒ G(L)

▶ **A Royal Worcester candle extinguisher,** entitled 'Granny Snow', c1890, 3in (7.5cm) high.
£95–110 / €135–160
$170–190 ⊞ WAC

Continental 18th & 19thC

A pair of Montelupo maiolica figures of angels, restored, Italian, c1600, 13in (33cm) high.
£8,600–10,300 / €12,400–14,800
$15,100–18,000 S(O)

◄ A Nevers maiolica **group of a putto and a dolphin,** slight restoration, French, 18thC, 6¾in (17cm) high.
£230–270 / €330–390
$400–470 DN

A porcelain figure of a gardener, slight damage, French, 18thC, 6¼in (16cm) high.
£500–600 / €720–860
$880–1,050 WW

► **A Delft figure of a woman,** probably Dutch, early 18thC, 7in (18cm) high.
£260–310 / €380–450
$460–540 L

A silver-mounted Paris porcelain pill box, modelled as a mouse, the cover painted with rats, the interior painted with a weasel and a chicken, slight damage, French, silver mount London 1797, 2½in (6.5cm) high.
£2,400–2,850 / €3,450–4,100
$3,750–4,200 SWO

A Doccia figure of an Eastern gentleman, losses, Italian, 1750–1800, 5¾in (14.5cm) high.
£1,300–1,550
€1,850–2,200
$2,300–2,700 S(Mi)

A Ludwigsburg porcelain figure of a lady with a cat on her shoulder, damaged, blue painted mark, German, 18thC, 6in (15cm) high.
£200–240 / €290–340
$350–420 DMC

A Vienna figure of Autumn, in the form of a man seated on wheatsheaves, slight damage, painted and incised marks, impressed 'O', Austrian, c1760, 7¼in (18.5cm) high.
£840–1,000 / €1,200–1,450
$1,450–1,750 S(O)

CONTINENTAL

A Ludwigsburg figure of a butcher, by J. J. Louis, slight damage, painted mark, German, 1762–72, 4½in (11.5cm) high.
£1,100–1,300
€1,600–1,900
$1,950–2,300 ⚖ S(O)

A Vienna figural group of two gardeners, restored, conjoined shields mark, Austrian, c1765, 8¾in (22cm) high.
£730–880 / €1,050–1,250
$1,300–1,550 ⚖ DORO

A Ludwigsburg figure of a farmer's wife, restored, marked, German, c1770, 5¾in (14.5cm) high.
£340–400 / €490–580
$600–710 ⚖ G(L)

A Volkstedt figural group of bird nesters, slight damage and restoration, German, 1770, 10¾in (27.5cm) high.
£1,400–1,650
€2,000–2,400
$2,450–2,900 ⚖ S

A Tournai figure of a young girl, losses, slight damage, French, c1770, 4¾in (12cm) high.
£600–720 / €870–1,050
$1,050–1,250 ⚖ S(O)

◀ **A Frankenthal figural group of an old man and a young woman,** by Karl Gottlieb Lück, restored, incised marks, German, 1770–75, 6in (15cm) high.
£1,650–1,950 / €2,350–2,800
$2,900–3,400 ⚖ S(O)

A Closter Veildorf group of a leopard attacking a mule, by Pfränger, German, c1775, 8¼in (21cm) wide.
£1,100–1,300 / €1,600–1,900
$1,950–2,300 ⚖ S(O)
This is a very rare group, but the gruesome subject may have been the reason for the modest price realized.

A Niderviller figure of an apple seller, restored, marked, French, c1775, 6in (15cm) high.
£220–260 / €320–380
$390–460 ⚖ G(L)

A Limbach figure of Autumn, from a set of the Four Seasons, slight damage, German, c1775, 6¾in (17cm) high.
£400–480 / €580–690
$700–840 ⚒ G(L)

A biscuit porcelain group, probably Niderviller, modelled as four rustic figures around a tree, the base with a later gilt-metal mount, slight damage and losses, French, late 18thC, 14¼in (36cm) high.
£300–360 / €430–520
$530–630 ⚒ DN

A Ludwigsburg figure of Plenty, restored, painted marks, German, late 18thC, 11in (28cm) high.
£200–240 / €290–350
$350–420 ⚒ ROS

A Limbach figure of Autumn, from a set of The Seasons, restored, German, c1780, 5½in (13.5cm) high.
£950–1,100
€1,350–1,600
$1,650–1,950 ⚒ S(O)

◀ **A tin-glazed jug,** in the form of a seated cat, with sponged decoration, Continental, 19thC, 11½in (29cm) high.
£130–155
€185–220
$230–270
⚒ WW

▶ **A majolica figure of a grape picker,** Continental, 19thC, 7½in (19cm) high.
£70–80
€100–115
$125–140
⊞ ACAC

A Sèvres biscuit porcelain figural group of wrestling cherubs, after a model by Falconet, slight damage, marked, French, 19thC, 8in (20.5cm) high.
£165–195 / €240–280
$290–340   DN(BR)

▶ **A terracotta figure of a woman,** German, 19thC, 10½in (26.5cm) high.
£270–300 / €390–430
$470–530   MFB

A Nymphenburg biscuit porcelain figure of a woman with a lyre, her right foot resting on a dolphin, restored, German, c1800, 15in (38cm) high.
£1,100–1,300 / €1,600–1,900
$1,950–2,300   DORO

A pottery model of a dog, with a moulded collar and glass eyes, impressed mark 'LL', Continental, 19thC, 31in (78.5cm) wide.
£900–1,050 / €1,300–1,550
$1,600–1,900   AH

A creamware figural group, of a man and a woman beneath a tree with birds, Italian, c1800, 13¾in (35cm) high.
£900–1,050
€1,300–1,550
$1,600–1,900   S

A Berlin porcelain figure of Amphiaraus, German, 19thC, 9in (23cm) high.
£165–185 / €230–270
$280–320   SER

◀ **A pair of porcelain figures of a gentleman and a lady,** losses, 'Kozloff's' factory marks, Russian, mid-19thC, 8¾in (22cm) high.
£1,300–1,550 / €1,850–2,200
$2,300–2,700   NSal

A figural match holder, in the form of a girl beside a wheelbarrow, German, c1870, 2¼in (5.5cm) wide.
£40–45 / €60–70
$75–85 ➚ **SAS**

A porcelain tobacco jar, in the form of a pug dog with a collar and bells, German, c1870, 11in (28cm) high.
£720–800 / €1,050–1,200
$1,250–1,400 ⌗ **RdeR**

A Berlin porcelain figural group, in the form of a bacchanalian couple and two leopards, restored, underglaze sceptre mark, late 19thC, 9¾in (25cm) high.
£110–130 / €160–190
$195–230 ➚ **ROS**

A pair of porcelain figures of a gallant and his lady, with encrusted decoration, on associated rococo plinths, late 19thC, 16½in (42cm) high.
£580–650 / €840–940
$1,000–1,200 ➚ **G(B)**

A pair of figures of a gallant and his lady, with encrusted decoration, incised 'JG', French, late 19thC, 19in (48.5cm) high.
£1,000–1,200 / €1,600–1,800
$1,750–2,100 ➚ **TEN**
'JG' is probably Jean Gille of Paris, who made large figures, often in biscuit porcelain.

A Volkstedt figure of a cherub on a chariot, c1880, 4in (10cm) wide.
£120–135 / 175–195
$210–240 ⌗ **OAK**

An Onnaing jug, modelled as a duck, French, 1880, 9in (23cm) high.
£310–350 / €450–500
$540–610 ⌗ **MLL**

A Sitzendorf porcelain figural group, of a couple with sheep, German, c1890, 6in (15cm) high.
£240–270 / €350–390
$420–470 ⌗ **MRA**

An Ernst Bohne porcelain figural candelabra, c1890, 16in (40.5cm) high.
£310–350 / €450–500
$540–610 ⌗ **MRA**

A figural match striker, in the form of a monkey with a basket on his back, probably German, late 19thC, 3in (7.5cm) high.
£50–60 / €75–85
$110–115 ⊞ JOA

A porcelain figural group of a harlequin and a lady, slight damage, 19thC, 6in (15cm) high.
£260–310 / €380–450
$460–540 ✎ BWL

A majolica stick stand, in the form of a heron with a fish, damaged, stamped '7764/12', 19thC, 31in (78.5cm) high.
£450–540 / €650–780
$790–950 ✎ SWO

▶ **A pair of piano babies,** one holding a rabbit, No. 7480, the other a doll, No. 7394, German, c1900, 7½in (19cm) wide.
£190–220 / €270–320
$330–390 ✎ G(L)

A porcelain figural group, modelled as a Scotsman and a boy seated on rocks, inscribed 'Ye Maunna Tramp on the Scotch Thistle Laddie', 19thC, 7½in (19cm) wide.
£200–240 / €290–350
$35–429 ✎ SWO

A Dutch Delft model of a bear, initialled 'AG', late 19thC, 3½in (9cm) long.
£90–100 / €130–145
$170–190 ✎ SWO

◀ **A Vienna porcelain figure of a boy,** Austrian, c1900, 14in (35.5cm) high.
£380–430 / €550–620
$670–750 ⊞ OAK

▶ **A Volkstedt porcelain candle extinguisher,** German, c1900, 2¾in (7cm) high.
£360–400 / €520–580
$630–700 ⊞ TH

Dresden

◀ **A set of three Dresden singing and dancing female figures,** painted marks, German, late 19thC, 9¼in (23.5cm) high.
£110–130
€160–190
$195–230
⚒ **G(L)**

▶ **A Dresden figure of a young man,** German, late 19thC, 6in (15cm) high.
£50–55 / €70–80
$85–95 ⊞ **MRA**

◀ **A pair of Dresden porcelain figures of a boy and a girl,** German, c1890, 3in (7.5cm) high.
£75–85 / €105–120
$130–150 ⊞ **MRA**

A Dresden figure of a boy with a flower, German, c1890, 3in (7.5cm) high.
£50–60 / €75–85
$90–105 ⊞ **MRA**

▶ **A pair of Dresden figural candlesticks,** one a man, the other a woman picking fruit, on scrolled bases with gilt detail, German, 19thC, 15in (38cm) high.
£800–960 / €1,200–1,400
$1,450–1,700 ⚒ **BWL**

A Dresden model of a budgerigar, German, c1890, 6in (15cm) high.
£75–85 / €105–120
$130–150 ⊞ **MRA**

Fairings

A Victorian fairing box and cover,
in the form of figures on horseback,
7¼in (18.5cm) high.
£65–75 / €95–110
$125–145 ⚒ SAS

A Victorian fairing figural inkwell,
in the form of a mother and child
with a dog, restored,
7¼in (18.5cm) high.
£95–110 / €135–160
$165–195 ⚒ SAS

A fairing, entitled 'Little Boy Blue',
1850–1914, 4in (10cm) wide.
£90–100 / €130–145
$170–190 ⊞ DHJ

CONTINENTAL

A fairing, entitled 'More Free than
Welcome', 1850–1914,
4in (10cm) high.
£4,500–5,000 / €6,500–7,200
$7,900–8,800 ⊞ DHJ
This is an extremely rare fairing.

A fairing, entitled 'A Long Pull and a Strong Pull', 1850–1914, 4in (10cm) wide.
£360–400 / €520–580
$630–700 ⊞ DHJ

◄ **A fairing,** entitled 'Don't Awake
the Baby', 1850–1914,
4in (10cm) wide.
£220–250 / €320–360
$390–440 ⊞ DHJ

▶ **A fairing,** entitled 'Hark Jo,
somebodys coming', 1850–1914,
4in (10cm) wide.
£180–200 / €260–290
$310–350 ⊞ DHJ

A fairing, entitled 'Kiss Me Quick',
1850–1914, 4in (10cm) wide.
£135–150 / €195–220
$230–260 ⊞ **DHJ**

A fairing, entitled 'The Last in Bed
to Put Out the Light', 1850–1914,
4in (10cm) wide.
£45–50 / €65–75
$85–95 ⊞ **DHJ**

A fairing, entitled 'That's Funny!
Very Funny!, Very, Very Funny!', slight
damage, 1850–1914, 4in (10cm) wide.
£70–80 / €100–115
$135–155 ⚒ **SAS**

A fairing, entitled 'After Marriage',
c1870, 2½in (6.5cm) wide.
£310–350 / €450–500
$540–610 ⊞ **Cas**

◄ **A fairing,** by Conta & Boehme,
entitled 'Slack', c1870,
4in (10cm) wide.
£310–350 / €450–500
$540–610 ⊞ **Cas**

◄ **A fairing,**
entitled 'Landlord
in Love', c1870,
4in (10cm) wide.
£450–500
€650–720
$790–880 ⊞ **Cas**

► **A fairing,** by
Conta & Boehme,
entitled 'Three
o'clock in the
Morning', c1870,
3in (7.5cm) wide.
£45–50 / €65–75
$85–95 ⊞ **Cas**

A fairing, entitled 'Ladies of Llangollen', c1870, 6in (15cm) high.
£45–50 / €65–75
$85–95 ⊞ Cas

A fairing, entitled 'Very Much Frightened', c1870, 3in (7.5cm) high.
£100–110 / €145–160
$175–195 ⊞ Cas

A fairing, entitled 'Five o'clock Tea', slight damage, c1870,
2¼in (5.5cm) wide.
£75–90 / €110–130
$135–160 ⚒ SAS

A fairing, entitled 'To Let', c1870,
2¼in (5.5cm) wide.
£340–400 / €490–580
$600–700 ⚒ SAS

A fairing, entitled 'A Doubtful Case',
c1870, 4in (10cm) wide.
£430–480 / €620–690
$750–840 ⊞ Cas

◄ **A match striker fairing,** entitled 'How's Your Poor Feet', c1870, 4½in (1.5cm) wide.
£500–550
€720–800
$870–960
⊞ Cas

A fairing, entitled 'Pluck', c1870, 5½in (14cm) wide.
£165–185 / €230–260
$280–320 ⊞ Cas

A fairing, by Conta & Boehme, entitled 'The Orphans', c1870, 4in (10cm) wide.
£175–195 / €250–280
$300–340 ⊞ Cas

A fairing, entitled 'Now Mam – Say When', c1870, 4in (10cm) wide.
£115–130 / €165–185
$200–230 ⊞ Cas

A fairing, entitled 'After', c1870, 4in (10cm) wide.
£400–450 / €580–650
$700–790 ⊞ Cas

A fairing, entitled 'Tug of War', c1870, 5in (12.5cm) wide.
£125–140 / €180–200
$220–250 ⊞ Cas

A fairing, entitled 'Who is Coming', c1870, 3½in (9cm) wide.
£160–180 / €230–260
$280–320 ⊞ Cas

A fairing, entitled 'Oyster Day', c1870, 3½in (9cm) high.
£110–125 / €160–180
$195–220 ⊞ Cas

◀ **A fairing,** entitled 'Hark Tom, Somebody's Coming', c1870, 3in (7.5cm) wide.
£140–160 / €200–220
$250–280 ⊞ Cas

A fairing, by Conta & Boehme, entitled 'Baby's First Steps', c1870, 4in (10cm) wide.
£220–250 / €320–360
$390–440 ⊞ Cas

A fairing, entitled 'Who said Rats?', c1870, 3¾in (9.5cm) wide.
£150–170 / €220–250
$260–290 ⊞ Cas

A fairing, entitled 'The Wedding Night', c1870, 3½in (9cm) wide.
£125–140 / €180–200
$220–250 ⊞ Cas

CONTINENTAL

A fairing, entitled 'Checkmate', c1870, 4in (10cm) wide.
£330–370 / €480–530
$580–660 ⊞ Cas

A fairing, entitled 'After You, My Dear Alphonso', c1870, 4in (10cm) wide.
£310–350 / €450–500
$540–610 ⊞ Cas

A fairing, by Conta & Boehme, entitled 'Which is the Prettiest?', c1870, 4in (10cm) wide.
£115–130 / €165–185
$200–230 ⊞ Cas

▶ **A fairing,** entitled 'Can You Do This, Grandma?', c1870, 4in (10cm) wide.
£310–350 / €450–500
$540–610 ⊞ Cas

A fairing, entitled 'By Appointment, the First of April', c1870, 4in (10cm) wide.
£430–480 / €620–690
$750–840 ⊞ Cas

A fairing, entitled 'Please Sir What Would You Charge to Christen My Doll?', c1870, 4in (10cm) wide.
£310–350 / €450–500
$540–610 ⊞ Cas

A fairing, entitled 'Between Two Stools You Fall to the Ground', c1870, 3½in (9cm) high.
£360–400 / €520–580
$630–700 ⊞ Cas

A spill holder fairing, entitled 'The Welsh Tea Party', c1870, 3½in (9cm) wide.
£30–35 / €45–50
$55–65 ⊞ Cas

◀ A fairing, entitled 'English Neutrality 1870 Attending to the Sick and the Wounded', 1870, 4in (10cm) wide.
£450–500 / €650–720
$790–880 🔨 G(L)

A fairing, entitled 'Now they'll Blame Me for This', c1870, 2¼in (5.5cm) wide.
£120–140 / €170–200
$210–250 🔨 SAS

A fairing, entitled 'Little Boy Blue', late 19thC, 2¼in (5.5cm) wide.
£65–75 / €95–105
$110–130 🔨 SJH

◀ A fairing, entitled 'Welsh Tea Party', c1880, 4½in (11.5cm) high.
£55–65 / €80–95
$105–125 ⊞ ACAC

Gebrüder Heubach

A Gebrüder Heubach bisque figure of a baby in a boot, German, 1880–1900, 11in (28cm) high.
£990–1,100 / €1,450–1,600
$1,750–1,950 ⊞ OAK

A pair of Gebrüder Heubach bisque figures of a boy and a girl, sitting on stools, German, c1880, 12in (30.5cm) high.
£450–500 / €650–720
$790–880 ⊞ OAK

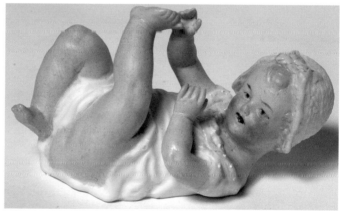

A Gebrüder Heubach bisque figure of a baby, entitled 'Stuart', c1890, 4in (10cm) wide.
£175–195 / €250–280
$300–340 ⊞ OAK

A Gebrüder Heubach bisque figure of a dancing girl, c1890, 12in (30.5cm) high.
£250–280 / €360–400
$440–490 ⊞ OAK

▶ **A pair of Gebrüder Heubach bisque figures of a boy and a girl with chickens,** c1890, 12in (30.5cm) high.
£270–300 / €390–430
$470–530 ⊞ OAK

Meissen

A Meissen figure of a lady selling potatoes, by J. J. Kändler, German, c1748, 7in (18cm) high.
£5,300–6,000 / €7,600–8,600
$9,200–10,500 ⊞ BHa

A Meissen figure of Cupid in disguise, by J. J. Kändler, German, c1750, 3½in (9cm) high.
£1,350–1,500 / €1,950–2,150
$2,350–2,650 ⊞ BHa

A Meissen figure of a street peddler, by J. J. Kändler, German, c1748, 7in (18cm) high.
£3,600–4,000 / €5,200–5,800
$6,300–7,000 ⊞ BHa

A Meissen figure of a lady, hat restored, German, 19thC, 6in (15cm) high.
£490–550 / €710–790
$860–960 ⊞ G&G

A Meissen figure of Cupid disguised as a lady, German, c1770, 4in (10cm) high.
£850–950 / €1,200–1,350
$1,500–1,650 ⊞ MAA

A Meissen figure of Cupid disguised as a musician, by Acier, German, c1775, 4in (10cm) high.
£850–950 / €1,200–1,350
$1,500–1,650 ⊞ MAA

◀ **A Meissen model of a Bolognese hound,** crossed swords mark, German, 19thC, 9¼in (23.5cm) high.
£520–620 / €750–890
$910–1,100 ⚒ SJH

A Meissen figural group of Winter, German, 19thC, 4½in (11.5cm) high.
£1,450–1,650 / €2,100–2,350
$2,550–2,900 ⊞ MAA

A Meissen figure of Sight, from the Five Senses series, German, c1840, 6in (15cm) high.
£1,100–1,250 / €1,600–1,800
$1,900–2,100 ⊞ MAA

A Meissen figural group, entitled 'Broken Bridge', first modelled by Acier, No. F63, crossed swords mark, German, c1850, 10in (25.5cm) high.
£2,450–2,750 / €3,500–4,000
$4,300–4,800 ⊞ DAV

A Meissen figural group of Aeneas carrying his father Anchise with his son Ascanius, first modelled by J. J. Kändler, No. 2030, crossed swords mark, German, c1850, 10in (25.5cm) high.
£1,400–1,600 / €2,000–2,200
$2,450–2,800 ⊞ DAV

▶ **A pair of Meissen models of golden orioles,** restored, crossed swords marks, German, 1850–90, 10in (25.5cm) high.
£1,100–1,300 / €1,600–1,900
$1,900–2,250 ⚒ WW

A Meissen figural group of Mars God of War and three cherubs, first modelled by Acier, No. D80, crossed swords mark, German, c1850, 9in (23cm) high.
£2,900–3,250 / €4,200–4,700
$5,100–5,700 ⊞ DAV

A Meissen figural water group, first modelled by Acier, No. D81, crossed swords mark, German, c1850, 10in (25.5cm) high.
£2,250–2,500 / €3,250–3,600
$4,000–4,400 ⊞ DAV

CONTINENTAL

A Meissen figural group of three putti astronomers, German, c1860, 5in (12.5cm) high.
£1,300–1,450 / €1,850–2,100
$2,250–2,550 ⊞ MAA

A Meissen figure of a cherub, German, c1860, 8½in (21.5cm) high.
£1,300–1,450 / €1,850–2,100
$2,250–2,550 ⊞ MAA

A Meissen group of two cherubs and a goat, German, c1860, 4in (10cm) high.
£850–950 / €1,200–1,350
$1,500–1,650 ⊞ MAA

A Meissen group, entitled 'Bird in a Hoop', German, c1860, 5in (12.5cm) high.
£1,300–1,450 / €1,850–2,100
$2,250–2,550 ⊞ MAA

A pair of Meissen figures of street traders, first modelled by J. J. Kändler, No. 2373 and No. 2350, crossed swords marks, German, c1860, 7in (18cm) high.
£990–1,100 / €1,400–1,600
$1,750–1,950 each ⊞ DAV

◄ **A pair of Meissen figural candlesticks,** first modelled by J. J. Kändler, Nos. F155 and F156, crossed swords marks, German, c1865, 14in (35.5cm) high.
£2,700–3,000 / €3,900–4,300
$4,700–5,200 ⊞ DAV

► **A Meissen figure of Venus on a chariot,** German, c1870, 7in (18cm) high.
£3,150–3,500 / €4,500–5,000
$5,500–6,100 ⊞ MAA

A Meissen figural group of a courting couple, German, c1860, 8in (20.5cm) high.
£2,300–2,600 / €3,300–3,750
$4,000–4,550 ⊞ BROW

A Meissen figure of a child with a doll, German, c1870, 5½in (14cm) high.
£1,300–1,450 / €1,850–2,100 $2,250–2,550 ⊞ MAA

A pair of Meissen figures of Day and Night, German, c1870, 7in (18cm) high.
£2,500–2,850 / €3,600–4,100 $4,400–5,000 ⊞ MAA

▶ **A Meissen figure of a Cupid disguised as a cripple,** German, c1870, 9in (23cm) high.
£1,100–1,250 / €1,600–1,800 $1,900–2,100 ⊞ MAA

A Meissen figure of a cherub, German, c1870, 4½in (11.5cm) high.
£670–750 / €960–1,100 $1,150–1,300 ⊞ MAA

A pair of Meissen figures of a girl with a cat and a boy with a dog, German, c1870, 5in (12.5cm) high.
£1,800–2,000 / €2,600–2,900 $3,150–3,500 ⊞ HKW

◀ **A Meissen figural group of two putti and a dog by an urn,** German, c1870, 8½in (21.5cm) high.
£2,250–2,550 / €3,250–3,650 $3,950–4,450 ⊞ MAA

▶ **A Meissen figural group,** entitled 'The Good Father', German, c1870, 8in (20.5cm) high.
£3,950–4,400 / €5,700–6,400 $6,900–7,700 ⊞ BROW

A pair of a Meissen figures with chickens, German, c1870, 6in (15cm) high.
**£2,350–2,650 / €3,400–3,800
$4,100–4,650** ⊞ BROW

A Meissen model of a hare, German, c1880, 6in (18cm) high.
**£1,050–1,200 / €1,500–1,700
$1,850–2,100** ⊞ K&M

A Meissen figure of Balance, first modelled by Acier, from a series of 16, No. F2, crossed swords mark, German, 1870, 6in (18cm) high.
**£900–1,000 / €1,300–1,450
$1,550–1,750** ⊞ DAV

▶ **A Meissen model of a parrot,** first modelled by J. J. Kändler, No. 63, crossed swords mark, German, c1880, 13in (33cm) high.
**£2,150–2,400 / €3,100–3,450
$3,750–4,200** ⊞ DAV

A Meissen figure of a cherub, German, c1880, 11in (28cm) high.
**£1,400–1,600 / €2,000–2,200
$2,450–2,800** ⊞ K&M

A Meissen group of a courting couple, German, c1880, 10in (25.5cm) high.
**£4,000–4,500 / €5,800–6,500
$7,000–7,900** ⊞ BROW

A Meissen figure of Touch, from the Senses series, German, c1880, 6in (15cm) high.
**£1,300–1,450 / €1,850–2,100
$2,250–2,550** ⊞ BROW

A Meissen frigural group of three children, German, c1880, 6in (15cm) high.
**£1,400–1,550 / €2,000–2,200
$2,450–2,800** ⊞ K&M

A Meissen figural group of a couple drinking wine, German, c1880, 7in (18cm) high.
£2,850–3,200 / €4,100–4,600
$5,000–5,600 ⊞ BROW

A Meissen model of a bullfinch, German, c1880, 3½in (9cm) high.
£300–340 / €430–490
$530–590 ⊞ BROW

A pair of Meissen figures, German, c1880, 7in (18cm) high.
£3,150–3,500 / €4,500–5,000
$5,500–6,100 ⊞ BHa

A Meissen figural group of Astronomy, German, c1880, 5in (12.5cm) high.
£1,300–1,450 / €1,850–2,100
$2,250–2,550 ⊞ MAA

A Meissen figural group of cherubs carrying a fox and a bird, German, c1880, 5¾in (14.5cm) high.
£1,100–1,250 / €1,600–1,800
$1,900–2,100 ⊞ MAA

A Meissen figural group of two cherubs with a ewer and a tambourine, German, c1880, 5in (12.5cm) high.
£1,650–1,850 / €2,400–2,650
$2,900–3,250 ⊞ MAA

A pair of Meissen figures of a girl and a boy feeding chickens and ducks, German, c1880, 5½in (14cm) high.
£2,250–2,500 / €3,250–3,600
$4,000–4,400 ⊞ MAA

A Meissen figure of a cherub, German, c1880, 5in (12.5cm) high.
£670–750 / €950–1,050
$1,150–1,300 ⊞ MAA

Royal Dux

A Royal Dux model of an elephant,
Bohemian, c1890, 15in (38cm) wide.
£450–500 / €650–720
$790–880 ⊞ GSA

A Royal Dux figure of a cavalier,
printed and painted marks, Bohemian,
19thC, 11½in (29cm) high.
£780–940 / €1,100–1,300
$1,350–1,600 ✎ SJH

▶ **A Royal Dux figural dish,** entitled
'Diana', slight damage, Bohemian,
c1900, 9in (23cm) high.
£160–190 / €230–270
$280–330 ✎ BWL

**A Royal Dux figure of
a shepherdess,** marked,
Bohemian, c1890, 24½in
(61cm) high.
£780–930 / €1,100–1,300
$1,350–1,600 ✎ TMA

**A Royal Dux figure of a man
carrying water,** Bohemian, c1900,
24in (61cm) high.
£490–550 / €710–790
$860–960 ⊞ JOA

A Royal Dux figural vase, Bohemian, c1900,
14in (35.5cm) high.
£900–1,000 / €1,300–1,450
$1,600–1,800 ⊞ HKW

Samson

A pair of Samson figures riding goats, entitled 'The Tailor' and 'The Tailor's Wife', based on Meissen models by Eberlein, *faux* Derby marks in red enamel, French, 19thC, 6¾in (17cm) high.
£440–520 / €630–750
$770–910 ⚒ G(L)

A Samson porcelain double scent bottle, in the form of a huntsman carrying a woman, French, 19thC, 3¼in (8.5cm) high.
£140–165 / €200–240
$250–300 ⚒ SWO

◀ **A Samson porcelain scent bottle,** French, c1870, 3½in (9cm) high.
£380–430 / €550–620
$670–750 ⊞ VK
The Samson company was founded in Paris in the early 19th century by Edmé Samson. They specialized in reproductions of ceramic pieces by named makers and their output included copies of 18th-century porcelain from such factories as Sèvres, Chelsea, Meissen and Derby and Chinese export-wares. Although often made 100 years or more after the originals, the early pieces are now antiques in their own right. The company is still in production today.

◀ **A Samson model of a hound,** after a Kutani original, with a gilded collar, French, 19thC, 15in (38cm) high.
£400–480 / €570–680
$700–840 ⚒ SWO
Kutani is a style of porcelain produced in Kaga, Japan, in the 17th century.

Decorative Arts

A model of a pig, by Alexander Lauder, c1890, 5in (12.5cm) wide.
£90–100 / €130–145
$155–175 ⊞ BKJL

A Brannam Pottery model of a cat, c1895, 10in (25.5cm) high.
£450–500 / €650–720
$790–880 ⊞ BKJL

A Watcombe Pottery model of a cat, c1900, 9in (23cm) high.
£220–250 / €320–360
$390–440 ⊞ BKJL

A Mosaic model of a dog, French, c1900, 5in (12.5cm) high.
£90–100 / €130–145
$160–180 ⊞ BKJL

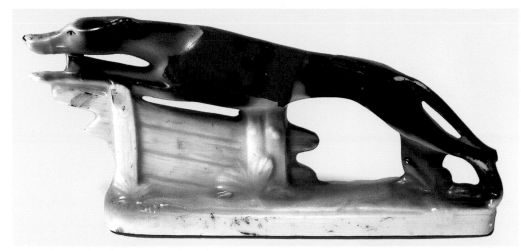

A porcelain model of a racing greyhound, c1900, 6in (15cm) wide.
£140–160 / €200–230
$250–280 ⊞ **BtoB**

A Reissner, Stellmacher & Kessel porcelain chamberstick, in the form of a girl on a lily pad, Austrian, c1910, 7½in (19cm) wide.
£720–800 / €1,050–1,200
$1,250–1,400 ⊞ **ASP**

A Mosanic model of a cat, French, c1900, 9in (23cm) high.
£110–130 / €160–185
$195–230 ⊞ **BKJL**

▶ **A Reissner, Stellmacher & Kessel porcelain centrepiece,** in the form of a girl on a lily pad, Austrian, c1910, 8in (20.5cm) high.
£900–1,000 / €1,300–1,450
$1,600–1,800 ⊞ **ASP**

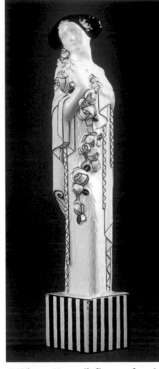

A Wiener Keramik figure of a girl holding roses, by Michael Powolny, impressed marks, c1910, 11½in (29cm) high.
£4,500–5,400 / €6,500–7,800 $7,900–9,400 ⚒ DORO

A porcelain lamp base, by Claire Volkhart, in the form of a dancing couple, Continental, dated 1913, 13in (33cm) high.
£360–400 / €520–580 $630–700 ⊞ StB

A pair of Ramvillers bookends, by A. Schneider, in the form of birds, French, c1915, 8in (20.5cm) high.
£130–150 / €185–220 $230–260 ⊞ StB

◄ **A Schwarzburger figural group,** by Schwartzkopf, entitled 'Ash Wednesday', German, c1920, 15in (38cm) high.
£1,350–1,500 / €1,950–2,150 $2,350–2,650 ⊞ CHO

A Gotha model of a French bulldog, German, c1920, 8in (20.5cm) wide.
£360–400 / €520–580
$630–700 ⊞ SRi

▶ **An Ipsen bisque figure of a girl,** signed 'FC', Danish, c1925,
8in (20.5cm) high.
£220–250 / €320–360
$390–440 ⊞ DSG
Ipsens Enke pottery was founded in Copenhagen in 1843 by Peter
Ipsen. After his death, his widow continued the business until his son
Bertel took over in 1865. The company was associated with many
internationally known artists including Kay Nielson and Georg
Jensen, and won countless awards from all over the world.

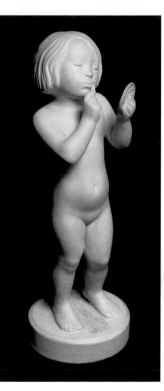

**A Bechyne porcelain figural group of a
woman and dogs,** Czechoslovakian, 1925,
21in (53.5cm) high.
£670–750 / €960–1,100
$1,150–1,300 ⊞ LLD

A Richard Ginori porcelain figure of a woman on a shell, by
Gio Ponti and Tommaso Buzzi, modelled by Italo Griselli, signed,
inscribed '27-10', Italian, 1926–28, 14in (35.5cm) high.
£12,100–14,400 / €17,400–20,800
$21,200–25,200 ✗ S(Mi)

DECORATIVE ARTS

A Richard Ginori earthenware figure, entitled 'The Tired Pilgrim', inscribed '363' and '1926', Italian, signed, designed 1922, 9½in (24cm) high.
£7,100–8,500 / €10,200–12,200
$12,400–14,900 ⚒ S(Mi)

A Gray's Pottery model of a toucan, by Nancy Catford, 1926, 8in (20.5cm) high.
£600–670 / €860–960
$1,050–1,200 ⊞ MMc

Auction or dealer?

All the pictures in our price guides originate from auction houses ⚒ and dealers ⊞. When buying at auction, prices can be lower than those of a dealer, but a buyer's premium and VAT will be added to the hammer price. Equally, when selling at auction, commission, tax and photography charges must be taken into account. Dealers will often restore pieces before putting them back on the market. Both dealers and auctioneers can provide professional advice, so it is worth researching both sources before buying or selling your antiques.

◀ **Two Richard Ginori porcelain figures,** by Gio Ponti, modelled by Geminiano Cibau, entitled 'The Poet' and 'The Dancing Teacher', signed, Doccia mark, Italian, dated 1927, larger 11in (28cm) high.
£3,350–3,950 / €4,800–5,700
$5,900–7,000 ⚒ S(Mi)

A porcelain half-doll pin cushion, 1920s, 4½in (11.5cm) high.
£220–250 / €320–360
$390–440 ⊞ SUW

An Ilmenau porcelain figure, probably designed by Schliepstein, German, 1920s, 8in (20.5cm) high.
£360–400 / €520–580
$630–700 ⊞ LLD

A Primavera figure of a harlequin, French, c1930, 13in (33cm) high.
£470–520 / €680–750
$820–910 ⊞ MI

A porcelain figure of a nude woman, standing on a gilt ball, German, c1930, 8½in (21.5cm) high.
£140–165 / €200–240
$250–300 ⋏ G(L)

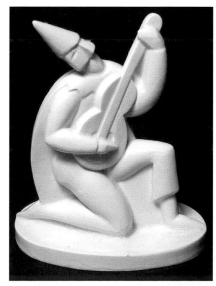

▶ **A crackle ware figure of a guitar player,** signed 'G. Conde', French, c1930, 10in (25.5cm) high.
£470–520 / €680–750
$820–910 ⊞ MI

A porcelain model of a dog,
Continental, c1930, 9in (23cm) high.
£120–140 / €175–200
$210–250 ⊞ HEW

**A Keramos earthenware figure
of a lady with a vase,** Austrian,
c1930, 16in (40.5cm) high.
£1,050–1,200 / €1,500–1,700
$1,800–2,050 ⊞ AnM

**A ROBJ ceramic figure of a
dancing woman,** French, 1930,
19in (48.5cm) high.
£540–600 / €780–860
$950–1,050 ⊞ JSG

▶ **A model of a deer,** probably French, c1930, 20in (51cm) wide.
£60–70 / €85–100
$105–125 ⊞ ASP

A ceramic napkin ring, in the form of a dog, 1930s, 3in (7.5cm) long.
£25–30 / €40–45
$50–55 ⊞ HeA

A Beswick model of a monkey, c1930, 7in (18cm) high.
£270–300 / €390–430
$470–530 ⊞ HEW

DECORATIVE ARTS

A porcelain figure of a lady, by Metzler & Ortloff, German, 1930s, 8in (20.5cm) high.
£130–150 / €185–220
$220–260 ⚒ DN(BR)

A Crown Ducal Spectria Flambé model of a clown, by E. R. Wilkes, c1935,
£200–230 / €290–330
$350–400 ⊞ DSG

◄ A porcelain figure, Continental, c1930, 9in (23cm) high.
£135–150 / €195–220
$230–260 ⊞ HEW

A Dutch Delft figural chess set, 1930s, king 4in (10cm) high.
£550–650 / €790–940
$960–1,150 ⚒ G(L)

◀ **An Essevi
figure of
a woman,**
by Sandro
Vacchetti, Italian,
c1935, 16in
(40.5cm) high.
£5,400–6,000
€7,200–8,600
$9,500–10,500
⊞ AnM

▶ **An Essevi
figure of
a woman,**
by Sandro
Vacchetti, Italian,
1930s, 16in
(40.5cm) high.
£9,000–10,000
€13,000–14,400
$15,700–17,500
⊞ AnM

A Carlton Ware model of a dog, No. 2600, 1930s, 6¼in (16cm) high.
£110–130 / €160–190
$195–230 ➶ DA

◄ **A pottery bust of a young girl,** by M. Blyth, 1930s, 3½in (9cm) high.
£105–120 / €150–170
$185–210 ⊞ StB

A model of a pelican, Czechoslovakian, mid-1930s, 10in (25.5cm) high.
£175–195 / €250–280
$300–340 ⊞ LLD

◄ **A Schlaggenwald dog,** German, mid-1930s, 4in (10cm) high.
£40–45 / €55–65
$70–80 ⊞ LLD

DECORATIVE ARTS

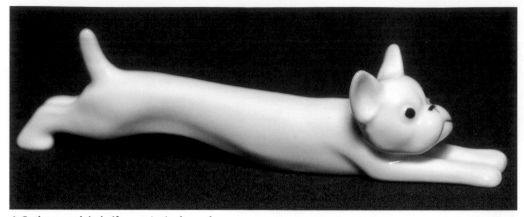

A Gotha porcelain knife rest, in the form of a dog, German, 1930s, 5in (12.5cm) wide.
£50–60 / €75–85
$90–105 ⊞ SRi

Prices

The price ranges quoted in this book reflect the average price a purchaser might expect to pay for a similar item. The price will vary according to the condition, rarity, size, popularity, provenance, colour and restoration of the item, and this must be taken into account when assessing values. Don't forget that if you are selling it is quite likely that you will be offered less than the price range.

A Wedgwood model of a deer, by John Skeaping, printed mark, 1930–40, 8in (20.5cm) high.
£90–105 / €130–155
$160–190 ⚒ PF

A Gebrüder Heubach figure of a pierrot, German, c1940, 4in (10cm) high.
£175–195 / €250–280
$300–340 ⊞ EAn

Ashtead Pottery

An Ashtead Pottery Stanley Baldwin character jug, by Percy Metcalf, No. 554 of edition of 1,000, facsimile signature, c1923, 7½in (19cm) diam.
£100–120 / €145–170
$200–240 ⚒ SAS

▶ An Ashtead Pottery figure, entitled 'Buster Boy', by Phoebe Stabler, 1930, 5½in (14cm) high.
£700–790 / €1,000–1,100
$1,250–1,400 ⊞ MMc

◀ An Ashtead Pottery figure of a girl holding a cane, by Phoebe Stabler, 1920s, 6in (15cm) high.
£770–880 / €1,100–1,250
$1,350–1,500 ⊞ MMc
Most of the figures produced by Ashtead Pottery were designed by leading artists of the day. The Phoebe Stabler figures were made under licence from Poole Pottery.

Bovey Pottery

A Bovey Tracey Pottery creamware model of a cat, c1880, 3¾in (9.5cm) long.
£570–640 / €820–920
$1,000–1,100 ⊞ RdV
The Bovey Pottery Co (1894–1957) was formerly the Bovey Tracey Pottery Co from 1842 to 1894.

▶ A Bovey Pottery figure of a pilot, c1940, 7in (18cm) high.
£170–190 / €240–270
$300–330 ⊞ BRT

A Bovey Pottery figure, entitled 'Scotty', c1940, 7in (18cm) high.
£170–190 / €240–270
$300–330 ⊞ BRT

DECORATIVE ARTS

Burmantofts

A Burmantofts Pottery spoon warmer, in the form of a toad, c1890, 6in (15cm) high.
£310–350 / €450–500
$540–610 ⊞ BKJL

A Burmantofts Pottery vase, in the form of a swan, c1880, 10in (25.5cm) high.
£360–400
€520–580
$630–700 ⊞ BKJL

▶ **A Burmantofts Pottery model of a monkey,** c1890, 3in (7.5cm) high.
£400–450
€580–650
$700–790 ⊞ BKJL

Denby

A Denby stoneware model of a terrier, c1935, 3in (7.5cm) long.
£85–95 / €120–135
$150–165 ⊞ StB

A Denby figure of a caddy with golf clubs, c1935, 5in (12.5cm) high.
£160–180 / €230–260
$280–320 ⊞ JSG

A **Denby ashtray,** in the form of a pig, c1936, 2in (5cm) high.
£220–250 / €320–360
$390–440 ⊞ KES

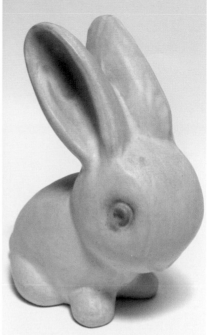

A **Denby model of a rabbit,** 1930s,
11in (28cm) high.
£250–290 / €360–410
$440–500 ⊞ BEV

A **Denby model of Byngo,** with trial glaze, late 1930s,
3½in (9cm) high.
£110–130 / €160–180
$195–230 ⊞ KES
Byngo is an Anglicized version of the popular 1920–40s dog,
Bonzo. Byngo came in a variety of sizes and colours and, if
marked at all, tends to be signed 'Danesby Ware' which
was part of Denby.

A **Denby model of a lamb,** size seven,
mid-20thC, 12in (30.5cm) high.
£130–145 / €185–210
$230–260 ⊞ HeA
Denby lambs, recognizable by their eerie,
cut-out eyes, heavy glazes and unglazed
feet are very popular. Sizes two and three
are most common, making the rarer larger
lambs more sought after and valuable.

Gallé

A Gallé model of a pug dog,
entitled 'Monsieur Le Marquis',
with gilded collar, c1900,
12in (30.5cm) high.
£2,250–2,500 / €3,250–3,600
$3,950–4,400 ⊞ RdeR

A Gallé faïence model of a cat,
with glass eyes, damaged, paw signed,
French, c1900, 12¾in (32.5cm) high.
£500–600 / €720–860
$880–1,050 ⚒ SWO

A faïence model of a cat,
attributed to Gallé, decorated with
mantilla and locket, French, c1900,
14in (35.5cm) high.
£1,800–2,000 / €2,600–2,900
$3,150–3,500 ⊞ RdeR

Goldscheider

◄ **A Gold-
scheider figure
of a dancing
lady,** No. 7855,
Austrian, early
19thC, 14in
(35.5cm) high.
£500–600
€720–860
$880–1,050
⚒ BWL

► **A Gold-
scheider figure
of a lady
carrying a
basket,** mono-
grammed 'GJ',
Austrian, late
19thC, 34½in
(87.5cm) high.
£1,000–1,200
€1,450–1,750
$1,750–2,100
⚒ G(L)

◀ **A Gold-scheider figure of a young man holding an urn,** lozenge mark, Austrian, 1885–1918, 19in (48.5cm) high.
£135–160
€195–230
$240–290
🔨 **MED**

▶ **A Goldscheider terracotta bust of a young woman,** Austrian, c1900, 24in (61cm) high.
£1,600–1,800
€2,300–2,600
$2,800–3,150 ⊞ **ASP**

A Goldscheider painted and bronzed terracotta bust of a young girl, by Montenave, the hairband set with glass stones, restored, Austrian, c1905, 26½in (67cm) high.
£1,500–1,800
€2,150–2,600
$2,650–3,150 🔨 **BUK**

A Goldscheider terracotta figure of a jockey, signed, Austrian, c1900, 21in (53.5cm) high.
£1,050–1,200 / €1,500–1,700
$1,850–2,100 ⊞ **OAK**

A Goldscheider terracotta bust of a young woman, impressed marks, signed, Austrian, c1900, 21in (53.5cm) high.
£700–840 / €1,000–1,200
$1,250–1,450 🔨 **TEN**

DECORATIVE ARTS

A Goldscheider terracotta bust of a woman,
Austrian, c1915, 26in (66cm) high.
£1,900–2,200 / €2,750–3,150
$3,350–3,850 ⊞ ASP

A Goldscheider figural group of two dancers,
Austrian, c1930, 15in (38cm) high.
£2,700–3,000 / €3,900–4,300
$4,750–5,300 ⊞ BD

A Goldscheider porcelain figure of a woman playing golf, by Stefan Dakon, Austrian, c1930, 10in (25.5cm) high.
£1,800–2,000 / €2,600–2,900
$3,150–3,500 ⊞ HEW

◄ A Goldscheider porcelain figure of a dancer, by Stefan Dakon, Austrian, c1930, 8in (20.5cm) high.
£490–550
€710–790
$860–960
⊞ HEW

► A Goldscheider figure of a woman, entitled 'Stockings', by Thomasch, Austrian, c1930, 18in (45.5cm) high.
£2,700–3,000
€3,900–4,300
$4,750–5,300
⊞ BD

A Goldscheider figural lamp base, in the form of a seated child, Austrian, c1930, 13in (33cm) high.
£210–250 / €300–360
$370–440 ♪ DORO

A Goldscheider porcelain figure of a woman, Austrian, c1930, 13in (33cm) high.
£1,500–1,700 / €2,150–2,450
$2,650–3,000 ⊞ HEW

A Goldscheider figure of a woman, by Stefan Dakon, impressed marks, restored, signed, Austrian, c1930, 15⅞in (40cm) high.
£1,050–1,250 / €1,500–1,800
$1,850–2,200 ♪ WW

A Goldscheider porcelain figure of a dancer, by Stefan Dakon, Austrian, c1935, 8in (20.5cm) high.
£540–600 / €780–860
$950–1,050 ⊞ LLD

A Goldscheider ceramic figure of a traveller seated on a trunk, by Stefan Dakon, restored, marked, impressed model No. 736/42/19, Austrian, c1935, 10in (25.5cm) high.
£1,350–1,600 / €1,950–2,300
$2,350–2,800 ⚒ DORO

A Goldscheider ceramic figure of a dancer, by Josef Lorenzl, entitled 'Butterfly Girl', restored, signed, factory mark, Austrian, c1937, 16in (40.5cm) high.
£1,450–1,700 / €2,100–2,500
$2,550–3,000 ⚒ SK

A Goldscheider ceramic figure of a dancer, factory mark, impressed model No. 8088/11, Austrian, 1938–39, 13in (33cm) high.
£420–500 / €600–720
$740–870 ⚒ DORO

A Goldscheider porcelain figure of a woman, by Josef Lorenzl, factory mark, impressed model No. 8493/22/7, Austrian, 1938–39, 16¾in (42.5cm) high.
£1,750–2,100 / €2,550–3,050
$3,100–3,700 ⚲ DORO

A Goldscheider figural group of a girl and a dog, by Stefan Dakon, factory marks, Austrian, c1939, 12¾in (32.5cm) high.
£1,250–1,500 / €1,800–2,150
$2,200–2,650 ⚲ DORO

◄ **A Goldscheider porcelain figure of a lady with a parasol,** Austrian, 1930s, 13in (33cm) high.
£720–800
€1,050–1,200
$1,250–1,400
⊞ MiW

A Goldscheider figure of a girl playing golf, Austrian, 1930s, 10in (25.5cm) high.
£850–950 / €1,200–1,350
$1,500–1,650 ⊞ AnM

▶ **A Goldscheider porcelain figure of a lady,** Austrian, 1930s, 7in (18cm) high.
£250–280 / €360–400
$440–490 ⊞ MiW

A Goldscheider figure of a woman, Austrian, 1930s,
9in (23cm) high.
£250–280 / €360–400
$440–490 ⊞ MiW

A Goldscheider figural group, entitled 'The Dolly
Sisters', Austrian, 1930s, 16in (40.5cm) high.
£3,150–3,500 / €4,500–5,000
$5,500–6,100 ⊞ GaL

A Goldscheider figure of a lady, Austrian, 1930s,
11in (28cm) high.
£1,250–1,400 / €1,800–2,000
$2,200–2,450 ⊞ AnM

A Goldscheider figure of a woman, Austrian, 1930s,
14in (35.5cm) high.
£1,250–1,400 / €1,800–2,000
$2,200–2,450 ⊞ AnM

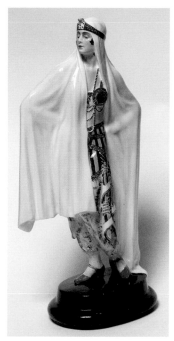

A Goldscheider figural group of a boy and a girl, Austrian, 1930s, 9in (23cm) high.
£400–450 / €580–650
$700–790 ⊞ AnM

▶ **A Goldscheider figure,** entitled 'Mephistopheles', Austrian, 1930s, 14in (35.5cm) high.
£1,050–1,200 / €1,500–1,700
$1,850–2,100 ⊞ AnM

A Goldscheider figure of a harem girl, Austrian, 1930s, 19in (48.5cm) high.
£2,150–2,400 / €3,100–3,450
$3,750–4,200 ⊞ AnM

A Goldscheider figural group, entitled 'The Dolly Sisters', Austrian, 1930s, 15in (38cm) high.
£4,900–5,500 / €7,100–7,900
$8,600–9,600 ⊞ AnM

A Goldscheider figure, entitled 'The Captured Bird' and 'The Butterfly Girl', Austrian, 1930s, 15in (38cm) high.
£2,300–2,600 / €3,300–3,750
$4,050–4,550 ⊞ AnM

A Goldscheider figure of a lady,
Austrian, 1930s, 19in (48.5cm) high.
£1,950–2,200 / €2,800–3,150
$3,400–3,850 ⊞ AnM

**A Goldscheider figural group of
a woman and a dog,** Austrian,
1930s, 15in (38cm) high.
£1,100–1,250 / €1,600–1,800
$1,950–2,200 ⊞ AnM

**A Goldscheider figure of a girl
with a suitcase,** Austrian,1950s,
6in (15cm) high.
£250–280 / €360–400
$440–490 ⊞ SCH

Hutschenreuther

**A Hutschenreuther porcelain figural group
of Pan and Psyche,** slight damage, German,
c1920, 12½in (32cm) high.
£760–850 / €1,100–1,250
$1,350–1,500 ⊞ ANO

A Hutschenreuther porcelain figure of a woman, by Karl
Tutter, German, 1920s, 11in (28cm) high.
£450–500 / €650–720
$780–870 ⊞ LLD

A Hutschenreuther porcelain figure, by Karl Tutter, German, 1920s, 7in (18cm) high.
£580–650 / €840–940
$1,000–1,150 ⊞ LLD

A Hutschenreuther figure of a woman, by Karl Tutter, German, c1930, 11in (28cm) high.
£450–500 / €650–720
$790–880 ⊞ EAn

A Hutschenreuther porcelain figure, by Karl Tutter, entitled 'The Goose Girl', German, c1930, 4in (10cm) high.
£130–150 / €195–220
$220–260 ⊞ CHO

▶ **A Hutschenreuther porcelain figural group,** by Karl Tutter, entitled 'The Two Girls Dancing', German, c1930, 7in (18cm) high.
£360–400 / €520–580
$630–700 ⊞ CHO

A Hutschenreuther porcelain model of a deer, by Hans Achtziger, German, c1930, 9in (23cm) high.
£450–500 / €650–720
$800–880 ⊞ EAn

A Hutschenreuther porcelain figural group of a boy and a girl dancing, German, mid-1930s, 11in (28cm) high.
£540–600 / €780–860
$950–1,050 ⊞ LLD

A Hutschenreuther porcelain figure, by Karl Tutter, entitled 'The Sun Child', German, c1940, 9in (23cm) high.
£220–250 / €320–360
$390–440 ⊞ CHO

A Hutschenreuther porcelain figure, by Karl Tutter, entitled 'The Ball Player', German, c1940, 9in (23cm) high.
£310–350 / €450–500
$540–610 ⊞ CHO

A Hutschenreuther porcelain figure of an ice skater, German, c1940, 5in (12.5cm) high.
£400–450 / €580–650
$700–790 ⊞ Bel

Katzhütte

A Katzhütte earthenware figure of a dancer, printed mark, German, 1920s, 12½in (32cm) high.
£360–430 / €520–620
$630–750 ⚒ G(L)

A Katzhütte porcelain figure of a snake dancer, printed marks, German, c1920, 6¾in (17cm) high.
£160–190
€230–270
$280–330
⚒ SWO

▶ A Katzhütte porcelain figure of a woman, German, 1920s, 6in (15cm) high.
£360–400
€520–580
$630–700 ⊞ LLD

A Katzhütte figure of a dancer, printed mark, German, 1920s, 11¼in (28.5cm) high.
£200–240 / €290–350
$350–420 ⚒ G(L)

A Katzhütte figural group of two dancers, German, c1930, 20½in (52cm) high.
£600–720 / €870–1,050
$1,050–1,250 ⚒ AH

A Katzhütte figure of a woman and a fawn, German, c1935, 14in (35.5cm) high.
£760–850 / €1,050–1,200
$1,350–1,500 ⊞ HEW

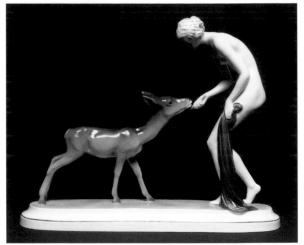

A Katzhütte figure of a woman and a fawn, German, c1935, 7in (18cm) high.
£760–850 / €1,050–1,200
$1,350–1,500 ⊞ HEW

A Katzhütte figure of a woman, German, c1935, 10in (25.5cm) high.
£430–480 / €620–690
$750–840 ⊞ HEW

► A Katzhütte figure of a woman with a fan, German, 1930s, 20in (51cm) high.
£890–1,000
€1,300–1,450
$1,550–1,750 ⊞ LLD

Lenci

A Lenci figure of a woman, entitled 'Il Vento', Italian, c1930, 16in (40.5cm) high.
£4,250–4,750
€6,100–6,800
$7,400–8,300 ⊞ BD

A Lenci figural group of a girl, a bird and a hippopotamus, Italian, 1935, 11in (28cm) high.
£4,500–5,000 / €6,500–7,200
$7,900–8,800 ⊞ AnM

◄ **A Lenci figure of a woman,** Italian, c1930, 7in (18cm) high.
£1,500–1,700 / €2,150–2,450
$2,650–3,000 ⊞ HEW

A Lenci figural group, by A. Jacopi, entitled 'Tritons', Italian, c1935, 22in (56cm) wide.
£4,500–5,000 / €6,500–7,200
$7,900–8,800 ⊞ AnM

► **A Lenci figure of a woman,** Italian, 1935, 16in (40.5cm) long.
£4,500–5,000 / €6,500–7,200
$7,900–8,800 ⊞ AnM

DECORATIVE ARTS

A Lenci figure of a woman and a rabbit, Italian, 1936, 13in (33cm) high.
£4,000–4,500 / €5,800–6,400
$7,000–7,800 ⊞ AnM

A Lenci model of a fish, by Elena Scavini, Italian, 1930s, 11in (28cm) high.
£2,700–3,000 / €3,900–4,300
$4,750–5,300 ⊞ AnM

A Lenci figure, entitled 'Don Quixote', Italian, 1937, 22in (56cm) high.
£5,800–6,500 / €8,400–9,400
$10,200–11,400 ⊞ AnM

A Lenci figure of a girl standing beside a vase, painted marks, Italian, dated 1936, 17¾in (45cm) high.
£480–570 / €690–820
$840–1,000 ♪ S(O)

▶ **A Lenci pottery figure of the Madonna,** black painted marks and '11-XII-E', Italian, c1950, 11½in (29cm) high.
£450–540 / €650–780
$790–950 ♪ DN

Martin Brothers

◄ **A Martin Brothers stoneware jar,** in the form of a Wally bird, 1900, 9½in (24cm) high.
£15,700–17,500
€22,600–25,200
$27,500–31,000 ⊞ POW

A Martin Brothers stoneware figure, entitled 'Mr Pickwick', 1914, 2in (5cm) high.
£2,000–2,300 / €2,900–3,300
$3,500–4,000 ⊞ POW

◄ **A Martin Brothers stoneware tobacco jar,** in the form of a Wally Bird, damaged and repaired, the cover inscribed and dated 1903, 10in (25.5cm) high.
£5,500–6,500 / €7,900–9,400
$9,600–11,400 ⚒ GAK

Poole Pottery

A Carter, Stabler & Adams model of a cockerel, by Harold Stabler, c1922, 10in (25.5cm) wide.
£1,750–1,950 / €2,500–2,800
$3,050–3,400 ⊞ MMc

A Carter, Stabler & Adams figure, entitled 'Picardy Peasant Man', by Phoebe Stabler, 1920s, 10in (25.5cm) high.
£1,800–2,000 / €2,600–2,900
$3,150–3,500 ⊞ MMc

DECORATIVE ARTS

A Carter, Stabler & Adams figure, entitled 'Madonna of the Square', by Phoebe Stabler, 1920s, 8in (20.5cm) high.
£1,150–1,300 / €1,650–1,850
$2,000–2,200 ⊞ MMc

A Carter, Stabler & Adams figural candlestick, by Harold Brownsword, in the form of a cherub, 1928–30, 5in (12.5cm) high.
£270–300 / €390–430
$470–530 ⊞ MMc

◀ **A Carter, Stabler & Adams figure,** by Phoebe Stabler, entitled 'Buster Boy', 1930, 7in (18cm) high.
£750–850 / €1,100–1,250
$1,350–1,500 ⊞ MMc

A Carter, Stabler & Adams book end, by Harold Brownsword, in the form of an elephant, 1930, 5½in (14cm) long.
£310–350 / €450–500
$540–610 ⊞ MMc

▶ **A Carter, Stabler & Adams prototype figure,** attributed to Phoebe Stabler, c1935, 9in (23cm) high.
£1,100–1,250 / €1,600–1,800
$1,950–2,200 ⊞ MMc

Royal Dux

A Royal Dux figural group of two lovers, Bohemian, c1925, 13in (33cm) high.
£350–420 / €500–600 $610–730 ↗ DN(EH)

A Royal Dux figural group of two dancers, Bohemian, c1929, 16in (40.5cm) high.
£670–750 / €960–1,100 $1,150–1,300 ⊞ HEW

◄ **A Royal Dux figure of a girl with an accordian,** Bohemian, c1930, 10in (25.5cm) high.
£490–550 / €700–790 $860–960 ⊞ OAK

A Royal Dux figure, entitled 'The Goose Girl', Bohemian, 1920s, 14in (35.5cm) high.
£720–800 / €1,000–1,150 $1,250–1,400 ⊞ OAK

A Royal Dux figure of a woman with an apple, by Schaff, Bohemian, 1930, 21in (53.5cm) wide.
£990–1,100 / €1,400–1,600 $1,700–1,900 ⊞ LLD

A Royal Dux figure of a woman and a deer, Bohemian, c1930, 14in (35.5cm) high.
£540–600 / €780–860
$950–1,050 ⊞ **ASP**

A Royal Dux figure , Bohemian, c1930, 12in (30.5cm) high.
£540–600 / €780–860
$950–1,050 ⊞ **LLD**

A Royal Dux figure of a Spanish dancer, Bohemian, 1930s, 14in (35.5cm) high.
£350–400 / €500–570
$610–700 ⊞ **OAK**

A Royal Dux figure of a woman, Bohemian, c1932, 12in (30.5cm) high.
£350–400 / €500–570
$610–700 ⊞ **LLD**

A Royal Dux figural group of children spinning, Bohemian, 1930s, 6in (15cm) high.
£110–125 / €160–180
$190–220 ⊞ **LLD**

A Royal Dux figure of a woman,
Bohemian, c1933, 7in (30.5cm) high.
£220–250 / €320–360
$380–440 ⊞ HEW

► A Royal Dux figure of a
woman, by Schaff, Bohemian,
c1933, 13in (33cm) high.
£540–600 / €780–860
$950–1,050 ⊞ LLD

A Royal Dux figure, entitled
'The Lily Girl', Bohemian, 1930s,
6in (15cm) high.
£380–430 / €550–620
$670–750 ⊞ OAK

A Royal Dux figural centrepiece, Bohemian,
c1935, 12in (30.5cm) high.
£780–880 / €1,100–1,250
$1,350–1,550 ⊞ HEW

► A Royal Dux figure of a woman feeding
ducks, Bohemian, 1930s, 14in (35.5cm) high.
£540–600 / €780–860
$950–1,050 ⊞ LLD

A Royal Dux figure of a snake
charmer, pipe missing, Bohemian,
1930s, 9in (23cm) high.
£270–300 / €390–430
$470–520 ⊞ LLD

DECORATIVE ARTS

A Royal Dux model of a Pekinese, Bohemian, c1935, 8in (20.5cm) wide.
£105–120 / €150–170
$180–210 ⊞ SRi

▶ **A Royal Dux figure of a woman,** by Schaff, Bohemian, c1935, 8in (20.5cm) high.
£400–450 / €570–650
$700–790 ⊞ HEW

A Royal Dux figure of a discus thrower, Bohemian, 1930s, 9in (23cm) high.
£450–500 / €650–720
$790–870 ⊞ LLD

▶ **A Royal Dux figural group of two dancers,** entitled 'Dolly Sisters', Bohemian, 1930s–40s, 16in (40.5cm) high.
£350–400 / €500–570
$610–700 ⊞ LLD

Wade

A **Wade figure of a dancer,** entitled 'Dawn', slight restoration, printed marks, early 20thC, 8½in (21.5cm) high.
£230–270 / €330–390
$400–470 ⚒ SWO

A **Wade figure of a dancing woman,** entitled 'Mimi II', slight damage, printed marks, early 20thC, 7¼in (18.5cm) high.
£220–260 / €320–380
$390–460 ⚒ SWO

A **Wade figure of a woman,** entitled 'Lotus', slight damage, printed marks, early 20thC, 9½in (24cm) high.
£230–270 / €330–390
$400–470 ⚒ SWO

A **Wade figure of a woman,** entitled 'Grace', slight damage, printed marks, c1930, 9½in (24cm) high.
£220–260 / €320–380
$390–460 ⚒ SWO

A **Wade figure of a dancing woman,** entitled 'Conchita', printed marks, c1930, 8¾in (22cm) high.
£260–310 / €370–440
$460–540 ⚒ SWO

Zsolnay Pecs

A Zsolnay Pecs model of a bird, by Lajos Mack, Hungarian, 1913, 8in (20.5cm) wide.
£1,600–1,800 / €2,300–2,600
$2,800–3,150 ⊞ **POW**

▶ **A Zsolnay Pecs model of an exotic bird,** by Lajos Mack, Hungarian, 1914, 10in (25.5cm) long.
£1,800–2,000 / €2,600–2,900
$3,150–3,500 ⊞ **POW**

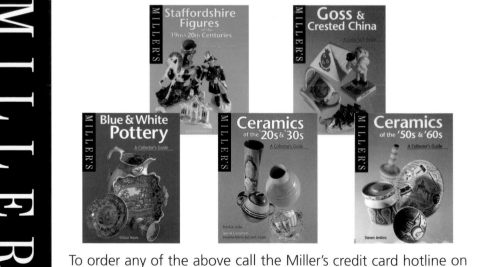

◄ **A Zsolnay Pecs lustre figure,** Hungarian, 1916, 14in (35.5cm) high.
£880–980 / €1,250–1,400
$1,500–1,700 ⊞ ANO

A Zsolnay Pecs model of a **cockerel,** Hungarian, 1926, 6in (15cm) high.
£220–250 / €320–360
$390–440 ⊞ POW

► **A Zsolnay Pecs model of an owl,** Hungarian, c1950, 3in (7.5cm) high.
£65–75 / €95–105
$115–130 ⊞ DSG

► **A Zsolnay Pecs figure of a woman,** entitled 'Coiffeure', Hungarian, 1960s, 9in (23cm) high.
£140–165 / €200–240
$250–300 ↗ TMA

A Zsolnay Pecs lustre model of a dog, Hungarian, 1950, 5in (12.5cm) wide.
£95–110 / €135–160
$165–190 ⊞ DSG

20th Century

A faïence model of a rabbit, with glass eyes, damaged, c1900, 11½in (29cm) high.
£320–380 / €460–550
$560–670 ⚒ WW

A figure of a cherub, Continental, early 20thC, 14in (35.5cm) high.
£150–180 / €220–260
$260–310 ⚒ G(L)

A majolica model of a duck, c1900, 6in (15cm) wide.
£155–175 / €220–250
$270–310 ⊞ MLL

◄ **A majolica model of a chick,** 1900, 7in (18cm) high.
£150–165 / €210–240
$260–290 ⊞ MLL

◀ **A set of five Sitzendorf monkey orchestra figures,** comprising a conductor, violinist, cellist, flautist, and a bugle player, on gilt-scrolled bases, losses, maker's mark, German, early 20thC, largest 5¼in (13.5cm) high.
£420–500 / €600–720 $740–880 ⚒ DN(BR)

A pair of Staffordshire models of spaniels, decorated with copper lustre, early 20thC, 9¼in (23.5cm) high.
£90–105 / €130–155 $160–190 ⚒ SWO

A porcelain monkey orchestra, comprising nine pieces, early 20thC, 7in (18cm) high.
£600–720 / €850–1,000 $1,050–1,250 ⚒ G(L)

A Gustavsberg porcelain model of the Spinario, after the antique, impressed marks, Swedish, early 20thC, 10¾in (27.5cm) high.
£380–450 / €550–650 $670–790 ⚒ WW
The Spinario is a bronze Roman masterpiece of the late first century BC. It depicts the intense concentration of a boy in the act of extracting a thorn from his foot. One of the first ancient sculptures to be copied, it has had a profound influence on artists over the centuries.

Two bisque figures of bathing belles, with hair wigs, one with a linen costume, German, early 20thC, larger 2½in (6.5cm) high.
£700–840 / €1,000–1,200 $1,250–1,500 ⚒ G(L)

20TH CENTURY

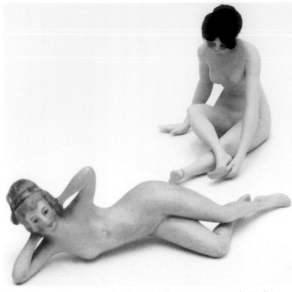

Two bisque figures of bathing belles, German, early 20thC, larger 5in (12.5cm) high.
£650–780 / €940–1,100
$1,150–1,350 ↗ G(L)

A Robinson & Leadbeater porcelain bust of Edward VII, 1901, 8in (20.5cm) high.
£160–180 / €230–260
$280–320 ⊞ JAK

Reissner & Kessel porcelain bust of a lady wearing a bonnet, printed mark, c1905, 18in (45.5cm) high.
£270–300 / €390–430
$470–520 ↗ SWO

A bisque figure of a boy, c1910, 3in (7.5cm) high.
£105–120 / €150–170
$185–210 ⊞ YC

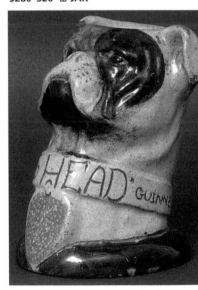

A pottery match striker, in the form of a dog's head, inscribed 'Bass Dog's Head, Guinness', impressed 'Read Bros, London', early 20thC, 4¼in (11cm) high.
£200–240 / €290–350
$350–420 ↗ BWL

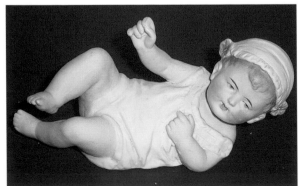

◄ **A bisque piano baby,** c1910, 4in (10cm) wide.
£90–105 / €130–155
$160–190 ⊞ JOA

◄ **A pair of porcelain figures,** of a cricketer and a tennis player, impressed '1838', Continental, 1910, 9¾in (25cm) high.
£210–250
€300–360
$370–440 ⚒ SJH

▶ **A bisque figure of a boy,** representing Faith, Hope and Charity, German, 1910, 1½in (4cm) high.
£40–45 / €60–70
$70–80 ⊞ CCs

A bisque figure of a cherub, 1910, German, 1½in (4cm) high.
£50–60 / €75–85
$90–105 ⊞ CCs

A bisque figure, in the form of a cherub playing an instrument, German, 1910, 4in (10cm) high.
£65–75 / €95–110
$115–130 ⊞ CCs

A porcelain figure of a rugby player, impressed '1838', Continental, 1910, 9¾in (25cm) high.
£150–180 / €220–260
$260–310 ⚒ SJH

◄ **A porcelain figural scent bottle,** with a crown stopper, Continental, c1910, 3¼in (8.5cm) high.
£150–170 / €220–250
$270–300 ⊞ VK

An Eichwald porcelain figure of a girl wearing a crinoline dress, by Bernard Bloch, with painted decoration, stamped '9333', 1910–15, 12¼in (31cm) high.
£350–420 / €500–600
$610–730 ⚒ **DORO**

A bisque figure of a cherub, German, 1910–20, 2½in (6.5cm) high.
£65–75 / €95–110
$115–130 ⊞ **CCs**

A Wilkinson character jug, by Carruthers Gould, in the form of King George V, 1910–36, 12in (30.5cm) high.
£260–310 / €370–440
$460–540 ⚒ **SAS**

A bisque figure of a cherub in a canoe, German, 1910–20, 3in (7.5cm) wide.
£70–80 / €100–115
$125–140 ⊞ **CCs**

◄ **A Hewitt & Leadbeater bust of Queen Mary,** 1911, 7in (18cm) high.
£140–160 / €200–230
$250–280 ⊞ **JAK**

► **A majolica Tit-Bits Toby jug,** by William Ault, commemorating WWI, c1917, 10in (25.5cm) high.
£360–400 / €520–580
$630–700 ⊞ **JBL**

A bisque piano baby, c1920, 3in (7.5cm) wide.
£25–30 / €35–40
$45–50 ⊞ YC

A bisque match striker, German, c1920, 3½in (9cm) high.
£60–70 / €85–100
$105–125 ⊞ MRW

A bisque figure of a girl, German, c1920, 4in (10cm) high.
£35–40 / €50–60
$60–70 ⊞ YC

▶ A pair of Staffordshire models of sheep, No.
2279, c1920, 5in (12.5cm) high.
£280–320 / €400–450
$490–560 ⊞ SER

◄ **A porcelain figure of a putto,** damaged, incised and painted monograms, Continental, c1925, 17¾in (45cm) high.
£7,100–8,500
€10,200–12,200
$12,400–14,900 ⚒ LJ

► **A Keramos figure of a girl,** by Stehendes Podany, restored, marked, inscribed '317/34899', Austrian, Vienna, c1925, 13¾in (35cm) high.
£220–260 / €320–380
$380–450 ⚒ DORO

An Ipsen bisque figure of a boy, signed 'KK', Danish, c1925, 8in (20.5cm) high.
£270–300 / €390–430
$470–530 ⊞ DSG

◄ **An Ipsen figure of a girl,** by M. Kursten, c1925, 8½in (21.5cm) high.
£220–250 / €320–360
$390–440 ⊞ DSG

A Muller & Co model of a dachshund,
1920s, 15in (38cm) wide.
£780–880 / €1,100–1,300
$1,350–1,550 ⊞ SRi

A pair of bisque models of dachshunds, 1920s, 1in (2.5cm) high.
£30–35 / €45–50
$55–60 ⊞ CCs

A Brentleigh Ware figure of a pixie, c1930, 6in (15cm) high.
£75–85 / €105–120
$130–150 ⊞ BEV

◄ **A lustre figure of a Welsh lady,** inscribed 'A Present from Bangor', Welsh, c1930, 5½in (14cm) high.
£15–20 / €20–30
$25–35 ⊞ ACAC

A collection of Goss Mabel Lucie Attwell wedding figures, mid-1930s, 4in (10cm) high.
£1,500–1,700 / €2,150–2,450
$2,650–3,000 ⊞ MEM
These rare wedding figures are made by a very collectable designer.

◀ **A Radford model of a humming bird,** c1935, 6in (15cm) high.
£135–150 / €195–220
$230–260 ⊞ BEV

A Burleigh ware character jug, in the form of Winston Churchill, c1940, 11in (28cm) high.
£340–400 / €490–580
$600–710 ⚲ SAS

◀ **A Midwinter model of a dog,** c1940, 3in (7.5cm) wide.
£50–60 / €75–85
$90–105 ⊞ BEV

A Wilton Pottery character jug, in the form of Winston Churchill, 1940, 7½in (19cm) high.
£220–250 / €320–360
$390–440 ⊞ BtoB

▶ **A Quimper figure of St Anne,** c1940, 3in (7.5cm) high.
£45–50 / €65–75
$80–90 ⊞ SER

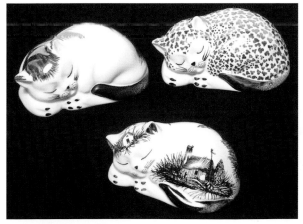

A set of four Piero Fornasetti models of cats, 1950s, 4in (10cm) wide.
£65–75 / €95–105
$115–130 each ⊞ MARK

A Samson figural group of a couple playing chess, French, c1950, 6in (15cm) high.
£130–145 / €185–210
$220–250 ⊞ MRA

A Hornsea model of a Pekinese dog, marked, 1956, 4in (10cm) high.
£90–105 / €130–155
$160–190 🔨 **BBR**

◄ **A Delphin Massier lamp,** in the form of a fish, French, Vallauris, 1950, 12in (30.5cm) high.
£70–80 / €100–115
$135–155 ⊞ **MLL**

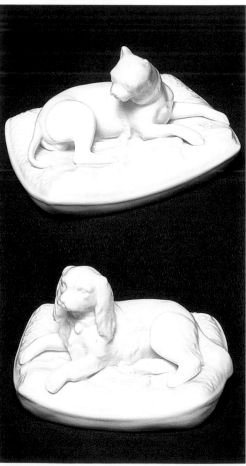

A Rye Pottery model of a chicken, 1960s, 7¾in (19.5cm) high.
£15–20 / €22–29
$29–38 ⊞ **HEI**

► **A pair of Belleek porcelain models of dogs,** Irish, Sixth period, 1965–80, 4in (10cm) wide.
£220–250 / €320–360
$390–440 ⊞ **MLa**

A David Sharp Pottery model of a dog,
1974–80, 7in (18cm) high.
£70–80 / €100–115
$135–155 ⊞ MARK

A Coalport figure of a lady, by Jenny Oliver, entitled 'Crystal',
c1982, 5½in (14cm) high.
£30–35 / €45–50
$50–60 ⊞ TAC

**An Enesco Memories of Yesterday figural
group of two children,** by Mabel Lucie
Attwell, 1987, 5in (12.5cm) high.
£35–40 / €50–60
$60–70 ⊞ SAA

**A collection of Enesco Memories of Yesterday bisque
figures,** by Mabel Lucie Attwell, 1988–99, 6in (15cm) high.
£20–25 / €30–35
$35–40 each ⊞ MEM

◀ **A Schmid Beatrix Potter musical figure of Tom Kitten,** 1988, 6in (15cm) high.
£50–55 / €70–80
$85–95 ⊞ SAA

A Belleek porcelain model of an Irish Wolfhound, limited edition, Irish, 1988, 7in (18cm) high.
£280–310 / €400–450
$490–540 ⊞ DeA

An Enesco Memories of Yesterday figural group, by Mabel Lucie Attwell, 1993, 5in (12.5cm) high.
£135–150 / €195–220
$230–260 ⊞ MEM

Four Enesco Memories of Yesterday hinged boxes, by Mabel Lucie Attwell, 1997, 3¾in (9.5cm) high.
£20–25 / €30–35
$35–40 each ⊞ MEM

Beswick

A Beswick model of a Dalmatian, entitled 'Arnoldene',
No. 961, 1941–93, 5¾in (14.5cm) high.
£50–60 / €75–85
$100–115 ⚒ MED

A Beswick Toby Jug, in the form of Winston
Churchill, with the Union flag and a scroll,
c1943, 8in (20.5cm) high.
£300–360 / €430–520
$530–630 ⚒ SAS

◄ **A Beswick model of an English setter,**
No. 1220, c1950, 8in (20.5cm) high.
£380–450 / €550–650
$670–790 ⚒ CHTR

A Beswick model of an Ayrshire cow, 'Ch. Ickham Bessie',
No. 1350, 1954–90, 4¾in (12cm) long.
£90–100 / €130–145
$170–190 ⚒ MED

A Beswick Babycham advertising figure,
c1955, 5in (12.5cm) high.
£50–60 / €75–85
$100–115 ⊞ HUX

20TH CENTURY

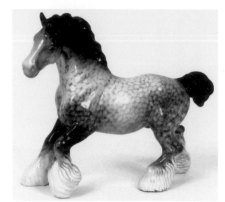

A Beswick model of a shire horse, No. 975, 1961–89, 8¾in (22cm) high.
£600–720 / €850–1,000
$1,050–1,250 ⚒ **CHTR**

A Beswick model of a trout, by Arthur Gredington, 1955–75, 7in (18cm) high.
£165–185 / €230–270
$280–320 ⊞ **ACAC**

A Beswick model of a fantail pigeon, by Arthur Gredington, No. 1614, restored, c1965, 5in (12.5cm) high.
£260–310 / €370–440
$460–540 ⚒ **CHTR**

A Beswick model of a girl on a pony, No. 1499, c1960, 5½in (14cm) high.
£180–210 / €260–310
$320–380 ⚒ **CHTR**

▶ **A Beswick model of a rabbit,** by Albert Hallam and Graham Tongue, No. 2131, 1967–73, 2½in (6.5cm) high.
£50–60 / €70–80
$85–105 ⚒ **BBR**

A Beswick model of a Sussex cockerel, by Arthur Gredington, No. 1899, c1968, 7in (18cm) high.
£550–650 / €790–950
$960–1,150 ↗ CHTR

A set of Beswick model animals, comprising Winnie the Pooh No. 2193, Eyore No. 2196, Piglet No. 2214, Rabbit No. 2215, Owl No. 2216, Kanga No. 2217 and Tigger No. 2394, Christopher Robin missing, 1968–90, tallest 3¼in (8.5cm) high.
£300–360 / €430–520
$530–630 ↗ CHTR

A Beswick model of a seated Dalmatian, No. 2271, 1969–96, 13¾in (35cm) high.
£150–180 / €220–260
$260–310 ↗ MED

◄ **A Beswick golden eagle Beneagles Scotch Whisky decanter,** 1969–84, 10½in (26.5cm) high.
£110–125 / €160–180
$195–220 ⊞ TAC

A Beswick model of a huntsman, No. 1501, c1970, 8¼in (21cm) long.
£220–260 / €320–380
$390–460 🔨 **CHTR**

A Beswick bar figure, entitled 'The Colonel', c1970, 9½in (24cm) high.
£145–160 / €200–230
$250–280 ⊞ **PrB**

A Beswick model of a huntswoman, c1970, 8¼in (21cm) high.
£550–650 / €790–940
$960–1,150 🔨 **CHTR**

A Beswick bar figure, entitled 'The Couple', c1970, 9½in (24cm) high.
£145–160 / €200–230
$250–280 ⊞ **PrB**

◄ **A Beswick bar figure,** entitled 'The Rugby Players', c1970, 9½in (24cm) high.
£145–160 / €200–230
$250–280 ⊞ **PrB**

A Beswick model of a game cock, No. 2059, c1970, 9¼in (23.5cm) high.
£1,250–1,500
€1,800–2,150
$2,200–2,650 ↗ **CHTR**

A Beswick model of a song thrush, by Albert Hallam, No. 2308, impressed mark, 1970–89, 5¾in (14.5cm) high.
£70–80 / €100–115
$125–140 ↗ **BBR**

A Beswick model of Beatrix Potter's Aunty Pettitoes, painted back-stamp, 1970–93, 4in (10cm) high.
£60–70 / €85–100
$115–135 ⊞ **BAC**

A Beswick model of a fox, No. 2348, 1970–83, 12¼in (31cm) high.
£170–200 / €240–290
$300–360 ↗ **MED**

A Beswick model of a labrador, No. 2314, 1970–96, 13¾in (35cm) high.
£90–100 / €130–145
$170–190 ↗ MED

A Beswick model of a highwayman on a horse, No. 2210, c1973, 13¾in (35cm) high.
£780–930 / €1,100–1,300
$1,350–1,600 ↗ CHTR

A Beswick model of a huntswoman, No. 1730, c1975, 8¼in (21cm) high.
£480–570 / €690–820
$840–1,000 ↗ CHTR

A Beswick model of Beatrix Potter's Duchess With Pie, No. BP6, 1979–82, 4in (10cm) high.
£270–300 / €390–430
$470–530 ⊞ BAC

A Beswick model of Beatrix Potter's Chippy Hackee, painted backstamp, 1979–93, 4in (10cm) high.
£60–70 / €85–10
$115–135 ⊞ BAC

A Beswick model of Beatrix Potter's Ginger, painted backstamp, 1976–82, 4in (10cm) high.
£400–450 / €580–650
$700–790 ⊞ BAC

A Beswick model of Beatrix Potter's Old Mr Bouncer, painted backstamp, 1986–95, 3in (7.5cm) high.
£60–70 / €85–100
$115–135 ⊞ BAC

A Beswick model of an Native American on a pony, No. 1391, c1980, 8½in (21.5cm) high.
£500–600 / €720–860
$880–1,050 ⤢ CHTR

20TH CENTURY

A Beswick model of Queen Elizabeth II on Imperial, No. MN1546, 1981, 10½in (26.5cm) high.
£150–180 / €220–260
$260–310 ✣ **Pott**

A Beswick model of a Nigerian pot-bellied pygmy goat, 1990–2002, 5in (12.5cm) high.
£45–50 / €65–75
$85–95 ⊞ **ACAC**

▶ **A Beswick model of Beatrix Potter's Head Gardener,** 2002, 4in (10cm) high.
£360–400 / €520–580
$630–700 ⊞ **BAC**

A Beswick character jug model of Beatrix Potter's Mr Jeremy Fisher, painted backstamp, 1987–92, 3in (7.5cm) high.
£115–130 / €165–185
$200–220 ⊞ **BAC**

A Beswick model of an Afghan hound, entitled 'Hajbah of Daulen', discontinued in 1993, 6in (15cm) high.
£65–75 / €95–105
$125–145 ⊞ **TAC**

Bing & Grøndahl

A Royal Copenhagen Bing & Grøndahl figure of horsewoman, Danish, c1948, 8in (20.5cm) high.
£150–170 / €220–250
$260–290 ⊞ PSA

A Royal Copenhagen Bing & Grøndahl model of a bull, Danish, c1948, 14in (35.5cm) wide.
£460–520 / €660–750
$810–910 ⊞ PSA

A Bing & Grøndahl figural group, entitled 'Fisherman's Friend', Danish, c1952, 12½in (23cm) high.
£520–580 / €750–840
$900–1,000 ⊞ PSA
This figure is no longer in production, making this piece highly collectable.

A Bing & Grøndahl model of a polar bear, Danish, c1952, 9in (23cm) high.
£330–370 / €480–530
$580–650 ⊞ PSA

Carlton Ware

A Carlton Ware model of a jockey on a racehorse, with Newmarket crest, c1925, 4½in (11.5cm) high.
£85–95 / €125–140
$165–185 ⊞ BtoB

◄ **A Carlton Ware model of a Pears advertising boy,** inscribed 'I'm Forever Blowing Bubbles', with arms of Bournemouth, 1902–30, 4¼in (11cm) high.
£70–80 / €100–115
$135–155 ⊞ G&CC

A Carlton Ware figure of a Welsh lady, with Mold crest, c1902, 6in (15cm) high.
£70–80 / €100–115
$135–155 ⊞ ACAC

A Carlton Ware Guinness advertising model of a kangaroo, 1960s, 4in (10cm) high.
£90–100 / €130–145
$170–190 ⌁ G(L)

▶ **A Bairstow Manor and Carlton Ware character jug,** by Ray Noble, in the form of John Prescott, edition of 500, 2002, 8in (20.5cm) high.
£75–85 / €110–120
$130–150 ⊞ IQ

Crown Devon

A Crown Devon figural ashtray, decorated with a golfer, c1930, 3in (7.5cm) high.
£135–150 / €195–220
$240–270 ⊞ BEV

◀ **A Crown Devon doorstop,** in the form of a dog, c1930, 10in (25.5cm) long.
£90–100 / €130–145
$170–190 ⊞ BD

Dresden

A Dresden figural group, advertising Yardley's Old English Lavender, c1910, 12in (30.5cm) high.
£400–450 / €580–650
$700–790 ⊞ HUX

◀ **A Dresden figural group of a boy and a girl,** c1900, 7in (18cm) high.
£45–50 / €65–75
$80–90 ⊞ MRA

A Dresden figure of a young woman, c1930, 7in (18cm) high.
£75–85 / €110–120
$130–150 ⊞ MRA

20TH CENTURY

Gebrüder Heubach

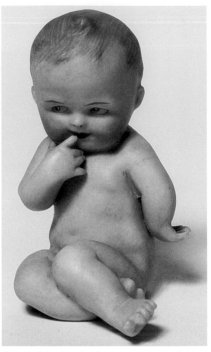

A Gebrüder Heubach bisque figure of a baby and an egg, German, c1910, 5in (12.5cm) high.
£310–350 / €450–500
$540–610 ⊞ OAK

A Gebrüder Heubach figure of a 'Cutie' baby, German, 1910–20, 4in (10cm) high.
£110–125 / €160–180
$195–220 ⊞ OAK

A pair of Gebrüder Heubach figures, German, c1920, 8in (20.5cm) high.
£720–800 / €1,000–1,150
$1,200–1,400 ⊞ YC

▶ **A Gebrüder Heubach piano baby,** German, c1920, 10¼in (26cm) high.
£630–700 / €900–1,000
$1,100–1,250 ⊞ YC

Goebel

A Goebel figure of a lady holding flowers, German, 1930s, 7½in (19cm) high.
£50–60 / €75–85
$90–105 ⊞ TAC

A Goebel figure of a lady holding a fan, German, 1930s, 7½in (19cm) high.
£50–60 / €75–85
$90–105 ⊞ TAC

A Goebel Hummel figure, entitled 'Sensitive Hunter', German, 1940–59, 4¾in (12cm) high.
£105–120 / €150–170
$185–210 ⊞ SAA
This figure was first called 'The Timid Hunter' when it was released along with 46 other Hummels. The biggest variation is the 'H' shape of the suspenders used with the lederhosen. This variation is associated with all of the figures marked with a crown and most of those marked with a full bee. The 'H' variation will add approximatley 30 per cent to the value when compared with the 'X' variation. The 'Sensitive Hunter' can also be marked with a decimal point which adds another ten per cent.

◄ **A Goebel honey pot,** in the form of a bee, German, 1940s, 4¾in (12cm) high.
£65–75 / €95–110
$115–130 ⊞ BET

► **A pair of Goebel bisque figures,** German, Nos. 15 and 21, 1950s.
£180–210 / €250–300
$320–380 ⋏ LAY

A Goebel model of a horse, German, c1960, 4in (10cm) high.
£20–25 / €30–35
$35–45 ⊞ TAC

A Goebel Hummel figure, entitled 'School Boy', German, 1960–63, 5in (12.5cm) high.
£125–140 / €180–200
$220–250 ⊞ TAC

▶ **A Goebel Hummel figure,** entitled 'Chick Girl', German, 1960–72, 3¾in (9.5cm) high.
£100–115
€145–165
$175–200 ⊞ TAC

◀ **A Goebel Hummel figure,** entitled 'Retreat to Safety', German, 1960–72, 4¼in (11cm) high.
£130–145
€185–210
$220–250 ⊞ TAC

A Goebel Hummel figure, entitled 'For Father', German, 1960–72, 6in (15cm) high.
£60–70 / €85–100
$105–125 ⊞ SAA

◄ **A Goebel Hummel figure,** entitled 'Little Goat Herder', German, 1960–72, 4½in (11.5cm) high.
£145–165 / €210–240
$240–290 ⊞ TAC

A Goebel Hummel figure, entitled 'Apple Tree Girl', German, 1960–72, 4in (10cm) high.
£95–110 / €135–160
$165–195 ⊞ TAC

A Goebel Hummel figure, entitled 'Village Boy', German, c1970, 3in (7.5cm) high.
£55–65 / €80–95
$95–115 ⊞ PrB

A Goebel Hummel figural advertising plaque, No. 187, German, 1970s, 6in (15cm) wide.
£165–185 / €240–270
$290–320 ⊞ TAC

◄ **A Goebel Hummel figure,** entitled 'Sign of Spring', German, 1990, 4in (10cm) high.
£110–125 / €160–180
$195–220 ⊞ SAA

A Goebel Hummel figure, entitled 'Be Patient', German, 1972–79, 5in (12.5cm) high.
£60–70 / €85–100
$105–125 ⊞ SAA

20TH CENTURY

Goss & Crested China

A Grafton model of a fledgling, with Aberdeen crest, 1900–33, 2½in (6.5cm) high.
£25–30 / €40–45
$50–55 ⊞ G&CC

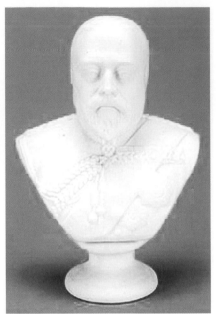

A Goss parian bust of King Edward VII, printed Goshawk mark, dated 1901, 3½in (9cm) high.
£180–210 / €250–300
$310–370 ⚒ DN

An Arcadian model of a Staffordshire bull terrier, with Broadstairs crest, 1903–33, 3¼in (8.5cm) high.
£20–25 / €30–35
$40–50 ⊞ G&CC

A Grafton figure of a golfer, inscribed 'The Colonel', with crest, early 20thC, 3½in (9cm) high.
£55–65 / €80–90
$90–100 ⊞ G&CC

A model of the Margate Surf Boat Memorial, with Margate crest, c1912, 13in (33cm) high.
£280–330 / €400–480
$490–580 ➚ SAS

An Arcadian model of a hen, with Ramsgate crest, c1920, 3in (7.5cm) high.
£20–25 / €30–35
$40–50 ⊞ SAAC

◄ An Arcadian model of a sailor winding a capstan, 1914–18, 4¼in (11cm) high.
£120–135 / €175–195
$210–240 ⊞ G&CC

A Goss model of a Shetland pony, with Lerwick, Shetland Isles crest, 1924–29, 4½in (11.5cm) wide.
£210–240 / €300–350
$370–420 ⊞ G&CC

An Arcadian model of a cat on a jug, with Grange Over Sands crest, Registered Series, 1 of 24, 1924–33, 2½in (6.5cm) high.
£60–70 / €85–100
$115–135 ⊞ G&CC

20TH CENTURY

An Arcadian model of a cat on a bicycle, with Lands End crest, Registered Series, No. 18, 1924–39, 3in (7.5cm) high.
£195–220 / €280–320
$340–390 ⊞ G&CC

A Swan model of a pig, with Newcastle-upon-Tyne crest, discontinued in 1925, 2½in (6.5cm) high.
£25–30 / €40–45
$50–55 ⊞ JMC

A Goss model of Lady Betty, 1929–39, 6½in (16.5cm) high.
£220–250 / €320–360
$390–440 ⊞ G&CC

◄ **An Arcadian cigarette holder,** with Worcester crest, 1925–33, 4in (10cm) high.
£140–160 / €200–220
$250–280 ⊞ G&CC

A Goss model of a garden gnome, 1929–39,
4¾in (12cm) high.
£360–400 / €520–580
$630–700 ⊞ G&CC

A model of a bulldog, with Blackpool crest, 1920s,
4in (10cm) long.
£30–35 / €45–50
$55–65 ⊞ HeA

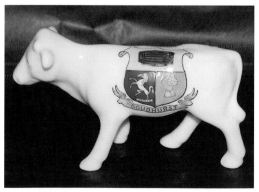

A Grafton model of a calf, with Goudhurst crest, the
reverse with Isle of Wight verse, 1920s,
2in (5cm) high.
£40–45 / €60–70
$75–85 ⊞ JMC

▶ **A Savoy model of a grotesque bird,** with Paignton
crest, 1920s, 4in (10cm) high.
£10–15 / €15–22
$19–28 ⊞ TWO

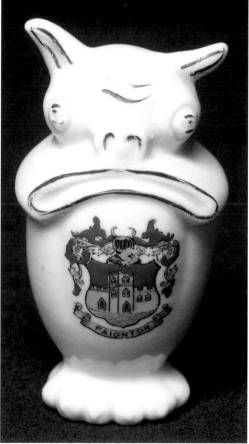

20TH CENTURY

Lladro

A Lladro porcelain figure of a boy holding snails, Spanish, discontinued in 1979, 9in (23cm) high.
£200–230 / €290–330
$350–400 ⊞ SAA

A Lladro model of two ducks, Spanish, c1980, 4in (10cm) high.
£25–30 / €35–40
$45–50 ⊞ TAC

A Lladro model of a duck, Spanish, c1982, 3in (7.5cm) high.
£15–20 / €20–25
$25–35 ⊞ TAC

◄ **A Lladro model of two birds,** Spanish, discontinued in 1985, 9in (23cm) high.
£175–195 / €250–280
$300–340 ⊞ SAA

► **A Lladro figure of a shepherd and his dog,** Spanish, discontinued in 1985, 8in (20.5cm) high.
£165–185 / €240–270
$290–320 ⊞ SAA

A Lladro figure, entitled 'Little Lady', limited edition, 2004, 8½in (21.5cm) high.
£110–125 / €160–180
$195–220 ⊞ BOP

A Lladro figure, entitled 'Time to Sew', 2004, 8in (20.5cm) high.
£60–70 / €85–100
$105–125 ⊞ BOP

A Lladro figure, entitled 'Natural Beauty', limited edition, 2005, 8½in (21.5cm) high.
£100–115 / €145–165
$175–200 ⊞ BOP
This figure was only available between 18 and 30 June 2005 .

Meissen

◄ **A Meissen porcelain figure of a girl,** by A. König, crossed swords mark, model No. Y140, German, c1908, 7in (18cm) high.
£1,100–1,250
€1,600–1,800
$1,950–2,200 ⊞ DAV

► **A Meissen porcelain model of a turkey,** by Paul Walther, model No. F279, signed, impressed marks, German, 1919, 14in (35.5cm) high.
£2,850–3,200
€4,100–4,600
$5,000–5,600 ⊞ DAV

20TH CENTURY

A Meissen porcelain model of a badger, by Max Esser, from Reineke Fuchs series, model No. H244, crossed swords mark, German, 1920–28, 11in (28cm) high.
£2,450–2,750
€3,550–3,950
$4,300–4,800 ⊞ DAV

A Meissen porcelain model of an Alsatian, by Eric Hosel, model No. V188, crossed swords mark, German, 1928, 7¼in (18.5cm) high.
£1,100–1,250 / €1,600–1,800
$1,950–2,200 ⊞ DAV

A Meissen porcelain model of Diana the Huntress, model No. A1046, crossed swords mark, German, c1949, 12in (30.5cm) high.
£2,200–2,450 / €3,150–3,550
$3,850–4,300 ⊞ DAV

Rosenthal

A Rosenthal porcelain model of a fawn, by Theodore Karner, German, 1905–15, 7in (18cm) wide.
£560–630 / €810–910
$980–1,100 ⊞ Scot

A Rosenthal figure, modelled by A. Caasmann, entitled 'The Snail Ride', German, dated 1910, 5in (12.5cm) high.
£530–600 / €760–860
$930–1,050 ⊞ CHO

◄ **A Rosenthal figural group,** by A. Caasmann, entitled 'The Gliding Flight', German, c1910, 4in (10cm) high.
£530–600 / €760–860
$930–1,050 ⊞ CHO

A Rosenthal figure of a child riding a snail, by A. Caasmann, German, c1914, 4in (10cm) high.
£400–450 / €580–650
$700–790 ⊞ Bel

A Rosenthal model of a squirrel, by Theodore Karner, German, c1920, 4in (10cm) high.
£105–120 / €150–175
$185–210 ⊞ CHO

A Rosenthal figural group, entitled 'Boy and Bear', German, c1920, 4½in (11.5cm) high.
£110–125 / €160–180
$195–220 ⊞ CHO

20TH CENTURY

A Rosenthal model of two birds, German, c1920, 4in (10cm) wide.
£220–250 / €320–360
$390–440 ⊞ **Scot**

A Rosenthal figure, by Richard Aigner, entitled 'Spring of Love', German, dated 1923, 10in (25.5cm) high.
£620–700 / €890–1,000
$1,100–1,250 ⊞ **CHO**

A Rosenthal figure, entitled 'Salambo', German, c1928, 11in (28cm) high.
£540–600 / €780–860
$950–1,050 ⊞ **Bel**

A Rosenthal figure, by D. Charol, entitled 'Spring', German, c1930, 8in (20.5cm) high.
£360–400 / €520–580
$630–700 ⊞ **CHO**

▶ **A Rosenthal model of two bears,** German, c1930, 4in (10cm) high.
£360–400 / €520–580
$630–700 ⊞ **Bel**

A Rosenthal model of a dachshund, by Heidenreich, German, c1930, 10in (25.5cm) wide.
£450–500 / €650–720
$790–880 ⊞ Scot

A Rosenthal figure, by K. Lysek, entitled 'After the Bath', German, c1930, 9in (23cm) high.
£450–500 / €650–720
$790–880 ⊞ CHO

A Rosenthal model of a fawn, German, c1930, 4in (10cm) wide.
£270–300 / €390–430
$470–530 ⊞ Scot

◄ **A Rosenthal model of a hedgehog,** German, 1930s, 3in (7.5cm) wide.
£120–135
€175–195
$210–240
⊞ Scot

A Rosenthal figure, by Franz Nagy, entitled 'Young Boy on a Ball', dated 1931, 6in (15cm) high.
£270–300 / €390–430
$470–530 ⊞ CHO

20TH CENTURY

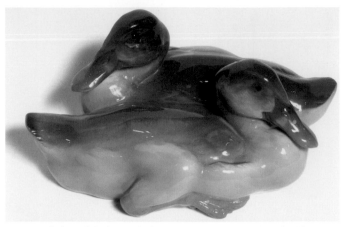

A Rosenthal model of two ducks, German, c1937, 7in (18cm) wide.
£360–400 / €520–580
$630–700 ⊞ Scot

A Rosenthal figure, by Gustav
Oppel, entitled 'The Prayer Dancer',
German, c1936, 8in (20.5cm) high.
£540–600 / €780–860
$950–1,050 ⊞ CHO

A Rosenthal figure, by Max
D. H. Fritz, entitled 'Liana', German,
dated 1937, 6in (15cm) high.
£310–350 / €450–500
$540–610 ⊞ CHO

◀ **A Rosenthal figure,** by Gustav
Oppel, entitled 'Dancer in Blue
Tunic', restored, German, dated
1937, 12in (30.5cm) high.
£360–400 / €520–580
$630–700 ⊞ CHO

▶ **A Rosenthal model of an
Alsatian,** German, 1930s,
11in (28cm) high.
£620–700 / €890–1,000
$1,100–1,250 ⊞ Scot

A **Rosenthal model of a fox,** by T. Karner, No. 1248, German, c1940, 10in (25.5cm) high.
£530–590 / €760–850
$930–1,050 ⊞ Scot

▶ A **Rosenthal model of a fox,** German, c1940, 16in (40.5cm) wide.
£510–570 / €730–820
$890–1,000 ⊞ Scot

A **Rosenthal figure,** by Ferdinand Liebermann, entitled 'The Two Princesses', German, c1940, 5in (12.5cm) high.
£450–500 / €650–720
$790–880 ⊞ CHO

A **Rosenthal model of a deer and fawn,** by Rempel, German, c1944, 7in (18cm) high.
£360–400 / €520–580
$630–700 ⊞ Bel

A **Rosenthal model of two foxes,** by Heidenreich, c1946, 6in (15cm) wide.
£270–300 / €390–430
$470–530 ⊞ Bel

20TH CENTURY

Royal Albert

A Royal Albert model of Beatrix Potter's **Little Black Rabbit,** printed backstamp, 1977–97, 4in (10cm) high.
£35–40 / €50–60
$65–75 ⊞ BAC

▶ A Royal Albert model of Beatrix Potter's Goodie and Timmy Tiptoes, printed backstamp, 1986–96, 4in (10cm) high.
£65–75
€95–105
$125–145
⊞ BAC

◀ A Royal Albert model of **Mr Toadflax,** No. DBH10B, from Brambly Hedge, without cushion, 1980s, 11in (28cm) high.
£180–210
€250–300
$310–370
⚲ Pott

◀ A Royal Albert model of Beatrix Potter's **Mother Ladybird,** printed backstamp, 1989–96, 3in (7.5cm) high.
£45–50 / €65–75
$85–95 ⊞ BAC

▶ A Royal Albert model of Beatrix Potter's **Jemima Puddleduck,** 1989–98, 4in (10cm) high.
£25–30 / €40–45
$50–55 ⊞ ACAC

◄ A Royal
Albert model of
Beatrix Potter's
Miss Moppet,
1989–98, 3in
(7.5cm) high.
£25–30
€40–45
$50–55 ⊞ ACAC

► A Royal
Albert model
of Beatrix
Potter's Mittens
& Moppet,
printed back-
stamp, 1990–94,
4in (10cm) high.
£110–125
€160–180
$195–220
⊞ BAC

A Royal Albert model of Beatrix Potter's Christmas Stocking,
printed backstamp, 1991–94, 4in (10cm) high.
£160–180 / €230–260
$280–320 ⊞ DAC

**A Royal Albert model of Beatrix Potter's
Jemima Puddleduck with the Foxy
Whiskered Gentleman,** printed backstamp,
1990–99, 5in (12.5cm) high.
£50–60 / €75–85
$100–115 ⊞ BAC

► **A Royal Albert model of Beatrix
Potter's Benjamin Wakes Up,** printed
backstamp, 1991–97, 4in (10cm) wide.
£30–35 / €45–50
$55–65 ⊞ BAC

Royal Copenhagen

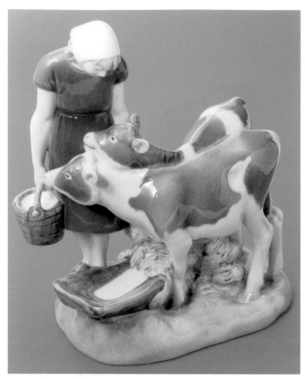

A Royal Copenhagen group of a milkmaid and calves,
Danish, c1915, 8½in (21.5cm) high.
£360–400 / €520–580
$630–700 ⊞ PSA

A Royal Copenhagen figure of Columbine,
Danish, c1915, 7in (18cm) high.
£350–400 / €500–560
$610–680 ⊞ PSA

A Royal Copenhagen model of a kid, Danish, c1923,
3½in (9cm) high.
£85–100 / €120–145
$150–180 ⊞ PSA

**A Royal Copenhagen figural group of
Pan playing with a bear,** Danish, c1944,
7½in (19cm) high.
£320–360 / €460–520
$560–630 ⊞ PSA
This figure of Pan is no longer in production,
making it a highly collectable piece.

A Royal Copenhagen model of a partridge, Danish, c1950, 8in (20.5cm) wide.
£170–190 / €240–270
$300–330 ⊞ PSA

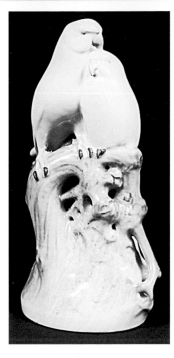

◀ **A Royal Copenhagen figure of a herder and a dog,** c1945, 8in (20.5cm) high.
£180–210 / €120–145
$150–180 ⊞ PSA

▶ **A royal Copenhagen model of a pair of budgerigars,** c1964, 8in (20.5cm) high.
£100–125 / €145–175
$175–210 ⊞ PSA

A Royal Copenhagen model of a pair of geese, Danish, c1958, 9in (23cm) high.
£350–400 / €500–560
$610–680 ⊞ PSA
This figure is no longer in production, making it a highly collectable piece.

A pair of Royal Copenhagen models of bear cubs, by Knud Kyhn, Danish, 1960s, 3in (7.5cm) wide.
£65–75 / €95–110
$115–130 each ⊞ MARK

Royal Crown Derby

A Royal Crown Derby figure of a Spanish guitar player, red factory mark, c1932, 7¾in (19.5cm) high.
£240–280 / €340–400
$420–500 ⚒ WW

A Royal Crown Derby figure, entitled 'Marjorie', c1933, 7in (18cm) high.
£250–280 / €360–400
$440–490 ⊞ Bel

▶ **A Royal Crown Derby figure of Peter Pan,** by Miss M. R. Locke, c1937, 9in (23cm) high.
£450–500 / €650–720
$790–880 ⊞ Bel

▶ **A Royal Crown Derby Barn Owl paperweight,** 2003, 5½in (14cm) high.
£80–90
€115–130
$155–175 ⊞ TAC

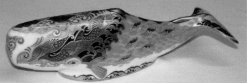

A Royal Crown Derby Cottage Garden Cat paperweight, 2001, 4½in (11.5cm) long.
£75–85 / €110–125
$145–165 ⊞ TAC

A Royal Crown Derby Oceanic Whale paperweight, made for Collectors' Guild, 2003, 8½in (21.5cm) long.
£110–125 / €160–180
$195–220 ⊞ TAC

Royal Doulton

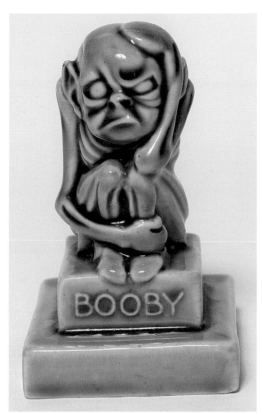

A Doulton figure, entitled 'Booby', c1900,
4in (10cm) high.
£450–500 / €650–720
$790–880 ⊞ BWDA

A Doulton Lambeth stoneware paperweight, by
Mark Marshall, 1905–10, 3in (7.5cm) high.
£450–500 / €650–720
$790–880 ⊞ BWDA

A Royal Doulton model of a bulldog, entitled 'Old
Bill', wearing a tin hat and uniform, damaged, 1918–25,
6½in (16.5cm) high.
£85–95 / €125–140
$165–185 ⚒ G(L)

◄ A Royal Doulton model of a fox, No. HN100,
slight damage, painted and printed marks, 1913–42,
6in (15cm) high.
£500–600 / €720–860
$880–1,050 ⚒ CDC

◀ A Royal Doulton figure, entitled 'The Scribe', No. HN305, inscribed 'C. J. Noke', 1918–36, 6in (15cm) high.
£980–1,150
€1,400–1,650
$1,700–2,000
🔨 BWL

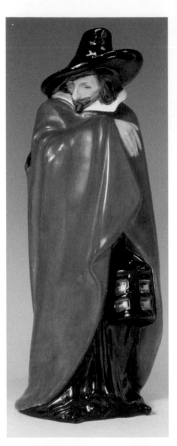

▶ A Royal Doulton figure, entitled 'Guy Fawkes', No. HN98, 1918–49, 11in (28cm) high.
£950–1,100
€1,350–1,600
$1,650–1,950
🔨 SWO

A Royal Doulton figure, entitled 'Sairey Gamp', No. HN558, slight damage, painted and printed marks, 1923–39, 7½in (19cm) high.
£95–110 / €135–160
$165–195 🔨 FHF

A Royal Doulton figure, entitled 'Pickwick', No. HN556, 1923–39, 7¼in (18.5cm) high.
£160–190 / €230–270
$280–330 🔨 SWO

▶ A Royal Doulton figure, entitled 'Micawber', No. HN557, 1923–39, 7¼in (18.5cm) high.
£160–190 / €230–270
$280–330 🔨 SWO

A Royal Doulton figure, entitled 'The Bather', No. HN687, 1924–49, 7¾in (19.5cm) high.
£700–840 / €1,000–1,200
$1,250–1,450 ⚒ G(L)

A Royal Doulton stoneware soap dish, by Harry Simeon, decorated with a model of a bird, c1925, 5in (12.5cm) high.
£360–400 / €520–580
$630–700 ⊞ StB

A Royal Doulton double-sided figure, entitled 'Mephistopheles and Marguerite', No. HN755, on a mahogany base, 1925–45, 7¾in (19.5cm) high.
£750–900 / €1,100–1,300
$1,300–1,550 ⚒ CDC

A Doulton 'Chinese jade' model of two cockatoos, by Harry Nixon, 1920s, 5in (12.5cm) high.
£1,250–1,400 / €1,800–2,000
$2,200–2,450 ⊞ BWDA

A Royal Doulton figure, entitled 'Biddy', c1930, 6in (15cm) high.
£135–150 / €195–220
$240–270 ⊞ SAA

20TH CENTURY

A Royal Doulton figure, entitled 'Little Child So Rare and Sweet', No. HN1542, 1933–49, 5¼in (13.5cm) high.
£200–240 / €290–350
$350–420 ⚖ **DN**

A Royal Doulton figure, by C. J. Noke, entitled 'Calumet', No. HN1689, 1935–49, 6¾in (17cm) high.
£300–360 / €430–520
$530–630 ⚖ **SWO**

A Royal Doulton figure, entitled 'Do You Wonder Where Fairies Are That Folks Declare Have Vanished', No. HN1544, printed, impressed and painted marks, 1933–49, 5in (12.5cm) high.
£260–310 / €370–440
$460–540 ⚖ **FHF**

A Royal Doulton figure, entitled 'Gladys', No. HN1740, 1935–49, 5in (12.5cm) high.
£280–330 / €400–480
$490–580 ⚖ **SWO**

◀ **A Royal Doulton figure,** entitled 'Nell Gwynn', No. HN1887, 1938–49, 6¾in (17cm) high.
£400–480 / €580–690
$700–840 ⚖ **L&E**

A Royal Doulton figure, entitled 'Daffy Down Dilly', No. HN1712, 1935–75, 8¼in (21cm) high.
£25–30 / €40–45
$50–55 ➚ SJH

▶ **A Royal Doulton figure,** entitled 'Maureen', No. HN1770, 1936–59, 9in (23cm) high.
£200–240 / €290–350
$350–420 ➚ G(L)

A Royal Doulton figure, by Leslie Harradine, entitled 'Windflower', No. HN1920, slight damage, 1939–49, 11in (28cm) high.
£700–840 / €1,000–1,200
$1,250–1,500 ➚ SWO

A Royal Doulton brooch, in the form of a spaniel's head, 1930s, 1½in (4cm) high.
£190–220 / €270–320
$330–390 ➚ Pott

A Royal Doulton character jug, by H. Fenton, entitled 'Drake', No. D6115, 1940–41, 6in (15cm) high.
£1,600–1,900 / €2,300–2,750
$2,800–3,350 ➚ DA

20TH CENTURY

A Royal Doulton Bols Distilleries flask, in the form of a dog, 1940s, 6½in (16.5cm) high.
£850–950 / €1,200–1,350
$1,500–1,650 ⊞ SRi

◀ **A Royal Doulton character jug,** entitled 'Field Marshall Smuts', No. D6198, 1946–48, 6½in (16.5cm) high.
£450–540 / €650–780
$790–950 ⚒ CHTR

A Royal Doulton figure, by L. Harradine, entitled 'Fortune Teller', No. HN2159, 1955–67, 6½in (16.5cm) high.
£150–180 / €220–260
$260–310 ⚒ L

A Royal Doulton figure, entitled 'Sir Walter Raleigh', No. HN2015, 1948–55, 11¾in (30cm) high.
£210–250 / €300–360
$370–440 ⚒ SWO

◀ **A Royal Doulton figure,** entitled 'Marianne', No. HN2074, painted and printed marks, 1951–53, 5in (12.5cm) high.
£260–310 / €370–440
$460–540 ⚒ FHF

A Royal Doulton earthenware figure, entitled 'The Cellist', No. HN2226, 1960–67, 8in (20.5cm) high.
£180–210 / €260–310
$320–380 ✗ G(L)

A Royal Doulton model of a monkey, No. HN2657, Chatcull series, 1960–69, 4in (10cm) high.
£110–130 / €160–190
$195–230 ✗ SWO

A Royal Doulton figure, entitled 'A Gentleman from Williamsburg', No. HN2227, 1960–83, 6¾in (17cm) high.
£75–85 / €110–125
$145–165 ✗ L&E

A Royal Doulton figure, entitled 'Soiree', No. HN2312, printed mark, 1967–84, 7½in (19cm) high.
£35–40 / €50–60
$65–75 ✗ L&E

A Royal Doulton figure, entitled 'Masque', No. HN2554, 1973–75, 8¾in (22cm) high.
£55–65 / €80–95
$105–125 ⚒ **AMB**

A Royal Doulton figure, entitled 'HM Queen Elizabeth II', HN2502, 1973–76, 7¾in (19.5cm) high.
£150–180 / €220–260
$260–310 ⚒ **WilP**

A Royal Doulton model, by Harry Sales, entitled 'Jogging Bunnykins', No. DB22, marked, 1983–89, 2½in (6.5cm) high.
£50–60 / €75–85
$90–105 ⚒ **BBR**

▶ **A Royal Doulton Oompa Bunnykins band,** comprising five pieces, commemorating the jubilee of Queen Elizabeth II, 1984, tallest 4in (10cm) high.
£260–310
€370–450
$460–540 ⚒ **G(L)**

◀ **A Royal Doulton model,** by Harry Sales, entitled 'Old Vole', No. DBH13, marked, 1985–92, 13½in (34.5cm) high.
£80–100
€115–145
$145–175 ⚒ **BBR**

A Royal Doulton model of a horse, entitled 'Desert Orchid', No. DA134, with certificate, 1990, 14in (35.5cm) long.
£200–240 / €290–350
$350–420 ⚒ **CHTR**

A **Royal Doulton model,** by Graham Tongue, entitled 'Bride Bunnykins', No. DB101, maker's mark, 1991, 4¼in (11cm) high, with box.
£25–30 / €35–45
$45–55 ✗ **BBR**

A **Royal Doulton model of a horse,** entitled 'Red Rum', No. DA218, with certificate, 1993, 12in (30.5cm) high.
£600–720 / €860–1,000
$1,050–1,250 ✗ **CHTR**

A **Royal Doulton model,** entitled 'Gardener Bunnykins', No. 08521, c1995, 4½in (11.5cm) high.
£30–35 / €45–50
$55–65 ⊞ **TAC**

▶ A **Royal Doulton model,** entitled 'Bunnykins Boy Skater', No. 08512, 1994, 4in (10cm) high, with box.
£25–30 / €40–45
$50–55 ⊞ **TAC**

A Royal Doulton model, entitled 'Humpty Dumpty', No. 957 of edition 1,500, 1998, 5¼in (13.5cm) high, with box.
£30–35 / €45–50
$55–65 ⚒ **L&E**

A Royal Doulton Guinness advertising model of Big Chief Toucan, limited edition of 2,000, 2001.
£180–200 / €260–290
$320–350 ⊞ **MCL**

Royal Dux

A Royal Dux model of a pig, Bohemian, 20thC, 4in (10cm) wide.
£40–45 / €55–65
$70–80 ⊞ **TAC**

▶ **A pair of Royal Dux figures of water carriers,** by Hampdel, marked, stamped '1433/1434', Bohemian, early 20thC, 31½in (80cm) high.
£2,000–2,400 / €2,900–3,450
$3,500–4,200 ⚒ **AH**

Shelley

▶ **A Shelley model of a camel,** with arms of Black-pool, 1903–23, 4in (10cm) long.
£20–25
€30–35
$40–50 ⊞ **G&CC**

A Shelley porcelain shop advertising figure of a lady holding a cup of tea, c1920, 12in (30.5cm) high.
£1,750–2,100 / €2,500–3,000
$3,050–3,650 ➶ **AH**

◀ **A Shelley figure,** by Mabel Lucie Attwell, entitled 'The Curate', 1930s, 7in (18cm) high.
£900–1,000 / €1,300–1,450
$1,600–1,800 ⊞ **GaL**

A pair of Shelley figures, entitled 'Lilbet' and 'Lil Bill', 1997, 5¾in (14.5cm) high, with certificates and box.
£120–140 / €175–210
$210–250 ➶ **BBR**
These figures were made for the Shelley China Club in America.

20TH CENTURY

SylvaC

A SylvaC model of a squirrel, No. 1144, 1930s, 8in (20.5cm) high.
£80–90 / €115–130
$140–155 ⊞ JFME

A SylvaC model of a rabbit, No. 1028, c1930, 10in (25.5cm) high.
£170–190 / €240–270
$300–330 ⊞ HarC

A SylvaC model of a poodle, 1940s, 3½in (9cm) high.
£40–45 / €60–70
$75–85 ⊞ JFME

A SylvaC model of a dog, 1940s, 6½in (16.5cm) high.
£80–90 / €115–130
$140–155 ⊞ JFME

► A SylvaC
model of a polar
bear, 1940s,
6in (15cm) wide.
£50–55 / €70–80
$90–100 ⊞ JFME

A SylvaC model of a lamb, 1940s,
4in (10cm) long.
£50–60 / €75–85
$100–115 ⊞ JFME

► A SylvaC model of
a poodle, mid-20thC,
5in (12.5cm) high.
£45–50 / €65–75
$85–95 ⊞ TAC

A SylvaC model of
a dog, mid-20thC,
5½in (14cm) high.
£35–40 / €50–60
$65–75 ⊞ TAC

A SylvaC model of a lamb, 1960s,
4in (10cm) high.
£30–35 / €45–50
$55–65 ⊞ ACAC

► A SylvaC model
of a rabbit, 1975,
5in (12.5cm) high.
£35–40 / €50–60
$65–75 ⊞ ACAC

20TH CENTURY

Volkstedt

A Volkstedt porcelain figure of a cherub, German,
c1920, 5in (12.5cm) high.
£155–175 / €220–250
$270–310 ⊞ OAK

A Volkstedt Karl Ens figure of a child, German, c1930,
6in (15cm) high.
£490–550 / €710–790
$860–960 ⊞ EAn

A Volkstedt Karl Ens figure, entitled 'The Turban Girl', German,
late 1930s, 7in (18cm) high.
£310–350 / €450–500
$540–610 ⊞ CHO

◄ A Volkstedt Karl Ens porcelain figure of a child, German,
c1930, 6in (15cm) high.
£400–450 / €580–650
$700–790 ⊞ EAn

Wade

A Wade model of a rhinoceros, 1950–60,
5¼in (13.5cm) high.
£160–190 / €230–270
$280–330 ⚒ BBR

A Wade Heath teapot, in the form of Donald Duck, 1930s,
7in (18cm) high.
£600–680 / €860–980
$1,050–1,200 ⊞ SCH

▶ A Wade Pex Nylons figure of a fairy, c1952,
2½in (6.5cm) high.
£200–240 / €290–350
$350–420 ⚒ BBR

A Wade porcelain model of a swallow, Irish, 1956–59,
2¾in (7cm) high.
£15–20 / €22–29
$29–38 ⊞ TAC

▶ A Wade porcelain model of an Alsatian, from a set of seven,
1957, 2in (5cm) wide.
£20–25 / €30–35
$40–50 ⊞ UD

A Wade Disney Blow Up model of Am,
c1960, 2in (5cm) high.
£30–35 / €45–50
$55–65 ⊞ UD

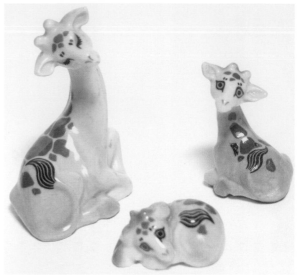

A Wade Happy Families giraffe family, 1960–65,
tallest 2in (5cm) high.
£35–40 / €50–60
$65–75 ⊞ UD

◄ **A Wade
Disney Blow Up
model of Lady,**
1961, 4¼in
(11cm) high.
£50–60 / €75–85
$90–105 🔨 BBR

**A Wade Nursery Favourites figure of
Humpty Dumpty,** 1972, 2½in (6.5cm) high.
£10–15 / €15–22
$19–28 ⊞ UD

**A set of five Wade National Westminster Bank pottery pig
money boxes,** c1983, tallest 7½in (19cm) high.
£130–145 / 185–210
$230–260 ⊞ TAC

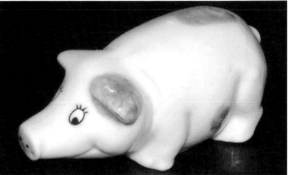

◄ A Wade
Family Favourites
model of Priscilla
the Pig, 2000,
2½in (6.5cm) long.
£10–15 / €15–22
$19–28 ⊞ JMC

A Wade Collectables model of a panda,
1998, 8in (20.5cm) high.
£35–40 / €50–60
$65–75 ⊞ LAS

► A Wade Pocket Pals model of Truffles
the Pig, 2000, 2½in (6.5cm) long.
£3–7 / €4–10
$6–13 ⊞ JMC

Winstanley

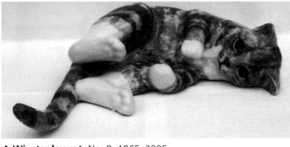

A Winstanley cat, No. 8, 1965–2005.
£45–50 / €65–75
$85–95 ⊞ CP

A Winstanley cat, No. 7, c1990,
12in (30.5cm) long.
£40–45 / €60–70
$75–85 ⊞ HEI

◄ A Winstanley cat, No. 7, 1998,
16in (40.5cm) long.
£55–65 / €80–95
$105–125 ⊞ RIA

20TH CENTURY

Worcester

A **Royal Worcester figure,** entitled 'Monday's Child is Fair of Face', c1902, 7in (18cm) high.
£160–180 / €230–260
$280–320 ⊞ WAC

A **collection of four Worcester *netsuke*,** early 20thC, 3in (7.5cm) wide.
£360–400 / €520–580
$630–700 ⊞ HKW

A **Royal Worcester model of two bears,** c1930, 3in (7.5cm) high.
£850–950 / €1,200–1,350
$1,500–1,650 ⊞ WAC

A **Royal Worcester Sabrina Ware model of a fish,** c1930, 5in (12.5cm) long.
£200–230 / €290–330
$350–400 ⊞ DSG

A **Royal Worcester model of a dog,** dated 1933, 3in (7.5cm) wide.
£130–150 / €185–220
$230–260 ⊞ WAC

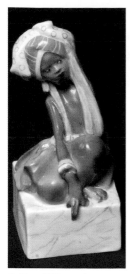

A Royal Worcester figure, by Gwendoline Parnell, entitled 'The Thief', 1942–49, 4½in (11.5cm) high.
£130–145 / €185–210
$230–260 ⊞ DEB

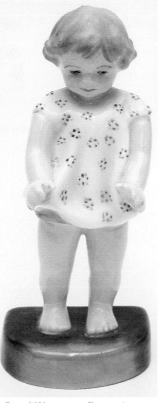

A Royal Worcester figure, by D. Doughty, entitled 'Joan', 1951, 4½in (11.5cm) high.
£90–105 / €130–150
$160–185 ⚒ G(L)

A Royal Worcester candle extinguisher, entitled 'Jenny Lind The Swedish Nightingale', dated 1953, 4¼in (11cm) high.
£180–210 / €260–310
$320–380 ⚒ SWO

A Royal Worcester prototype figure of a boy holding a toy galleon, by Freda Doughty, entitled 'Mayflower', No. RW3656, repaired, painted 'Please Return', signed, c1958, 7¾in (19.5cm) high.
£150–180 / €220–260
$260–310 ⚒ Bea

A Royal Worcester equestrian group, by Doris Lindner, entitled 'HRH Duke of Edinburgh on his polo pony', printed marks, c1968, with stand and certificate.
£200–240 / €290–350
$350–420 ⚒ DN

A Royal Worcester equestrian group, by Doris Lindner, entitled 'Stroller and Marion Coakes', printed marks, c1970, 10¼in (26cm) high, with stand and certificate.
£280–330 / €400–480
$490–580 ⚒ DN

20TH CENTURY

Directory of Specialists

If you require a valuation for an item it is advisable to check whether the dealer or specialist will carry out this service, and whether there is a charge. Please mention Miller's when making an enquiry. Having found a specialist who will carry out your valuation, it is best to send a description and photograph of the item to them, together with a stamped addressed envelope for the reply. A valuation by telephone is not possible. Most dealers are only too happy to help you with your enquiry, however, they are very busy people and consideration of the above points would be welcomed.

UK & IRELAND
Berkshire
Dreweatt Neate,
Donnington Priory, Donnington,
Newbury, RG14 2JE
Tel: 01635 553553
donnington@dnfa.com
www.dnfa.com/donnington
*Regular specialist antique and fine
art sales*

Law Fine Art
Tel: 01635 860033
info@lawfineart.co.uk
www.lawfineart.co.uk
Specialist ceramics auctioneers

M & K Antiques
Tel: 0031 624240 467
*English and continental porcelain and
decorative antiques*

Special Auction Services,
Kennetholme, Midgham,
Reading, RG7 5UX
Tel: 0118 971 2949
www.antiquestradegazette.com/sas
*Specialist auctions of commemoratives,
pot lids & Prattware, fairings,
Goss & Crested*

Derbyshire
Roger de Ville Antiques,
Bakewell Antiques Centre,
King Street, Bakewell,
DE45 1DZ
Tel: 01629 812496 or 07798 793857
contact@rogerdeville.co.uk
www.rogerdeville.co.uk
*Specialising in 18th & 19th century
British pottery, particularly Prattware,
creamware, saltglaze, Delft, blue &
white printed wares, Masons Ironstone
& political & Royal commemoratives*

Devon
Bearnes, St Edmund's Court,
Okehampton Street,
Exeter, EX4 1DU
Tel: 01392 207000
enquiries@bearnes.co.uk
www.bearnes.co.uk
Fine art auctioneers and valuers

Mere Antiques,
13 Fore Street, Topsham,
Exeter, EX3 0HF
Tel: 01392 874224
Oriental porcelain

Dorset
Box of Porcelain, 51d Icen Way,
Dorchester, DT1 1EW
Tel: 01305 267110
www.boxofporcelain.com
*Moorcroft, Lladro, Royal Doulton,
Beswick, Spode, Coalport, Royal
Worcester, Wedgwood, Beatrix Potter*

Charterhouse, The Long Street
Salerooms, Sherborne, DT9 3BS
Tel: 01935 812277
enquiry@charterhouse-auctions.co.uk
www.charterhouse-auctions.co.uk
Auctioneers and valuers

Hardy's Collectables
Tel: 07970 613077
www.poolepotteryjohn.com
Poole pottery

Essex
Sworders,
14 Cambridge Road,
Stansted Mountfitchet,
CM24 8BZ
Tel: 01279 817778
auctions@sworder.co.uk
www.sworder.co.uk
Fine art auctioneers

Gloucestershire
Dreweatt Neate, Bristol Saleroom Two,
Baynton Road, Ashton,
Bristol, BS3 2EB
Tel: 0117 953 1603
bristol@dnfa.com
www.dnfa.com/bristol
Auctioneers and valuers

Clive & Lynne Jackson
Tel: 01242 254375
Parian ware

David March,
Abbots Leigh, Bristol, BS8
Tel: 0117 937 2422
Porcelain

Hampshire
Gazelles Ltd, Stratton Audley,
Ringwood Road, Stoney Cross,
Lyndhurst, SO43 7GN
Tel: 023 8081 1610
allan@gazelles.co.uk
www.gazelles.co.uk
1920s and 1930s Art Deco ceramics

The Goss & Crested China Club &
Museum, incorporating Milestone
Publications, 62 Murray Road, Horndean,
PO8 9JL Tel: (023) 9259 7440
info@gosschinaclub.demon.co.uk
Goss & Crested china

Millers Antiques Ltd,
Netherbrook House,
86 Christchurch Road, Ringwood,
BH24 1DR Tel: 01425 472062
mail@millers-antiques.co.uk
www.millers-antiques.co.uk
Majolica and Quimper

Herefordshire
Brightwells Fine Art,
The Fine Art Saleroom,
Easters Court, Leominster, HR6 0DE
Tel: 01568 611122
fineart@brightwells.com
www.brightwells.com
Auctioneers and valuers

Hertfordshire
Tring Market Auctions,
The Market Premises, Brook Street,
Tring, HP23 5EF Tel: 01442 826446
sales@tringmarketauctions.co.uk
www.tringmarketauctions.co.uk
Auctioneers and valuers

Kent
J & M Collectables
Tel: 01580 891657 or 077135 23573
jandmcollectables@tinyonline.co.uk
*Crested china, Osborne (Ivorex) plaques
and small collectables including
Doulton, Wade, etc.*

Derek H Jordan
chinafairings@aol.com
www.chinafairings.co.uk
Fairings

Pretty Bizarre,
170 High Street, Deal, CT14 6BQ
Tel: 07973 794537
1920s–1970s ceramics and collectables

Serendipity,
125 High Street, Deal, CT14 6BB
Tel: 01304 369165/366536
dipityantiques@aol.com
Staffordshire pottery

London
Aurea Carter, P.O. Box 44134,
SW6 3YX Tel: 020 7731 3486
aureacarter@englishceramics.com
www.englishceramics.com
Antique English porcelain, ceramics and pottery

Banana Dance Ltd,
155A Northcote Road,
Battersea, SW11 6QT
Tel: 01634 364539 or 07976 296987
jonathan@bananadance.com
www.bananadance.com
Decorative Arts of the 1920s and the 1930s

Beth, GO 43-44, Alfies Antique Market,
13-25 Church Street, Marylebone,
NW8 8DT Tel: 020 7723 5613
or 0777 613 6003
Specialising in Carltonware, Clarice Cliff, Shelley, Royal Doulton tea/coffee ware, Keith Murray, unusual figures, Royal Winton, Chintz

Beverley, 30 Church Street,
Marylebone, NW8 8EP
Tel: 020 7262 1576 or 07776136003
Specialising in 19th & 20th century ceramics

David Brower, 113 Kensington Church Street, W8 7LN Tel: 0207 221 4155
David@davidbrower antiques.com
www.davidbrower-antiques.com
Specialising in Meissen, KPM, european porcelain and Japanese works of art

Guest & Gray, 1-7 Davies Mews,
W1K 5AB Tel: 020 7408 1252
info@chinese-porcelain-art.com
www.chinese-porcelain-art.com
Antique Chinese porcelain & Japanese porcelain, european ceramics & works of art

Jonathan Horne, 66c Kensington
Church Street, W8 4BY
Tel: 020 7221 5658
JH@jonathanhorne.co.uk
www.jonathanhorne.co.uk
Early English pottery

Steve and Angela Hyder,
Saturdays at The Admiral Vernon
Arcade, Portobello Road, London
Tel: 01306 880976
or 07939 819 438
info@hyderantiques.co.uk
www.hyderantiques.co.uk
Specialising in Oriental ceramics and works of art, Staffordshire figures and English ceramics

Marion Langham Limited
Tel: 028 895 41247
marion@ladymarion.co.uk
www.ladymarion.co.uk
Belleek

Mario's Antiques,
75 Portobello Road, W11 2QB
Tel: 020 8902 1600
or 07919 254000
marwan@barazi.screaming.net
www.marios_antiques.com
Porcelain

Mike Weedon,
7 Camden Passage, Islington, N1 8EA
Tel: 020 7226 5319
info@mikeweedonantiques.com
www.mikeweedonantiques.com
Art Deco and Art Nouveau antiques

Sylvia Powell Decorative Arts,
Suite 400, Ceramic House,
571 Finchley Road, NW3 7BN
Tel: 020 8458 4543 or 07802 714998
dpowell909@aol.com
Doulton

Rogers de Rin,
76 Royal Hospital Road, SW3 4HN
Tel: 020 7352 9007
rogersderin@rogersderin.co.uk
www.rogersderin.co.uk
Wemyss

Santos, Old Court House,
21 Old Court Place,
London, W8 4PD
Tel: 020 7937 6000
Specialising in Chinese export porcelain from the 17th and 18th centuries

Sotheby's,
34-35 New Bond Street, W1A 2AA
Tel: 020 7293 5000
www.sothebys.com
Fine art auctioneers and valuers

Agnes Wilton,
3 Camden Passage,
London, N1 8EA
Tel: 020 7226 5679
Staffordshire figures

Norfolk
Cat Pottery,
1 Grammar School Road,
North Walsham,
NR28 9JH
Tel: 01692 402962
Winstanley cats

Keys, Off Palmers Lane, Aylsham,
NR11 6JA Tel: 01263 733195
www.aylshamsalerooms.co.uk
Fine art auctioneers

Nottinghamshire
Millennium Collectables Ltd,
P.O. Box 146, Newark,
NG24 2WR
Tel: 01636 703075
mail@millenniumcollectables.co.uk
www.millenniumcollectables.co.uk
Limited edition Royal Doulton & Coalport advertising icon figures

Oxfordshire
John Howard at Heritage,
6 Market Place, Woodstock,
OX20 1TA
Tel: 0870 4440678 or 07831 850544
john@johnhoward.co.uk
www.antiquepottery.co.uk
Staffordshire pottery, creamware, Lustreware and Gaudy Welsh pottery

Republic of Ireland
Delphi Antiques,
Powerscourt Townhouse Centre,
South William Street, Dublin 2
Tel: 1 679 0331
Specialists in Fine 19th century Irish, English and continental porcelain

Mitofsky Antiques,
8 Rathfarnham Road, Terenure,
Dublin 6 Tel: 1 492 0033
info@mitofskyantiques.com
www.mitofskyantiques.com
Ceramics by Doulton, Poole and others

Shropshire
Brettells Antiques & Fine Art,
Newport Saleroom,
Newport, Shropshire
Tel: 01952 815925
auction@brettells.com
www.brettells.com
Weekly auction sales

Somerset
Lawrence Fine Art Auctioneers,
South Street, Crewkerne, TA18 8AB
Tel: 01460 73041
www.lawrences.co.uk
Fine art auctioneers

Jeanne Schubert,
31 Old Market Centre,
Taunton, Somerset
Tel: 01823 251074
enquiries@jeanneschubert.co.uk
www.jeanneschubert.co.uk
Lilliput Lane, Lladro, Doulton, Robert Harrop, Worcester and Spode

Staffordshire
Potteries Specialist Auctions,
271 Waterloo Road, Cobridge,
Stoke-on-Trent, ST6 3HR
Tel: 01782 286622
www.potteriesauctions.com
Regular monthly sales in pottery and ceramics, specialising in 20th century collectable ceramics

Wade Ceramics Ltd,
Royal Victoria Pottery,
Westport Road, Burslem,
Stoke-on-Trent, ST6 4AG
Tel: 01782 577321
www.wade.co.uk

Suffolk
John Read,
29 Lark Rise, Martlesham Heath,
Ipswich, IP5 7SA
Tel: 01473 624897

Surrey
Bac to Basic Antiques
Tel: 07787 105609
bcarruthers@waitrose.com
Late 19th and early 20th century porcelain, Doulton and parian ware, Royal, military and exhibition commemoratives. Goss and Crested china

Judi Bland Antiques
Tel: 01276 857576 or 01536 724145
18th & 19th century English Toby jugs

Candice Horley Antiques
Tel: 01883 716056 or 0705 0044855
cjhorleyantiques@aol.com
Specialising in european figural sculpture

East Sussex
Dreweatt Neate,
46-50 South Street, Eastbourne,
BN21 4XB Tel: 01323 410419
eastbourne@dnfa.com
www.dnfa.com/eastbourne
Auctioneers and valuers

Gorringes Auction Galleries,
Terminus Road, Bexhill-on-Sea,
TN39 3LR Tel: 01424 212994
bexhill@gorringes.co.uk
www.gorringes.co.uk
Antiques, fine art and collectables auctions

Gorringes inc Julian Dawson,
15 North Street, Lewes, BN7 2PD
Tel: 01273 478221
clientservices@gorringes.co.uk
www.gorringes.co.uk

Tony Horsley,
P.O. Box 3127, Brighton, BN1 5SS
Tel: 01273 550770
Candle extinguishers, Royal Worcester and other fine porcelain

Jupiter Antiques,
P.O. Box 609, Rottingdean, BN2 7FW
Tel: 01273 302865
Specialising in English porcelain from 18th century factories and Royal Worcester and Royal Crown Derby

West Sussex
Rupert Toovey & Co Ltd,
Spring Gardens,
Washington, RH20 3BS
Tel: 01903 891955
auctions@rupert-toovey.com
www.rupert-toovey.com
Monthly specialist auctions of antiques, fine art and collectors' items

Wales
Peter Francis,
Curiosity Sale Room,
19 King Street, Carmarthen,
SA31 1BH
Tel: 01267 233456
nigel@peterfrancis.co.uk
www.peterfrancis.co.uk
Auctioneers and valuers

Islwyn Watkins,
Offa's Dyke Antique Centre,
4 High Street, Knighton,
Powys, LD7 1AT
Tel: 01547 520145
18th and 19th century pottery, 20th century country and Studio pottery

West Wales Antiques,
18 Mansfield Road,
Murton, Swansea, SA3 3AR
Tel: 01792 234318/01639 644379
info@westwalesantiques.co.uk
www.westwalesantiques.co.uk
Specialist dealers in Swansea and Nantgarw

West Midlands
Fellows & Sons,
Augusta House, 19 Augusta Street,
Hockley, Birmingham, B18 6JA
Tel: 0121 212 2131
info@fellows.co.uk www.fellows.co.uk
Auctioneers and valuers

Wiltshire
Andrew Dando,
34 Market Street,
Bradford on Avon, BA15 1LL
Tel: 01225 865444
andrew@andrewdando.co.uk
www.andrewdando.co.uk
English, oriental and continental porcelain

Typically English Antiques,
By appointment only
Tel: 01249 721721 or 07818 000204
TypicallyEng@aol.com
www.typicallyenglishantiques.co.uk
English 18th & 19th century pottery and porcelain

Woolley & Wallis,
Salisbury Salerooms,
51-61 Castle Street,
Salisbury,
SP1 3SU
Tel: 01722 424500/411854
enquiries@woolleyandwallis.co.uk
www.woolleyandwallis.co.uk
Fine art auctioneers and valuers

Worcestershire
Art Nouveau Originals,
The Bindery Gallery,
69 High Street, Broadway,
WR12 7DP
Tel: 01386 854645
or 07774 718 096
cathy@artnouveauoriginals.com
www.artnouveauoriginals.com

Yorkshire
BBR, Elsecar Heritage Centre,
Elsecar, Barnsley, S74 8HJ
Tel: 01226 745156
sales@onlinebbr.com
www.onlinebbr.com
Specialist auctions including Doulton, Beswick, Wade & other 20th century pottery

Dee, Atkinson & Harrison,
The Exchange Saleroom,
Driffield, YO25 6LD
Tel: 01377 253151
info@dahauctions.com
www.dahauctions.com
Auctioneers and valuers

Andrew Hartley,
Victoria Hall Salerooms,
Little Lane, Ilkley, LS29 8EA
Tel: 01943 816363
info@andrewhartleyfinearts.co.uk
www.andrewhartleyfinearts.co.uk
Fine art auctioneers and valuers

Muir Hewitt Art Deco Originals,
Halifax Antiques Centre,
Queens Road Mills, Queens Road
Gibbet Street, Halifax, HX1 4LR
Tel: 01422 347377
muir.hewitt@virgin.net
muir.hewitt@btconnect.com
www.muirhewitt.com
Clarice Cliff

Brenda Kimber & John Lewis,
The Victoria Centre,
3-4 Victoria Road,
Saltaire, Shipley
Tel: 01274 611478 or 01482 442265
*Specialists in Bermantofts and British
Art pottery*

Tennants,
The Auction Centre,
Harmby Road, Leyburn, DL8 5SG
Tel: 01969 623780
enquiry@tennants-ltd.co.uk
www.tennants.co.uk
Auctioneers and valuers

U.S.A.
Ancient & Classic Inc.,
54 Franklin St, New York,
NY 10013 Tel: 212 393 9696 or
646 812 3693
info@ancientclassic.com
www.ancientclassic.com
Chinese ceramics

Arroyo Arts,
191 S. Oak Park Blvd,
Suite 4, Grover Beach, CA 93433
Tel: (805) 481 0374
Toll Free (800) 970 9198
info@arroyoarts.com
www.arroyoarts.com
*Wall sculptures and figurines in floral
and aquatic themes*

Back Alley Antiques,
128 E. Kings Hwy,
Shreveport, La. 71104
Tel: (318) 219 7440
www.backalleyantiques.com
*Selection of Hull, McCoy, Redwing,
Goebel and Hummel brands of pottery*

Bishop and Daughter Antiques,
P.O. Box 519, Newtown Square,
PA 19073 Tel: 610 359 1908
www.bishopantiques.com
*Victorian Staffordshire pottery animals,
figures and children's dishes,
Royal Winton chintz and cottageware,
Royal Doulton figures, jugs, and plates,
as well as Clarice Cliff and Susie
Cooper items*

Elizabeth Bradley Antiques,
1115 W. Green Tree Road,
Milwaukee, WI 53217
By appointment only
Tel: 414 352 1521
Staffordshire figures, Canton and Imari

Brickwood Antiques,
103 Woodlawn Drive,
Gloversville, New York 12078
Tel: 518 725 0230 Mail enquiries and
appointments only

Brian Cullity,
18 Plesant Street,
P.O. Box 595, Sagamore,
MA 02561
By appointment only
Tel: 508 888 8409
bcullity@adelphia.net
www.briancullity.com
American and English ceramics

Goodfaith Antiques and Fine Art,
By appointment
Tel: 518 854 7844
ntk@goodfaithantiques.com
www.goodfaithantiques.com
Pottery and porcelain

Samuel Herrup,
435 Sheffield Plain Road (Route 7),
Sheffield, MA 01257
Tel: 413 229 0424
herrup@verizon.net
*Always a good selection of PA and
New England redware. Also European
decorative arts including ceramics*

JMW Gallery,
144 Lincoln Street,
Boston, MA02111
Tel: 617 338 9097
www.jmwgallery.com
*American Arts & Crafts, Decorative
Arts, American Art Pottery*

La Verrerie d'Art,
P.O. Box 757, Bowie,
MD 20718-0757
Tel: 301 464 3251
mail@decoesque.com
www.decoesque.com
*European Decorative Arts from the Art
Nouveau and Deco eras, specializing in
20th century european art glass and
pottery, with emphasis on the works of
Charles Schneider*

Mellin's Antiques,
P.O. Box 1115, Redding, CT 06875
Tel: 203 938 9538
reMellin@aol.com
Specializing in Chinese export porcelain

*with a focus on Canton. We buy, sell
and appraise Canton. We also offer a
nice selection of decorative arts items.
Open by appointment only*

Mimi's Antiques
Tel: 410 381 6862
or 443 250 0930
mimisantiques@comcast.net
www.mimisantiques.com
www.trocadero.com/mimisantiques
*18th and 19th century Chinese Export
porcelain, Continental porcelain*

Elinor Penna,
P.O. Box 324, Old Westbury,
NY 11568
Tel: 800 294 0324
www.elinorpenna.com
*19thc Staffordshire animals, cottages
and historical figures*

Rago Arts & Auction Center,
7 South Main Street,
Lambertville,
New Jersey 08530
Tel: 609 397 9374
www.ragoarts.com
Arts and auction center

The Sign of the Lyne,
Monte and Margaret Bourjaily,
Alexandria, Virginia
Tel: 703 548 6438 or
703 549 2322
www.signofthelyne.com
Staffordshire figures, fairings, etc

Skinner Inc.,
The Heritage On The Garden,
63 Park Plaza, Boston,
MA 02116
Tel: 617 350 5400
www.skinnerinc.com
*Auctioneers and appraisers of antiques
and fine art*

Sotheby's,
1334 York Avenue at 72nd St,
New York, NY 10021
Tel: 212 606 7000
www.sothebys.com

Philip Suval, Inc.,
John P. Suval,
1501 Caroline Street,
Fredericksburg, VA 22401
Tel: 540 373 9851
*Chinese and China trade porcelain and
British and continental ceramics*

Directory of Collectors' Clubs

UK & IRELAND

**Age of Jazz Ceramic Circle
(Linking Art Deco Websites)**
Fantasque House, Tennis Drive,
The Park, Nottingham, NG7 1AE

The UK Beatrix Potter Society
Registered Charity No. 281198,
c/o Membership Secretary, 9 Broadfields,
Harpenden, Hertfordshire, AL5 2HJ
info@beatrixpottersociety.org.uk
www.beatrixpottersociety.org.uk

Belleek Collectors Group (UK)
The Hon Chairman Mr D. A. Reynolds,
7 Highfield Estate, Wilmslow, Cheshire,
SK9 2JR chairman@belleek.org.uk
www.belleek.org.uk

Beswick Collectors Club
Barry Hill, P.O. Box 310, Richmond,
TW10 7FU barryjhill@hotmail.com
www.collectingdoulton.com/

**British Equine Collectors Forum
(Model Horses)**
SAE to Membership Secretary
Miss Helen Cooke, 24 Coleridge Close,
Bletchley, Milton Keynes,
Buckinghamshire, MK3 5AF
www.worldofpaul.com/becf

**The Burleigh Ware International
Collectors Circle**
Tel: 01664 454570

**Carlton Ware Collectors
International**
Carlton Factory Shop, Carlton Works,
Copeland Street, Stoke on Trent,
Staffordshire, ST4 1PU
Tel: 01782 410504

Cat Collectables
297 Alcester Road, Hollywood,
Birmingham, West Midlands, B47 5HJ
Tel: 01564 826277
cat.collectables@btinternet.com
www.cat-collectables.co.uk

Charlotte Rhead Newsletter
c/o 49 Honeybourne Road, Halesowen,
West Midlands, B63 3ET
Tel: 0121 560 7386

Clarice Cliff Collectors' Club
Fantasque House, Tennis Drive,
The Park, Nottingham, NG7 1AE
www.claricecliff.com

**Commemorative Collectors' Society
and Commemoratives Museum**
c/o Steven Jackson, Lumless House,
77 Gainsborough Road, Winthorpe,
Newark, Nottinghamshire, NG24 2NR

Tel: 01636 671377
commemorativecollectorssociety
@hotmail.com

The Crested Circle
42 Douglas Road, Tolworth, Surbiton,
Surrey, KT6 7SA

Danesby Collectors Club
Fantasque House, Tennis Drive,
The Park, Nottingham, NG7 1AE
www.danesby.co.uk

**Derby Porcelain International
Society**
Box 6997, Coleshill, Warwickshire,
B46 2LF ich@soc.soton.ac.uk
www.derby-porcelain.org.uk/

Devon Pottery Collectors Group
Mrs Joyce Stonelake, 19 St Margarets
Avenue, Torquay, Devon, TQ1 4LW
Tel: 01803 327277
Virginia.Brisco@care4free.net

The Fairing Collectors Society
Stuart Piepenstock Tel: 01895 824830

**Fieldings Crown Devon
Collectors' Club**
P.O. Box 462, Manvers, Rotherham,
S63 7WT Tel: 01709 874433
fcdcc@tiscali.co.uk
www.fieldingscrowndevclub.com

Goss Collectors' Club (est 1970)
Brian Waller, 35 Felstead Way, Luton,
LU2 7LH Tel: 01582 732063
commercialofficer@gosscollectors
club.org

Hagen-Renaker Collectors Club (UK)
Chris and Derek Evans, 97 Campbell
Road, Burton, Christchurch, Dorset,
BH23 7LY ww.priorycollectables.co.uk

Honiton Pottery Collectors' Society
Ian McLellan (Chairman),
51 Cherryfields, Gillingham,
Dorset, SP8 4TJ Tel: 01747 835299
jandimclellan@btinternet.com
www.hpcs.info

**Hornsea Pottery Collectors' and
Research Society**
c/o Peter Tennant, 128 Devonshire
Street, Keighley, West Yorkshire,
BD21 2QJ
hornsea@pdtennant.fsnet.co.uk
www.hornseacollector.co.uk

**James Sadler International
Collectors Club**
Customer Services, Churchill China
PLC, High Street, Tunstall, Stoke on
Trent, Staffordshire, ST6 5NZ

Tel: 01782 577566
diningin@churchillchina.plc.uk
www.james-sadler.co.uk

**Legend Products International
Collector's Club**
Sheila Cochrane (Owner and club
founder), 1 Garden Villas, Wrexham
Road, Cefn Y Bedd, Flintshire,
LL12 9UT Tel: 01978 760800
sheila@legend-lane.demon.co.uk
www.legendproducts.co.uk

Limoges Porcelain Collectors Club
The Tannery, Park Stile, Haydon Bridge,
Hexham, NE47 6BP Tel: 01434 684444
www.limogesboxoffice.co.uk

**Memories UK, Mabel Lucie
Attwell Club**
Abbey Antiques, 63 Great Whyte,
Ramsey, Nr Huntingdon,
Cambridgeshire, PE26 1HL
Tel: 01487 814753
www.mabellucieatwellclub.com

Moorcroft Collectors' Club
W. Moorcroft PLC, Sandbach Road,
Burslem, Stoke-on-Trent, Staffordshire,
ST6 2DQ Tel: 01782 820510
cclub@moorcroft.com
www.moorcroft.com

Moorland Pottery Collectors Club
Moorland Road, Burslem, Stoke on
Trent, Staffordshire, ST6 1DY

**Keith Murray Collectors Club
(Patron Constance Murray)**
Fantasque House, Tennis Drive,
The Park, Nottingham, NG7 1AE
www.keithmurray.co.uk

**The Official International Wade
Ceramics Collectors Club**
Royal Victoria Pottery, Westport Road,
Burslem, Stoke on Trent, Staffordshire,
ST6 4AG www.wade.co.uk

Pen Delfin Family Circle
Pendelfin Studios Ltd, Townley Street,
Briercliffe Business Centre, Burnley,
Lancashire, BB10 2HG
Tel: 01282 432301
boswell@pendelfin.co.uk
www.pendelfin.co.uk

Poole Pottery Collectors Club
Poole Pottery Limited, Sopers Lane,
Poole, Dorset, BH17 7PP
Tel: 01202 666200 www.poolepottery.com

Potteries of Rye Society
Membership Secretary Barry Buckton,
2 Redyear Cottages, Kennington Road,

Ashford, Kent, TN24 0TF
Tel: 01233 647898
www.potteries-of-rye-society.co.uk

Quimper Association
Odin, Benbow Way, Cowley, Uxbridge,
Middlesex, UB8 2HD

Robert Harrop Collectors Club
Robert Harrop Designs Ltd, Coalport
House, Lamledge Lane, Shifnal,
Shropshire, TF11 8SD
www.robertharrop.com

**Royal Doulton International
Collectors' Club**
Royal Doulton, Sir Henry Doulton
House, Forge Lane, Stoke-on-Trent,
Staffordshire, ST1 5NN
www.icc@royal-doulton.com

**The Shelley Group, (for collectors
of Shelley and Wileman wares)**
Ruskin, 47 St Andrew's Drive, Perton,
Staffordshire, WV6 7YL
Tel: 01902 754245
shelley.group@shelley.co.uk
www.shelley.co.uk

The Soviet Collectors Club
P.O. Box 56, Saltburn by the Sea,
TS12 1YD collect@sovietclub.com
www.sovietclub.com

The SylvaC Collectors Circle
174 Portsmouth Road, Horndean,
Waterlooville, Hampshire, PO8 9HP
www.sylvacclub.com

The Wedgwood International Society
Admail 981, Stoke on Trent,
Staffordshire, ST12 9JW

**The Wedgwood Society of
Great Britain**
P.O. Box 5921, Bishop's Stortford,
Essex, CM22 7FB

U.S.A.
**Alice In Wonderland Collectors
Network**
Joel Birenbaum, 2765 Shellingham
Drive, Lisle, IL 60532-4245, U.S.A.

All God's Children Collector's Club
Kathy Martin, P.O. Box 5038, Gadsden,
AL 35905-0038, U.S.A.
Tel: 256 492 0221
info@missmarthaoriginals.com
www.missmarthaoriginals.com

American Art Pottery Association
Patti Bourgeois, P.O. Box 834, Westport,
MA 02790, U.S.A. Tel: 508 679 5910
amartpotassn@aol.com
www.amartpot.org/

American Ceramic Circle
Nancy K. Lester, 520 16th St, Brooklyn,
NY 11215, U.S.A. nlester@earthlink.net

**The Belleek Collectors' International
Society (USA)**
P.O. Box 1498, Great Falls, VA 22066,
U.S.A. Tel: 800 235 5335 or
703 272 6270 info@belleek.ie
www.belleek.ie/

The Boehm Porcelain Society
25 Princess Diana Lane, Trenton,
NJ 08638, U.S.A. Tel: 609 392 2207 or
800 257 9410 boehmporcelain@att.net
www.boehmporcelain.com/

Borsato Collectors Club
Allan Koskela, P.O. Box 104,
Webster City, IA 50595, U.S.A.
Tel: 515 832 2437
alankoskela@wmconnect.com
www.borsato.20m.com/

Dedham Pottery Collectors Society
Jim Kaufman, 248 Highland St,
Dedham, MA 02026-5833, U.S.A.
Tel: 800 283 8070 or 781 329 8070
dpcurator@aol.com
www.dedhampottery.com/

Delftware Collectors Association
Ed Goldgehn, P.O. Box 670673,
Marietta, GA 30066, U.S.A.
Tel: 770 499 8515
comments@delftware.org
www.delftware.org/

The Family Circle of Pen Delfin
Susan Beard, 230 Spring Street N.W.,
Suite 1238, Atlanta, Georgia 30303,
U.S.A.

Florence Ceramics Collectors Society
David Miller, 1971 Blue Fox Dr, Lansdale,
PA 19446, U.S.A.
FlorenceCeramics@aol.com

Friar Tuck Collectors Club
Carol Skaggs-Austin, 1076 Grays
Creek, Church Rd, Rutherfordton,
NC 28139, U.S.A. Tel: 828 248 3985
friartuckcollectorclub@webtv.net

Goebel Networkers
P.O. Box 355, Hamburg, PA 19526, U.S.A.

The Hagen-Renaker Collectors Club
Jenny Palmer, 3651 Polish Line Road,
Cheboygan, Mitchigan 49721, U.S.A.

Hummel Collector's Club, Inc.
Dorothy Dous, 1261 University Dr,
Yardley, PA 19067-2857, U.S.A.
Tel: 215 493 6705 or 888 5 HUMMEL
customerservice@hummels.com
www.hummels.com/

**Kevin Francis Toby Jug Collectors
Guild**
917 Chicago Ave, Evanston, IL 60202,
U.S.A. Tel: 800 634 0431 or
847 570 4867 Britcol@msn.com
www.britishcollectibles.com/

M.I. Hummel Club
Goebel Plaza, Rte. 31, P.O. Box 11,
Pennington, NJ 08534-0011, U.S.A.
Tel: 609 737 8777 or 800 666 2582
memsrv@mihummel.com
www.mihummel.com

National Shelley China Club
Rochelle Hart,
591 West 67th Ave,
Anchorage, AK 99518-1555, U.S.A.
Tel: 907 562 2124
imahart@alaska.net
www.nationalshelleychinaclub.com/

National Society of Lefton Collectors
Loretta DeLozier,
P.O. Box 50201,
Knoxville, TN 37950 0201, U.S.A.

Quimper Club International
Diane Robinson, 5316 Seascape Lane,
Plano, TX 75093, U.S.A.
Tel: 972 867 7839
dianerobinson@quimperclub.org
www.quimperclub.org/

Royal Bayreuth Collectors' Club
Karen Church, 110 Blackwood St,
Beaver Falls, PA 15010, U.S.A.
Tel: 507 645 5382
tenebrous@aol.com
www.royalbayreuth.com/

**Royal Bayreuth International
Collectors' Society**
Howard & Sarah Wade,
P.O. Box 325, Orrville,
OH 44667 0325, U.S.A.
Tel: 330 682 8551
RBCollectr@aol.com

**Royal Doulton International
Collectors' Club**
701 Cottontail Lane, Somerset,
NJ 08873, U.S.A. Tel: 732 356 7880
or 800 682 4462
usa@royal-doulton.com
www.royaldoulton.com

Stangl Bird Collectors Club
P.O. Box 3146, Patchogue, NY 11772,
U.S.A. Tel: 631 475 6537
stangl.bird@verizon.net
www.members.bellatlantic.net/~ljsdavis/

Stangl Fulper Collectors Club
Jonathan Nielsen, P.O. Box 538,
Flemington, NJ 08822, U.S.A.
Tel: 908 995 2696 or 908 782 9631
jonathannielsen@stanglfulper.com
www.stanglfulper.com/

Wade Attic
Carole Murdock,
8199 Pierson Ct,
Arvada, CO 80005, U.S.A.
carole@wadeattic.com
www.wadeattic.com

Museums & Websites

American Museum of Ceramic Arts
AMOCA, 340 S. Garey Avenue,
Pomona, CA 91766,
U.S.A.
Tel: 909 865 3146 or 3147
www.ceramicmuseum.org

Antique British Ceramics
www.abcir.org/

Arizona State University Art Museum
Tempe, AZ 85287-2911,
U.S.A.
Tel: 480 965 2787
www.asuartmuseum.asu.edu

Art Institute of Chicago
111 South Michigan Avenue,
Chicago, Illinois 60603,
U.S.A.
Tel: 312 443 3600
www.artic.edu

Ashmolean Museum of Art and Archaeology
Ceramics online @ the Ashmolean Museum
www.ashmol.ox.ac.uk/PotWeb/

Belleek Pottery Visitor Centre & Museum
Belleek, Co Fermanagh,
Northern Ireland
Tel: 028 6865 9300
visitorcentre@belleek.ie
www.belleek.ie

The Bennington Museum
75 Main Street,
Bennington, VT 05201,
U.S.A.
Tel: 802 447 1571
www.benningtonmuseum.com

The Bowes Museum
Barnard Castle, County Durham,
DL12 8NP, England
Tel: 01833 690606
www.bowesmuseum.org.uk

British Collectibles
US tel: 800 634 0431 overseas
Tel: 847 570 4867
www.britishcollectibles.com

Carnegie Museum of Art
4400 Forbes Avenue, Pittsburgh,
PA 15213-4080, U.S.A.
Tel: 412 622 3131
www.cmoa.org

Ceramics Today
www.ceramicstoday.com

Crocker Art Museum
216 O Street, Sacramento,
CA 95814, U.S.A.
Tel: 916 264 5423
www.crockerartmuseum.org

Etruria Industrial Museum
Lower Bedford Street,
Etruria, Stoke-on-Trent,
Staffordshire,
ST4 7AF, England
Tel: 01782 233144
museums@stoke.gov.uk

Everson Museum of Art
Syracuse, New York, U.S.A.
www.fmhs.cnyric.org/community/everson/

The Field Museum
1400 S. Lake, Shore Dr,
Chicago, IL 60605-2496, U.S.A.
Tel: 312 922 9410
www.fieldmuseum.org

Ford Green Hall
Ford Green Road,
Smallthorne, Stoke-on-Trent,
Staffordshire, England
Tel: 01782 233195
ford.green.hall@stoke.gov.uk

the-forum On-Line Antiques Mall
www.the-forum.com

The Gilbert Collection of Decorative Arts
The Gilbert Collection Trust,
Somerset House, Strand,
London WC2R 1LA,
England
Tel: 020 7420 9400
info@gilbert-collection.org.uk
www.gilbert-collection.org.uk

Gladstone Pottery Museum
Uttoxeter Road, Longton,
Stoke-on-Trent,
Staffordshire,
ST3 1PQ, England
Tel: 01782 319232 or 311378
gladstone@stoke.gov.uk

Kirkcaldy Museum and Art Gallery
War Memorial Gardens,
Kirkcaldy, KY1 1YG,
Scotland
Tel: 01592 412860
kirkcaldy.museum@fife.gov.uk
www.fifedirect.org.uk/museums

Lladró Museum
43 West, 57th Street,
New York, NY 10019,
U.S.A.
Toll free (only from USA)
800 785 3490 or 212 838 9356
newyork-museum@us.lladro.com

Meissen Porcelain Museum
Staatliche Porzellan-Manufaktur
Meissen GmbH, Besucherbüro,
Talstraße 9, 01662 Meißen,
Germany
Tel: 3521 468 208
www.meissen.de

The Metropolitan Museum of Art
1000 Fifth Avenue at 82nd Street,
New York 10028-0198, U.S.A.
Tel: 212 535 7710
www.metmuseum.org

Mint Museum of Art
Charlotte, NC, U.S.A.
Tel: 704 337 2101
www.tfaoi.com

Minton Museum
Royal Doulton, Minton House,
Stoke-on-Trent, Staffordshire,
ST4 7QD, England
Tel: 01782 292292

Model Horse Gallery
www.modelhorsegallery.info/

The Museum of Ceramics
400 East Fifth Street,
East Liverpool, Ohio 43920, U.S.A.
Tel: 330 386 6001 or 800 600 7180
www.themuseumofceramics.org

National Ceramic Museum & Heritage Center
7327 Ceramic Road NE,
Roseville, Ohio 43777,
U.S.A.
Tel: 740 697 7021
www.ceramiccenter.info

National Museum & Gallery
Cathays Park,
Cardiff, CF10 3NP,
Wales
Tel: 029 2039 7951
www.nmgw.ac.uk

Newark Museum
www.newarkmuseum.org

Ohio Ceramic Center
Ceramic Pottery Museum Association,
P.O. Box 200, Crooksville,
OH 43731, U.S.A.
Tel: 740 697 7021 or
800 752 2604

Overbeck Pottery Museum
Cambridge City Public Library,
33. W. Main Street,
Cambridge City,
IN 47327, U.S.A.
Tel: 765 478 3335 or 765 478 3335
www.overbeckmuseum.com

Paisley Museum and Art Galleries
High Street, Paisley, PA1 2BA,
Scotland
Tel: 0141 889 3151

**The Potteries Museum
& Art Gallery**
Bethesda Street,
Hanley, Stoke-on-Trent,
Staffordshire, ST1 3DW,
England
Tel: 01782 232323
museums@stoke.gov.uk
www2002.stoke.gov.uk

PotteryAuction.com
www.potteryauction.com

Royal Crown Derby Museum
The Royal Crown Derby Porcelain Co
Limited, 194 Osmaston Road,
Derby, DE23 8JZ, England
Tel: 01332 712800
www.royal-crown-derby.co.uk

Sainsbury Centre for Visual Arts
University of East Anglia,
Norwich, NR4 7TJ, England
Tel: 01603 593199
scva.marketing@uea.ac.uk
www.scva.org.uk

**The Schein-Joseph International
Museum of Ceramic Art**
New York State College of Ceramics

at Alfred University, U.S.A.
Tel: 607 871 2421
ceramicsmuseum.alfred.edu/

Ulster Museum
Botanic Gardens, Belfast,
BT9 5AB, Northern Ireland
Tel: 028 9038 3000
www.ulstermuseum.org.uk

Victoria & Albert Museum
V&A South Kensington,
Cromwell Road, London, SW7 2RL,
England Tel: 020 7942 2000
www.vam.ac.uk

Wedgwood Museum
Barlaston, Stoke on Trent,
Staffordshire, ST12 9ES,
England
Tel: 01782 282818
info@wedgwoodmuseum.org.uk
www.wedgwood.museum@
wedgwood.co.uk

The Worcester Porcelain Museum
Severn Street, Worcester, WR1 2NE,
England Tel: 01905 746000
www.worcesterporcelain
museum.org.uk

Directory of Markets & Centres

UK & IRELAND
Bedfordshire
Woburn Abbey Antiques Centre, Woburn, MK17 9WA
Tel: 01525 290666 antiques@woburnabbey.co.uk
www.discoverwoburn.co.uk
Furniture, porcelain, silver, paintings

Buckinghamshire
Marlow Antique Centre, 35 Station Road, Marlow, SL7 1NW
Tel: 01628 473223
Furniture, china, glass, cuff links, pens. A good secondhand book dept

Derbyshire
Alfreton Antique Centre, 11 King Street, Alfreton, DE55 7AF
Tel: 01773 520781
Antiques, collectables, furniture, books, militaria, postcards, silverware

Ashbourne Antiques Centre, 28A Church Street, Ashbourne, DE6 1AF Tel: 01335 300 820
barbara@acres120.freeserve.co.uk

Chappells Antiques Centre - Bakewell, King Street, Bakewell, DE45 1DZ Tel: 01629 812496
ask@chappellsantiquescentre.com
www.chappellsantiquescentre.com
Furniture, ceramics, silver, plate, metals, treen, clocks, barometers, books, pictures, maps, prints, textiles, kitchenalia, lighting and furnishing accessories from the 17th–20th century

Heanor Antiques Centre, 1–3 Ilkeston Road, Heanor, DE75 7AE Tel: 01773 531181/762783
sales@heanorantiquescentre.co.uk
www.heanorantiques.co.uk

Matlock Antiques, Collectables & Riverside Café, 7 Dale Road, Matlock, DE4 3LT Tel: 01629 760808
bmatlockantiques@aol.com
www.matlock-antiques-collectables.cwc.net
Wide range of items including collectables, mahogany, pine, oak, pictures, books, linen, kitchenalia, china, clocks, clothes and jewellery

Devon
Quay Centre, Topsham, Nr Exeter, EX3 0JA
Tel: 01392 874006 office@quayantiques.com
www.quayantiques.com

Essex
Debden Antiques, Elder Street, Debden, Saffron Walden, CB11 3JY Tel: 01799 543007
info@debden-antiques.co.uk
debden-antiques.co.uk
Large selection of 16th—20th century oak, mahogany and pine furniture, watercolours and oil paintings, rugs, ceramics, silver and jewellery

Gloucestershire
Alchemy Antiques, The Old Chapel, Long Street, Tetbury, GL8 8AA Tel: 01666 505281
Jewellery, clocks, antiquities, books, furniture, treen, flatware, glass, china, porcelain and decorative accessories

Antiques Centre Gloucester, 1 Severn Road, The Historic Docks, Gloucester, GL1 2LE Tel: 01452 529716
www.antiques.center.com

Durham House Antiques, Sheep Street, Stow-on-the-Wold, GL54 1AA Tel: 01451 870404
DurhamHouseGB@aol.com
www.DurhamHouseGB.com
Town and country furniture, metalware, books, ceramics, kitchenalia, sewing ephemera, silver, jewellery and samplers

Jubilee Hall Antiques Centre, Oak Street, Lechlade on Thames, GL7 3AY Tel: 01367 253777 sales@jubileehall.co.uk
www.jubileehall.co.uk

The Top Banana Antiques Mall, 1 New Church Street, Tetbury, GL8 8DS Tel: 0871 288 1102
info@topbananaantiques.com
www.topbananaantiques.com
Decorative antiques and interiors
Also at:
32 Long Street, Tetbury, GL8 8AQ Tel: 0871 288 1110
46 Long Street, Tetbury Tel: 0871 288 3058 and
48 Long Street, Tetbury Tel: 0871 288 3058

Hampshire
Dolphin Quay Antique Centre, Queen Street, Emsworth, PO10 7BU Tel: 01243 379994 chrisdqantiques@aol.com
Antique furniture, porcelain, clocks, watches, jewellery, silver

Hertfordshire
Home & Colonial, 134 High Street, Berkhamsted, HP4 3AT
Tel: 01442 877007 homeandcolonial@btinternet.com
www.homeandcolonial.co.uk
English, French period furniture, clocks, pine and country furniture, Arts & Crafts, painted furniture, garden antiques, jewellery, collectables

Kent
Castle Antiques, 1 London Road (opposite Library), Westerham, TN16 1BB Tel: 01959 562492
Antiques, small furniture, collectables, rural bygones, costume, glass, books, linens, jewellery, chandeliers, cat collectables

Copperfields Antiques & Craft Centre, 3c-4 Copperfields, Spital Street, Dartford, DA9 2DE Tel: 01322 281445
Antiques, bygones, collectables, stamps, Wade, Sylvac, Beswick, Royal Doulton, Victoriana, Art Deco, 1930's-60's, clocks, crafts, hand-made toys, dolls' Houses & miniatures, jewellery, glass, china, furniture, Kevin Francis character jugs, silk, lace and more

Nightingales, 89-91 High Street, West Wickham, BR4 0LS
Tel: 020 8777 0335
Antiques, furniture and collectors items, including ceramics, glass, silver, furniture and decorative ware

Tenterden Antiques Centre, 66-66A High Street, Tenterden, TN30 6AU Tel: 01580 765655/765885

Lancashire
The Antique & Decorative Design Centre, 56 Garstang Road, Preston, PR1 1NA Tel: 01772 882078
info@paulallisonantiques.co.uk

www.paulallisonantiques.co.uk
Antiques, objects d'art, clocks, pine, silverware, porcelain, upholstery, French furniture for the home and garden.

GB Antiques Centre, Lancaster Leisure Park (the former Hornsea Pottery), Wyresdale Road, Lancaster, LA1 3LA
Tel: 01524 844734
Porcelain, pottery, Art Deco, glass, books, linen, mahogany, oak and pine furniture

Leicestershire
Oxford Street Antique Centre, 16-26 Oxford Street, Leicester, LE1 5XU Tel: 0116 255 3006
osac.leicester@tiscali.co.uk www.oxfordstreetfurniture.co.uk

Lincolnshire
Hemswell Antique Centres, Caenby Corner Estate, Hemswell Cliff, Gainsborough, DN21 5TJ
Tel: 01427 668389 info@hemswell-antiques.com
www.hemswell-antiques.com

London
Alfie's Antique Market, 13 Church Street, Marylebone, NW8 8DT Tel: 020 7723 6066 www.alfiesantiques.com

Antiquarius Antiques Centre, 131/141 King's Road, Chelsea, SW3 5ST Tel: 020 7351 5353
neiljackson@atlantic100.freeserve.co.uk
www.antiquarius.co.uk

Atlantic Antiques Centres, Chenil House, 181-183 Kings Road, SW3 5EB Tel: 020 7351 5353 antique@dial.pipex.com

Bond Street Antiques Centre, 124 New Bond Street, W1Y 9AE Tel: 020 7351 5353 antique@dial.pipex.com

Bourbon-Hanby Antiques Centre, 151 Sydney Street, Chelsea, SW3 6NT Tel: 020 7352 2106

Grays Antique Markets, South Molton Lane, W1K 5AB
Tel: 020 7629 7034 grays@clara.net
www.graysantiques.com

The Mall Antiques Arcade, Camden Passage, 359 Upper Street, Islington, N1 8DU Tel: 020 7351 5353
antique@dial.pipex.com

Northcote Road Antique Market, 155a Northcote Road, Battersea, SW11 6QB Tel: 020 7228 6850
gillikins@ntlworld.com www.spectrumsoft.net/nam.htm
Jewellery, prints, pictures, glass, Victoriana, Art Deco, furniture, lighting, silver, plate, textiles

The Old Cinema, 160 Chiswick High Road, W4 1PR
Tel: 020 8995 4166 theoldcinema@antiques-uk.co.uk
www.antiques-uk.co.uk/theoldcinema

Palmers Green Antiques Centre, 472 Green Lanes, Palmers Green, N13 5PA Tel: 020 8350 0878
Furniture, jewellery, clocks, pictures, porcelain, china, glass, silver & plate, metalware, kitchenalia and lighting, etc

Norfolk
Tombland Antiques Centre, Augustine Steward House, 14 Tombland, Norwich, NR3 1HF Tel: 01603 761906
or 619129 www.tomblandantiques.co.uk

Northamptonshire
The Brackley Antique Cellar, Drayman's Walk, Brackley, NN13 6BE Tel: 01280 841841 antiquecellar@tesco.net
Ceramics, porcelain, clocks, glass, books, dolls, jewellery, militaria, linen, lace, victoriana, kitchenalia and furniture

Nottinghamshire
Dukeries Antiques Centre, Thoresby Park, Budby, Newark, NG22 9EX Tel: 01623 822252 dukeriesantiques@aol.com
Antique furniture, paintings, porcelain, glass, silver

Oxfordshire
Deddington Antiques Centre, Laurel House, Market Place, Bull Ring, Deddington, Nr Banbury, OX15 0TT
Tel: 01869 338968
Furniture, silver, porcelain, oils and watercolours, jewellery

Heritage, 6 Market Place, Woodstock, OX20 1TA
Tel: 01993 811332/0870 4440678
dealers@atheritage.co.uk www.atheritage.co.uk
Wide range of antiques including British pottery, silver, glassware, furniture, paintings, books, textile, decorative arts, lighting and other associated antique and decorative accessories all pre-dating 1940

Lamb Arcade Antiques Centre, High Street, Wallingford, OX10 0BX Tel: 01491 835166
Furniture, silver, porcelain, glass, books, boxes, crafts, rugs, jewellery, brass bedsteads and linens, pictures, curtains, Tin toys Diecast, sports and fishing items, decorative and ornamental items

The Swan at Tetsworth, High Street, Tetsworth, Nr Thame, OX9 7AB Tel: 01844 281777
antiques@theswan.co.uk www.theswan.co.uk
Large selection of furniture, Georgian through to Art Deco. Wonderful selection including silver, mirrors, rugs, glass, ceramics, jewellery, boxes and lots more

Scotland
Scottish Antique and Arts Centre, Carse of Cambus, Doune, Perthshire, FK16 6HG Tel: 01786 841203
sales@scottish-antiques.com www.scottish-antiques.com

Scottish Antique Centre, Abernyte, Perthshire, PH14 9SJ
Tel: 01828 686401 sales@scottish-antiques.com
www.scottish-antiques.com

Somerset
Bartlett Street Antique Centre, 5-10 Bartlett Street, Bath, BA1 2QZ Tel: 01225 466689 info@antiques-centre.co.uk
www.antiques-centre.co.uk

Surrey
Great Grooms Antiques Centre, 51/52 West Street, Dorking, RH4 1BU Tel: 01306 887076 dorking@greatgrooms.co.uk
www.greatgrooms.co.uk
General antiques, furnishings, country furniture, porcelain, clocks, silver, rugs, glass, bronzes, lighting, pictures

East Sussex
The Brighton Lanes Antique Centre, 12 Meeting House Lane, Brighton, BN1 1HB Tel: 01273 823121
www.brightonlanes-antiquecentre.co.uk
Furniture, silver, jewellery, glass, porcelain, clocks, pens, watches, lighting and decorative items

Church Hill Antiques Centre, 6 Station Street, Lewes, BN7 2DA Tel: 01273 474 842
churchhilllewes@aol.com
www.church-hill-antiques.com

Hastings Antique Centre, 59-61 Norman Road, St Leonards-on-Sea, TN38 0EG Tel: 01424 428561
www.hastingsantiquecentre.co.uk

Wales

Afonwen Craft & Antique Centre, Afonwen, Nr Caerwys,
Nr Mold, Flintshire, CH7 5UB Tel: 01352 720965
www.afonwen.co.uk
Antiques, china, silver, crystal, quality collectables, fine furniture, oak, walnut, mahogany, pine

Offa's Dyke Antique Centre, 4 High Street,
Knighton, Powys, LD7 1AT
Tel: 01547 528635/520145
Specialists in ceramics and glass, fine art of the 19th & 20th centuries, country antiques and collectables

Warwickshire

Granary Antiques Centre, Ansley Road (B4114),
Nuneaton, CV10 0QL Tel: 024 76395551
www.gbsgranary.com
Porcelain, pottery, kitchenware, collectables, Victorian and Edwardian furniture. Masons Ironstone specialist. Licensed tearooms

Worcestershire

Worcester Antiques Centre, Reindeer Court, Mealcheapen
Street, Worcester, WR1 4DF Tel: 01905 610680
WorcsAntiques@aol.com
Porcelain & pottery, furniture, silver & dining room accessories, jewellery, period watches & clocks, scientific instrumentation, Arts & Crafts, Nouveau, Deco, antique boxes, Mauchline & Tartan wares, books, ephemera, militaria & kitchenalia

Yorkshire

The Chapel Antiques Centre, 99 Broadfield Road, Heeley,
Sheffield, S8 0XQ Tel: 0114 258 8288
enquiries@antiquesinsheffield.com
www.antiquesinsheffield.com
Clocks, Art Deco, French furniture, books, pine, fabrics, porcelain, and much more

U.S.A.

Alhambra Antiques Center, 3640 Coral Way, Coral Cables,
Florida Tel: 305 446 1688

Antique Center I, II, III at Historic Savage Mill, Savage,
Maryland Tel: 410 880 0918 or 301 369 4650
antiquec@aol.com

Antique Village, North of Richmond, Virginia, on Historic
US 301, 4 miles North of 1-295 Tel: 804 746 8914
Art Pottery, country & primitives, Civil War artifacts, paper memorabilia, African art, toys, advertising, occupied Japan, tobacco tins, glassware, china, holiday collectibles, jewellery, postcards

Antiques at Colony Mill Marketplace, 222 West Street,
Keene, New Hampshire 03431 Tel: 603 358 6343
Period to country furniture, paintings and prints, Art Pottery, glass, china, silver, jewellery, toys, dolls, quilts, etc

Antique Centers-Charlestown, 200 W Washington St,
Charles Town, WV 25414-1532 Tel: 304 725 1009

Antiques USA, U.S. Route One, Arundel-Kennebunk,
Maine 04046 Tel: 207 985 7766 or 800-USA-1114
www.antiquesusamaine.com

Antique Warehouse, 1122 Tittabawassee Rd, Saginaw,
MI 48604 Tel: 989 753 5719
www.theantiquewarehouse.net/

Bay Antique Center, 1010 N. Water Street, Bay City,
MI 48708 Tel: 989 894 0400
bayantiquectr@bayantiquectr.com
www.bayantiquectr.com

Chesapeake Antique Center, Inc., Route 301, PO Box 280,
Queenstown, MD 21658 Tel: 410 827 6640
admin@chesapeakeantiques.com
www.chesapeakantiques.com

The Coffman's Antiques Markets, at Jennifer House
Commons, Stockbridge Road, Route 7, PO Box 592,
Great Barrington, MA 01230 Tel: 413 528 9282/9602
www.coffmansantiques.com

Fern Eldridge & Friends, 800 First NH Turnpike (Rte. 4),
Northwood, New Hampshire 03261 Tel: 603 942 5602/8131
FernEldridgeAndFriends@NHantiqueAlley.com

Goodlettsville Antique Mall, 213 N. Main St, Germantown,
Tennessee Tel: 615 859 7002

The Hayloft Antique Center, 1190 First NH Turnpike (Rte. 4),
Northwood, New Hampshire 03261 Tel: 603 942 5153
TheHayloftAntiqueCenter@NHantiqueAlley.com
Estate jewelry, sterling silver, rare books, glass, porcelain, pottery, art, primitives, furniture, toys, ephemera, linens, military, sporting collectibles and much more

Hermitage Antique Mall, 4144-B Lebanon Road, Hermitage,
Tennessee Tel: 615 883 5789

Howard's Flea Market, 6373 Suncoast Blvd. (US 19),
Homosassa Tel: 352 628 3532 www.howardsfleamarket.com

Madison Antique Mall, 320 Gallatin Rd, S. Nashville,
Tennessee Tel: 615 865 4677

Michiana Antique Mall, 2423 S. 11th Street, Niles, Michigan
49120 www.michianaantiquemall.com

Millington Antiques, Inc., 8549 State Street, Millington,
MI 48746 Tel: 989 871 4597 millington@tds.net
www.millingtonmichigan.com

Morningside Antiques, 6443 Biscayne Blvd., Miami, Florida
Tel: 305 751 2828

Nashville Wedgewood Station Antique Mall, 657
Wedgewood Ave., Nashville, Tennessee Tel: 615 259 0939

Parker-French Antique Center, 1182 First NH Turnpike (Rt.
4), Northwood, New Hampshire 03261 Tel: 603 942 8852
ParkerFrenchAntiqueCenter@NHantiqueAlley.com
Sterling silver, jewelry, glassware, pottery, early primitives

Quechee Gorge Antiques & Collectibles Center,
Located in Quechee Gorge Village Tel: 1 800 438 5565
Depression glass, ephemera, tools, toys, collectibles, Deco, primitives, prints, silver and fine china

R & J Needful Things Antique Center, 6398 West Pierson
Road, Flushing, MI 48433 Tel: 810 659 2663
info@antiqueit.com

Showcase Antique Center, P.O. Box 1122, Sturbridge,
MA 01566 Tel: 508 347 7190 www.showcaseantiques.com

Tennessee Antique Mall, 654 Wedgewood Ave., Nashville,
Tennessee Tel: 615 259 4077

Webster Westside Flea Market, Corner of Rt. 478 & NW 3rd
St., Webster Tel: 352 793 9877 www.websterfleamarket.net

Key to Illustrations

Each illustration and descriptive caption is accompanied by a letter code. By referring to the following list of Auctioneers (denoted by ⚒) and Dealers (⊞), the source of any item may be immediately determined. Inclusion in this edition in no way constitutes or implies a contract or binding offer on the part of any of our contributors to supply or sell the goods illustrated, or similar articles, at the prices stated. Advertisers in this year's directory are denoted by (†).

If you require a valuation for an item, it is advisable to check whether the dealer or specialist will carry out this service and if there is a charge. Please mention Miller's when making an enquiry. Having found a specialist who will carry out your valuation it is best to send a photograph and description of the item to the specialist together with a stamped addressed envelope for the reply. A valuation by telephone is not possible. Most dealers are only too happy to help you with your enquiry; however, they are very busy people and consideration of the above points would be welcomed.

ACAC ⊞ Afonwen Craft & Antique Centre, Afonwen, Nr Caerwys, Nr Mold, Flintshire, CH7 5UB, Wales Tel: 01352 720965 www.afonwen.co.uk

AH ⚒ Andrew Hartley, Victoria Hall Salerooms, Little Lane, Ilkley, Yorkshire, LS29 8EA Tel: 01943 816363 www.andrewhartleyfinearts.co.uk

AMB ⚒ Ambrose, Ambrose House, Old Station Road, Loughton, Essex, IG10 4PE Tel: 020 8502 3951

AnM ⚒ Andrew Muir Tel: 07976 956208 www.andrew-muir.com

ANO ⊞ Art Nouveau Originals, The Bindery Gallery, 69 High Street, Broadway, Worcestershire, WR12 7DP Tel: 01386 854645 www.artnouveauoriginals.com

ASP ⊞ Aspidistra Antiques, 51 High Street, Finedon, Wellingborough, Northamptonshire, NN9 9JN Tel: 01933 680196 www.aspidistra.antiques.com

AUC ⊞ Aurea Carter, P.O. Box 44134, London, SW6 3YX Tel: 020 7731 3486 www.englishceramics.com

BAC ⊞ The Brackley Antique Cellar, Drayman's Walk, Brackley, Northamptonshire, NN13 6BE Tel: 01280 841841

BBR ⚒ BBR, Elsecar Heritage Centre, Elsecar, Barnsley, S.Yorks, S74 8HJ Tel: 01226 745156 www.onlinebbr.com

BD ⊞ Banana Dance Ltd, 155A Northcote Road, Battersea, London, SW11 6QT Tel: 01634 364539 www.bananadance.com

Bea ⚒ Bearnes, St Edmund's Court, Okehampton Street, Exeter, Devon, EX4 1DU Tel: 01392 207000

Bel ⊞ Belvedere Antiques sic@waitrose.com

BET ⊞ Beth, GO 43-44, Alfies Antique Market, 13-25 Church Street, Marylebone, London, NW8 8DT Tel: 020 7723 5613

BEV ⊞ Beverley, 30 Church Street, Marylebone, London, NW8 8EP Tel: 020 7262 1576

BHa ⊞ Judy & Brian Harden, P.O. Box 14, Bourton-on-the-Water, Cheltenham, Gloucestershire, GL54 2YR Tel: 01451 810684 www.portraitminiatures.co.uk

BKJL ⊞ Brenda Kimber & John Lewis, The Victoria Centre, 3-4 Victoria Road, Saltaire, Shipley, West Yorkshire Tel: 01274 611478

BOP ⊞ Box of Porcelain, 51d Icen Way, Dorchester, Dorset, DT1 1EW Tel: 01305 267110 www.boxofporcelain.com

BROW ⊞ David Brower, 113 Kensington Church Street, London, W8 7LN Tel: 020 7221 4155 www.davidbrower-antiques.com

BRT ⊞ Britannia, Grays Antique Market, Stand 101, 58 Davies Street, London, W1Y 1AR Tel: 020 7629 6772

BtoB ⊞ Bac to Basic Antiques Tel: 07787 105609

BUK ⚒ Bukowskis, Arsenalsgatan 4, Stockholm, Sweden Tel: (8) 614 08 00 www.bukowskis.se

BWDA ⊞ Brightwells Decorative Arts Tel: 01744 24899

BWL ⚒ Brightwells Fine Art, The Fine Art Saleroom, Easters Court, Leominster, Herefordshire, HR6 0DE Tel: 01568 611122 www.brightwells.com

Cas ⊞ Castle Antiques www.castle-antiques.com

CCs ⊞ Coco's Corner, Unit 4, Cirencester Antique Centre, Cirencester, Gloucestershire Tel: 01452 556 308

CDC ⚒ Capes Dunn & Co, The Auction Galleries, 38 Charles Street, Off Princess Street, Greater Manchester, M1 7DB Tel: 0161 273 6060/1911

CHAC ⊞ Church Hill Antiques Centre, 6 Station Street, Lewes, East Sussex, BN7 2DA Tel: 01273 474842 www.church-hill-antiques.com

CHO ⊞† Candice Horley Antiques Tel: 01883 716056 or 0705 0044855

CHTR ⚒ Charterhouse, The Long Street Salerooms, Sherborne, Dorset, DT9 3BS Tel: 01935 812277 www.charterhouse-auctions.co.uk

CoS ⊞ Corrinne Soffe, Tel: 01295 730317

CP ⊞ Cat Pottery, 1 Grammar School Road, North Walsham, Norfolk, NR28 9JH Tel: 01692 402962

DA ⚒ Dee, Atkinson & Harrison, The Exchange Saleroom, Driffield, East Yorkshire, YO25 6LD Tel: 01377 253151 www.dahauctions.com

DAN ⊞ Andrew Dando, 34 Market Street, Bradford-on-Avon, Wiltshire, BA15 1LL Tel: 01225 865444 www.andrewdando.co.uk

DAV ⊞ Hugh Davies, The Packing Shop, 6-12 Ponton Road, London, SW8 5BA Tel: 020 7498 3255

DeA ⊞ Delphi Antiques, Powerscourt Townhouse Centre, South William Street, Dublin 2, Republic of Ireland Tel: 1 679 0331

DEB ⊞ Debden Antiques, Elder Street, Debden, Saffron Walden, Essex, CB11 3JY Tel: 01799 543007 www.debden-antiques.co.uk

DHA ⊞ Durham House Antiques, Sheep Street, Stow-on-the-Wold, Gloucestershire, GL54 1AA Tel: 01451 870404 www.DurhamHouseGB.com

DHJ ⊞ Derek H Jordan www.chinafairings.co.uk

DMa ⊞ David March, Abbots Leigh, Bristol, Gloucestershire, BS8 Tel: 0117 937 2422

DMC ⚒ Diamond Mills & Co, 117 Hamilton Road, Felixstowe, Suffolk, IP11 7BL Tel: 01394 282281

DN ⚒ Dreweatt Neate, Donnington Priory, Donnington, Newbury, Berkshire, RG14 2JE Tel: 01635 553553 www.dnfa.com/donnington

DN(BR) ⚒ Dreweatt Neate, The Auction Hall, The Pantiles, Tunbridge Wells, Kent, TN2 5QL Tel: 01892 544500 www.dnfa.com/tunbridgewells

DN(Bri)⚒ Dreweatt Neate, Bristol Saleroom Two, Baynton Road, Ashton, Bristol, Gloucestershire, BS3 2EB Tel: 0117 953 1603 www.dnfa.com/bristol

DN(EH)⚒ Dreweatt Neate, 46-50 South Street, Eastbourne, East Sussex, BN21 4XB Tel: 01323 410419 www.dnfa.com/eastbourne

DORO ⚒ Dorotheum, Palais Dorotheum, A-1010 Wien, Dorotheergasse 17, 1010 Vienna, Austria Tel: 515 60 229

DSG ⊞ Delf Stream Gallery Tel: 07816 781297 www.delfstreamgallery.com

EAn ⊞ Era Antiques ikar66@aol.com

F&F ⊞ Fenwick & Fenwick, 88-90 High Street, Broadway, Worcestershire, WR12 7AJ Tel: 01386 853227/841724

FHF ⚒ Fellows & Sons, Augusta House, 19 Augusta Street, Hockley, Birmingham, West Midlands, B18 6JA Tel: 0121 212 2131 www.fellows.co.uk

G(B) ⚒ Gorringes Auction Galleries, Terminus Road, Bexhill-on-Sea, East Sussex, TN39 3LR Tel: 01424 212994 www.gorringes.co.uk

G(L) ⚒ Gorringes inc Julian Dawson, 15 North Street, Lewes, East Sussex, BN7 2PD Tel: 01273 478221

G&CC ⊞ The Goss & Crested China Club & Museum, incorporating Milestone Publications, 62 Murray Road, Horndean, Hampshire, PO8 9JL Tel: (023) 9259 7440

G&G ⊞ Guest & Gray, 1–7 Davies Mews, London, W1K 5AB Tel: 020 7408 1252 www.chinese-porcelain-art.com

GAK ⚒ Keys, Off Palmers Lane, Aylsham, Norfolk, NR11 6JA Tel: 01263 733195 www.aylshamsalerooms.co.uk

GaL ⊞ Gazelles Ltd, Stratton Audley, Ringwood Road, Stoney Cross, Lyndhurst, Hampshire, SO43 7GN Tel: 023 8081 1610 www.gazelles.co.uk

GAU ⊞ Becca Gauldie Antiques, The Old School, Glendoick, Perthshire, PH2 7NR, Scotland Tel: 01738 860 870

GLB ⊞ Glebe Antiques, Scottish Antique Centre, Doune, FK16 6HG, Scotland Tel: 01259 214559

GSA ⊞ Graham Smith Antiques, 83 Fern Avenue, Jesmond, Newcastle upon Tyne, Tyne & Wear, NE2 2RA Tel: 0191 281 5065

HarC ⊞ Hardy's Collectables Tel: 07970 613077 www.poolepotteryjohn.com

HeA ⊞ Heanor Antiques Centre, 1–3 Ilkeston Road, Heanor, Derbyshire, DE75 7AE Tel: 01773 531181/762783 www.heanorantiques.co.uk

HEI NO LONGER TRADING

HEW ⊞ Muir Hewitt, Art Deco Originals, Halifax Antiques Centre, Queens Road Mills, Queens Road/Gibbet Street, Halifax, Yorkshire, HX1 4LR Tel: 01422 347377 www.muirhewitt.com

HKW ⊞ Hawkswood Antiques, P.O. Box 156, Goole, DN14 7FW Tel: 01757 638630

HOW ⊞† John Howard at Heritage, 6 Market Place, Woodstock, Oxfordshire, OX20 1TA Tel: 0870 4440678 www.antiquepottery.co.uk

HUX ⊞ David Huxtable, Saturdays at: Portobello Road, Basement Stall 11/12, 288 Westbourne Grove, London, W11 Tel: 07710 132200 www.huxtins.com

IQ ⊞ Cloud Cuckooland, 12 Fore Street, Mevagissey, Cornwall, PL26 6UQ Tel: 01726 842364 www.cloudcuckooland.biz

IW ⊞ Islwyn Watkins, Offa's Dyke Antique Centre, 4 High Street, Knighton, Powys, LD7 1AT, Wales Tel: 01547 520145

JAd ⚒ James Adam & Sons, 26 St Stephen's Green, Dublin 2, Republic of Ireland Tel: 1 676 0261 www.jamesadam.ie/

JAK ⊞ Clive & Lynne Jackson Tel: 01242 254375

JBL ⊞ Judi Bland Antiques Tel: 01276 857576 or 01536 724145

JFME ⊞ James Ferguson & Mark Evans Tel: 0141 950 2452 or 077 699 72935 and 01388 768108 or 07979 0189214 www.evanscollectables.co.uk

JHo ⊞ Jonathan Horne, 66c Kensington Church Street, London, W8 4BY Tel: 020 7221 5658 www.jonathanhorne.co.uk

JMC ⊞ J & M Collectables Tel: 01580 891657 or 077135 23573

JOA ⊞ Joan Gale, Tombland Antiques Centre, 14 Tombland, Norwich, Norfolk, NR3 1HF Tel: 01603 619129

JRe ⊞ John Read, 29 Lark Rise, Martlesham Heath, Ipswich, Suffolk, IP5 7SA Tel: 01473 624897

JSG ⊞ James Strang Tel: 01334 472 566 or 07950 490088

JUP ⊞ Jupiter Antiques, P.O. Box 609, Rottingdean, East Sussex, BN2 7FW Tel: 01273 302865

K&M ⊞ K & M Antiques, 369-370 Grays Antique Market, 58 Davies Street, London, W1K 5LP Tel: 020 7491 4310

KES ⊞ Keystones, P.O. Box 387, Stafford, ST16 3FG Tel: 01785 256648 www.keystones.co.uk

L ⚒ Lawrence Fine Art Auctioneers, South Street, Crewkerne, Somerset, TA18 8AB Tel: 01460 73041 www.lawrences.co.uk

L&E ⚒ Locke & England, 18 Guy Street, Leamington Spa, Warwickshire, CV32 4RT Tel: 01926 889100

LAS ⊞ Reasons to be Cheerful, Georgian Village, 30-31 Islington Green, London, N18 DU Tel: 0207 281 4600

LAY ⚒ David Lay ASVA, Auction House, Alverton, Penzance, Cornwall, TR18 4RE Tel: 01736 361414

LBr ⊞ Lynda Brine, By Appointment only lyndabrine@yahoo.co.uk www.scentbottlesandsmalls.co.uk

LFA ⚒ Law Fine Art Ltd: 01635 860033 www.lawfineart.co.uk

LJ ⚒ Leonard Joel Auctioneers, 333 Malvern Road, South Yarra, Victoria 3141, Australia Tel: 03 9826 4333 www.ljoel.com.au

LLD ⊞ Lewis & Lewis Deco Tel: 07739 904681

MAA ⊞ Mario's Antiques, 75 Portobello Road, London, W11 2QB Tel: 020 8902 1600 www.marios_antiques.com

MARK ⊞ 20th Century Marks, Whitegates, Rectory Road, Little Burstead, Near Billericay, Essex, CM12 9TR Tel: 01268 411 000 www.20thcenturymarks.co.uk

MCL ⊞ Millennium Collectables Ltd, P.O. Box 146, Newark, Nottinghamshire, NG24 2WR Tel: 01636 703075 www.millenniumcollectables.co.uk

MED ⚒ Medway Auctions, Fagins, 23 High Street, Rochester, Kent, ME1 1LN Tel: 01634 847444 www.medwayauctions.co.uk

MEM ⊞ Memories UK, Mabel Lucie Attwell Club, Abbey Antiques, 63 Great Whyte, Ramsey, Nr Huntingdon, Cambridgeshire, PE26 1HL Tel: 01487 814753 www.mabellucieatwellclub.com

MER ⊞ Mere Antiques, 13 Fore Street, Topsham, Exeter, Devon, EX3 0HF Tel: 01392 874224

MFB ⊞ Manor Farm Barn Antiques Tel: 01296 658941 or 07720 286607 btwebworld.com/mfbantiques

MI ⊞ Mitofsky Antiques, 8 Rathfarnham Road, Terenure, Dublin 6, Republic of Ireland Tel: 1 492 0033 www.mitofskyantiques.com

MiW ⊞ Mike Weedon, 7 Camden Passage, Islington, London, N1 8EA Tel: 020 7226 5319 www.mikeweedonantiques.com

ML ⊞ Memory Lane, Bartlett Street Antiques Centre, 5/10 Bartlett Street, Bath, Somerset, BA1 2QZ Tel: 01225 466689/310457

MLa ⊞ Marion Langham Limited Tel: 028 895 41247 www.ladymarion.co.uk

MLL ⊞ Millers Antiques Ltd, Netherbrook House, 86 Christchurch Road, Ringwood, Hampshire, BH24 1DR Tel: 01425 472062 www.millers-antiques.co.uk

MMc ⊞ Marsh-McNamara Tel: 07790 759162

MRA ⊞ Millroyale Antiques Tel: 01902 375006 www.whiteladiesantiques.com

MRW ⊞ Malcolm Russ-Welch, P.O. Box 1122, Rugby, Warwickshire, CV23 9YD Tel: 01788 810 616

NAW ⊞ Newark Antiques Warehouse Ltd, Old Kelham Road, Newark, Nottinghamshire, NG24 1BX Tel: 01636 674869 www.newarkantiques.co.uk

NSal ⚒ Netherhampton Salerooms, Salisbury Auction Centre, Netherhampton, Salisbury, Wiltshire, SP2 8RH Tel: 01722 340 041

OAK ⊞ Oakwood Antiques Tel: 01204 304309 or 07813 386415

PF ⚒ Peter Francis, Curiosity Sale Room, 19 King Street, Carmarthen, SA31 1BH, Wales Tel: 01267 233456 www.peterfrancis.co.uk

Pott ⚒ Potteries Specialist Auctions, 271 Waterloo Road, Cobridge, Stoke on Trent, Staffordshire, ST6 3HR Tel: 01782 286622 www.potteriesauctions.com

POW ⊞ Sylvia Powell Decorative Arts, Suite 400, Ceramic House, 571 Finchley Road, London, NW3 7BN Tel: 020 8458 4543

PrB ⊞ Pretty Bizarre, 170 High Street, Deal, Kent, CT14 6BQ Tel: 07973 794537

PSA ⊞ Pantiles Spa Antiques, 4, 5, 6 Union House, The Pantiles, Tunbridge Wells, Kent, TN4 8HE Tel: 01892 541377 www.antiques-tun-wells-kent.co.uk

RAN ⊞ Ranby Hall-Antiques, Barnby Moor, Retford, Nottinghamshire, DN22 8JQ Tel: 01777 860696 www.ranbyhall.antiques-gb.com

RdeR ⊞ Rogers de Rin, 76 Royal Hospital Road, London, SW3 4HN Tel: 020 7352 9007 www.rogersderin.co.uk

RdV ⊞ Roger de Ville Antiques, Bakewell Antiques Centre, King Street, Bakewell, Derbyshire, DE45 1DZ Tel: 01629 812496 www.rogerdeville.co.uk

RGa ⊞ Richard Gardner Antiques, Swanhouse, Market Square, Petworth, West Sussex, GU28 0AN Tel: 01798 343411 www.richardgardnerantiques.com

RIA ⊞ Riverside Antiques, 60 Ely Street, Stratford-upon-Avon, Warwickshire Tel: 01789 262090

ROS ⚒ Rosebery's Fine Art Ltd, 74/76 Knights Hill, London, SE27 0JD Tel: 020 8761 2522

RTo ⚒ Rupert Toovey & Co Ltd, Spring Gardens, Washington, West Sussex, RH20 3BS Tel: 01903 891955 www.rupert-toovey.com

S ⚒ Sotheby's, 34-35 New Bond Street, London, W1A 2AA Tel: 020 7293 5000 www.sothebys.com

S(Am) ⚒ Sotheby's Amsterdam, De Boelelaan 30, Amsterdam 1083 HJ, Netherlands Tel: 31 20 550 2200

S(Mi) ⚒ Sotheby's, Palazzo Broggi, Via Broggi, 19, Milan 20129, Italy Tel: 39 02 295 001

S(NY) ⚒ Sotheby's, 1334 York Avenue at 72nd St, New York NY 10021, U.S.A. Tel: 212 606 7000

S(O) ⚒ Sotheby's Olympia, Hammersmith Road, London, W14 8UX Tel: 020 7293 5555

SAA ⊞ Scottish Antique and Arts Centre, Carse of Cambus, Doune, Perthshire, FK16 6HG, Scotland Tel: 01786 841203 www.scottish-antiques.com

SAAC ⊞ Scottish Antique Centre, Abernyte, Perthshire, PH14 9SJ, Scotland Tel: 01828 686401 www.scottish-antiques.com

SAS ⚒ Special Auction Services, Kennetholme, Midgham, Reading, Berkshire, RG7 5UX Tel: 0118 971 2949 www.antiquestradegazette.com/sas

SCH ⊞ Scherazade Tel: 01708 641117 or 07855 383996

Scot ⊞ Scottow Antiques, Green Street Green, Orpington, Kent, BR6 6JY

SER ⊞ Serendipity, 125 High Street, Deal, Kent, CT14 6BB Tel: 01304 369165 or 366536

SJH ⚒ S.J. Hales, 87 Fore Street, Bovey Tracey, Devon, TQ13 9AB Tel: 01626 836684

SK ⚒ Skinner Inc., The Heritage On The Garden, 63 Park Plaza, Boston, MA 02116, U.S.A. Tel: 617 350 5400

SRi ⊞ Steve Ribbons Tel: 01484 684043

StB ⊞ Steven Bishop Antiques & Decorative Arts Tel: 07761563095 www.meridiangallery.co.uk

SUW ⊞ Sue Wilde at Wildewear Tel: 01395 577966 www.wildewear.co.uk

SWO ⚒ Sworders, 14 Cambridge Road, Stansted Mountfitchet, Essex, CM24 8BZ Tel: 01279 817778 www.sworder.co.uk

TAC ⊞ Tenterden Antiques Centre, 66-66A High Street, Tenterden, Kent, TN30 6AU Tel: 01580 765655/765885

TEN ⚒ Tennants, The Auction Centre, Harmby Road, Leyburn, Yorkshire, DL8 5SG Tel: 01969 623780 www.tennants.co.uk

TH ⊞ Tony Horsley, P.O. Box 3127, Brighton, East Sussex, BN1 5SS Tel: 01273 550770

TMA ⚒ Tring Market Auctions, The Market Premises, Brook Street, Tring, Hertfordshire, HP23 5EF Tel: 01442 826446 www.tringmarketauctions.co.uk

TWO ⊞ Two P'S Tel: 01252 647965 or 07710 277726

TYE ⊞ Typically English Antiques Tel: 01249 721721 or 07818 000704

UD ⊞ Upstairs Downstairs, 40 Market Place, Devizes, Wiltshire, SN10 1JG Tel: 01380 730266 or 07974 074220

VK ⊞ Vivienne King of Panache Tel: 01934 814759

WAA ⊞ Woburn Abbey Antiques Centre, Woburn, Bedfordshire, MK17 9WA Tel: 01525 290666 www.discoverwoburn.com

WAC ⊞ Worcester Antiques Centre, Reindeer Court, Mealcheapen Street, Worcester, WR1 4DF Tel: 01905 610680

WeW ⊞ West Wales Antiques, 18 Mansfield Road, Murton, Swansea, SA3 3AR, Wales Tel: 01792 234318/01639 644379 www.westwalesantiques.com

WilP ⚒ W&H Peacock, 26 Newnham Street, Bedford, MK40 3JR Tel: 01234 266366

WW ⚒ Woolley & Wallis, Salisbury Salerooms, 51-61 Castle Street, Salisbury, Wiltshire, SP1 3SU Tel: 01722 424500/411854 www.woolleyandwallis.co.uk

YC ⊞ Yesterday Child Tel: 020 7354 1601 or 01908 583403

Picture Acknowledgements

p.1 OPG/RS/SΛΛ (p.238 tl); p.3 OPG/RS/Scot (p.243 bl); p.5 OPG/RS/Bel (p.250 tc); p.6 OPG/RS/JSG (p.174 tr); p.11 l OPG/RS/ASP (p.184 tl), c OPG/RS/BWDA (p.126 cl), r OPG/RS/AnM (p188 br); p.15 OPG/RS/BRT (p.84 cr); p.16 OPG/RS/DAN; p.17 OPG/DN; p.18 OPG/DL; p.19 OPG/RS/JRe (p.122 bl); p.20 OPG/RS/TYE (p.125 tr); p.21 OPG/SWO (p.126 bl); p.22 3x OPG/RS/MLa (p.127 tl, cr & bc); p.23 OPG/RS/DMA (p.128 cl); p.25 t OPG/RS/DMA (p131 bl), b OPG/Bea; p.26 OPG/DN; p.27 OPG/CH/Bon; p.28 t & r OPG/RS/JAK (p.142 cr & bl), l OPG/RS/MRA (p.142 tc); p.29 OPG/G(L) (p.145 bl); p.30 t OPG/RS/MER (p.145 tr), bl OPG/RS/TH (p.145 tl), br OPG/RS/WAC; p.32 l OPG/ROS (p.150 tr), r OPG/S, b OPG/S(Mi) (p.146 b); p.33 l OPG/TEN, c OPG/S(O) (p.147 c), r OPG/CH/Bon; p.34 t OPG/CH/Bon, b OPG/S(O) (p.147 tl), r OPG/CH/Bon; p.35 t OPG/DORO (p.149 tr), b OPG/G(L); p.36 tr OPG/DORO, bl OPG/CH/Bon; p.37 l OPG/BWL (p.152 bc), r OPG/RS/MRA (p.152 br); p.38 t OPG/RS/Cas, b OPG/G(L); p.40 bl OPG/ST/JS, tr OPG/CH/Bon; p.41 t OPG/RS/GSA (p.166 tr), b OPG/CH/Bon; p.44 t OPG/RDu/PCo, b OPG/RS/BKJL (p.180 tl); p.45 l OPG/RS/KES (p.181 bl), r OPG/RS/BEV (p.181 tr); p.47 l OPG/TR/BEV, r OPG/WW, b OPG/RS/LLD (p.190 br); p.48 l OPG/RS/BD (p.195 tl), r OPG/RS/HEW (p.195 tc); p.49 OPG/RS/POW (p.197 tl); p.50 OPG/RS/MMc (p.198 br); p.51 OPG/RS/POW (p.204 tr); p.52 OPG/CHTR (p.221 tl); p.53 OPG/PFK; p.54 OPG/RDu/BBA; p.55 t OPG/RS/IQ (p.228 br), b OPG/Bea; p.56 t OPG/RS/BEV (p.229 tr), bl OPG/RS/SAA, br OPG/JAA; p.57 OPG/ST/LP; p.58 t OPG/JAA, b OPG/TR/BEV; p.59 l OPG/CH/Bon, r OPG/JM/PSA; p.60 t OPG/CH/Bon, bl OPG/LT, br OPG/RS/Bel (p.250 tl); p.61 OPG/G(L) (p.258 c); p.62 t OPG/CH/Bon, b OPG/CH/P; p.63 l OPG/TR/BEV, r OPG/RDu/BBA; p.64 OPG/BBR; p.65t OPG/RS/UD (p.265 br), l OPG/SWO (p.203 tr); p.66 t OPG/IB/NFM, b OPG/CP; p.67 l OPG/CH/Bon, r OPG/ST; p.68 OPG/G(L); p.69 l OPG/RS/POW (p.205 tr), c OPG/G(L) (p.78 tl), r OPG/RS/DAN (p.81 tl)
Key: OPG – @ Octopus Publishing Group
Photographers: IB – Ian Booth, RDu – Rish Durka, CH – Chris Halton, JM – Jeremy Martin, TR – Tim Ridley, RS – Robin Saker, ST – Steve Tanner
Please refer to the Key to Illustrations on pages 281–283 for source codes except for those shown below:
BBA – Bloomsbury, Bon – Bonhams, DL – Dr Laird, JAA – Jackson's, JS – John Sandon, LP – Lynda Pine, LT – Louis Taylor Auctioneers, NFM – Newhaven Flea Market, P – Phillips, PCo – Private collection, PFK – Penrith Farmers' & Kidds'

Bibliography

Godden, Geoffrey A., *Godden's New Guide to English Porcelain,* London: Octopus Publishing Group Ltd, 2004.

Knowles, Eric, *Miller's Antiques Checklist Art Deco,* London: London: Octopus Publishing Group Ltd, 1991.

Knowles, Eric, *Miller's Antiques Checklist: Art Nouveau,* London: London: Octopus Publishing Group Ltd, 1992.

Knowles, Eric, *Miller's Antiques Checklist: Victoriana,* London: London: Octopus Publishing Group Ltd, 1991.

Lang, Gordon, *Miller's Antiques Checklist: Porcelain,* London: London: Octopus Publishing Group Ltd, 1991.

Lang, Gordon, *Miller's Pottery Antiques Checklist*, London: Octopus Publishing Group Ltd, 2000.

Lang, Gordon, *Miller's Pottery and Porcelain Marks,* London: London: Octopus Publishing Group Ltd, 1995.

Marsh, Madeleine, *Miller's Collectables Price Guide 2005,* London, Octopus Publishing Ltd, 2005.

Miller, Judith, *Miller's Antiques Encyclopedia,* London: London: Octopus Publishing Group Ltd, 1998

Miller's Antiques Price Guide 2006, London:Octopus Publishing Group Ltd, 2005.

Miller's Art Nouveau and Art Deco Buyer's Guide, London: London: Octopus Publishing Group Ltd, 1995.

Miller's Buying Affordable Antiques Price Guide 2004, London: London: Octopus Publishing Group Ltd, 2004.

Miller's Collecting Pottery and Porcelain-The Facts at Your Fingertips, London:Octopus Publishing Group Ltd, 1997.

Miller's Kitchenware Buyer's Guide, London: Octopus Publishing Group Ltd, 2005.

Miller's Toys and Games Buyer's Guide, London: Octopus Publishing Group Ltd, 2004

Pearson, Sue, *Miller's Antiques Checklist: Dolls and Teddy Bears*, London: London: Octopus Publishing Group Ltd, 1992

Sandon, John, *Miller's Collecting Porcelain,* London: Octopus Publishing Group Ltd, 2002.

Index to Advertisers

Index

Bold numbers refer to information and pointer boxes